Dipladenia 'Amoena'

Concise
ENCYCLOPEDIA OF
HOUSEPLANTS

Asplenium nidus avis

Phalaenopsis hybrid

Concise
ENCYCLOPEDIA OF HOUSEPLANTS

Packed with practical advice on how to grow over 450
exciting and colorful plants to enhance your home

Peter Chapman • William Davidson • Margaret Martin

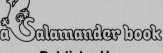

a Salamander book

Published by
CRESCENT BOOKS
New York

A Salamander Book

First English edition published by
Salamander Books Ltd.,
52 Bedford Row,
London WC1R 4LR,
United Kingdom

This 1987 edition
published by Crescent Books,
distributed by Crown Publishers, Inc.,
225 Park Avenue South,
New York,
New York 10003.

hgfedcba

ISBN 0 517 63368 X

Credits

Authors: William Davidson, Peter
Chapman and Margaret Martin. Special
contributions by Jack Kramer

Editor: Geoffrey Rogers

Designers: Roger Hyde, Barry Savage,
Stonecastle Graphics

Monochrome: Bantam Litho Ltd.,
England; Tenreck, England

Filmset: SX Composing Ltd, England

Color reproductions: Bantam Litho Ltd.,
England; Rodney Howe Ltd., England;
Scansets Ltd., England

Line drawings: Tyler/Camoccio Design
Consultants, Maureen Holt. © Salamander
Books Ltd.

Photographs: A full list of credits appears
on page 488

Printed in Belgium by Proost International
Book Production, Turnhout, Belgium

CONTENTS

Gymnocalycium horridspinum

Polyscias balfouriana 'Pinnochio'

INTRODUCTION

There is nothing quite so disappointing as watching a cherished houseplant slowly dying in your care. Despite all your efforts, it never seems to regain the vitality it once enjoyed in the plant shop. Not surprisingly, this experience may persuade you that you will never succeed with any plants in your home. This is regrettable, because with just a little encouragement and the suggestion of a plant more suited to your home conditions, you might well become a successful and even a fanatic houseplant grower.

Whether you are one of life's 'plant refugees' or able to grow a wide range of houseplants with consummate skill, this guide will give you the incentive to try something new. Here is a selection of over 450 plants, described with enthusiasm as well as accuracy, that can fill your home with colour all year through. The book is divided into three sections – flowering (non-succulent plants), foliage plants, and cacti and succulents – and each section is preceded by an index of scientific names followed by one of common names (where these exist). Within each section, the plants are presented in alphabetical order of Latin name and coded in words (not confusing symbols) according to the amount of light they need, their ideal growing temperature (for the orchids this is a winter night minimum), and a note about moisture and/or feeding. Clear instructions on the best way to grow each plant are followed by a special tip to promote growth, avoid injury to either you or your plant, or, in the case of flowering species, encourage blooming.

Each plant is illustrated by a clear line drawing and most are also shown in beautiful colour photographs, with text and photographs cross-referenced throughout as follows: 24♦.

Part One
FLOWERING HOUSEPLANTS

Aechmea chantinii

Author

William Davidson is involved with all aspects of houseplants, and has been employed by Rochfords, Europe's leading growers, for most of his working life. His interests encompass growing, exhibiting, writing, consultancy and lecturing, as well as radio and television programmes. He is the author of many successful books on houseplants.

Catharanthus roseus

Index of Scientific Names

The plants are arranged in alphabetical order of Latin name.
Page numbers in **bold** refer to text entries; those in *italics* refer to photographs.

Index of Common Names

Guzmania lingulata 'Minor Orange'

Introduction to Flowering Houseplants

With their delicate form and ability to create a wide range of colours throughout the year, flowering houseplants always bring beauty and interest to a home, whatever their size. Even the smallest apartment benefits from a floriferous cyclamen at Christmas, a bright-eyed primula at Easter or the dazzling yellow, pouch-like flowers of calceolarias during the summer.

Conditions

Flowering houseplants are not as tolerant as foliage types, totally disliking fluctuating temperatures, draughts and moisture variation in the compost. If abandoned to mistreatment when in flower the plants seldom fully recover, and, if just showing buds, fluctuating conditions may cause the buds to fall off. It is therefore important to take note of the temperatures indicated for the plants in this section, together with moisture, feeding and positioning requirements.

Orchids, in particular, require special conditions. For instance, it is important that the temperature does not fall below a certain level at night, for which reason the temperature quoted at the beginning of each orchid article is the winter night minimum rather than the ideal growing temperature. Some species also require a winter rest during which they should be placed in full light and kept mostly dry until the new growth is seen. Rest requirements are therefore shown for each species.

Potting

Many flowering houseplants are discarded after giving their display, but some are kept from year to year. Periodically, when their roots fill the pot, plants kept throughout the year need repotting into slightly larger containers. You should not be tempted to pot-up your plant into too large a pot, as it will then be difficult to keep the compost at the right moisture content – an important factor during winter. Some plants grow best in loam-based composts, while others need peat-based tyes, and these and other preferences are indicated.

Care in winter

Winter is the most difficult time to keep flowering houseplants in good condition. This is because temperatures either widely fluctuate with central heating or are just too cold, especially at night. Plants on window-sills are best removed at night to the centre of the room, and should never be left between windows and drawn curtains.

It is difficult to give plants the right amount of water during winter – a period when they are not actively growing. In summer, plants soon use up excess water in the compost, but during winter such moisture remains for a long time, causing stagnation, chills and decay, as well as facilitating the onset of diseases. Water splashed on the foliage or flowers also encourages diseases.

Above: **Abutilon 'Boule de Neige'**
Well known for their paper-thin
orange, yellow or red flowers,
abutilons are decorative plants
where a vertical accent is necessary.
Do stake plants so they do not
become unwieldy. 25♦

Left: **Acacia armata**
Grown more outdoors than indoors,
this beautiful yellow flowering plant is
a happy choice if you have space for
it. Flowers appear in early spring and
assure colour at the window. 25♦

Right: **Acalypha hispida**
The long chenillelike red catkins
make A. hispida a popular houseplant. The large leaves are
decorative as well, and when young
a fine plant for limited space. 26♦

Left: **Achimenes hybrids 'Paul Arnold'**
Dozens of attractive varieties come from this large gesneriad group, and all offer a wealth of colourful flowers for summer show. 26♦

Below left: **Aechmea chantinii**
Called the 'Queen of the Bromeliads'. A. chantinii has handsome broad leaves, rosette growth and an inflorescence that seems artificial, it is so vividly coloured. Bracts last for months. 27♦

Right: **Adenium obesum 'Multiflorum'**
An extraordinary succulent with rosettes of leaves and large white, crimson-edged flowers. The stems eventually become woody trunks of a sculpturesque form. 27♦

Below: **Aeschynanthus lobbianus**
Brilliant red flowers in tubular 'lipstick cases' adorn this plant in midsummer – a mature specimen may have over 50 flowers. The plant has pendent growth and is best grown in a basket container. 28♦

19

Left: **Anguloa clowesii**
*This yellow tulip orchid is aptly
named. Its fragrant blooms cluster at
the base of the plant, but are never
hidden from view because the
leaves are upright.* 30♦

Right: **Angraecum eburneum**
*Large white to pale green crystalline
flowers in winter make this orchid
highly desirable for indoor accent,
and the evergreen straplike leaves
are attractive as well.* 30♦

Below: **Alpinia purpurata**
*A fine ginger plant – though
somewhat large – with dense
clusters of red bracts; an excellent
touch of tropical atmosphere for a
spacious window.* 29♦

Above: **Aphelandra squarrosa
'Louisae'**
*This fine houseplant from South
America has stellar yellow flowers –
a brilliant display at any window. A
good plant for limited space.* 32♦

Right: **Anthurium andreanum**
*With its glossy green leaves this is a
glamorous subject for a shady part of
the indoor garden. It bears large
flower spathes and comes in white or
shades of pink and red.* 31♦

23

Above: **Begonia boweri**
Long a favourite, the eyelash begonia has spectacular foliage and white or pale pink flowers that are a delight throughout summer and autumn months of the year. 33♦

Left: **Azalea indica**
Here is a plant that can brighten any autumn day. A compact shrub, it can be in flower for many weeks. 33♦

Abutilon hybrids
(Bellflower; Flowering maple)
- **Good light**
- **Temp: 10-18°C (50-65°F)**
- **Keep moist and fed**

There are numerous varieties, with pendulous bell-shaped flowers in a range of colours, and some have colourful foliage. Many of the abutilons are worthy of a place in the houseplant collection for their foliage alone.

Most are of vigorous habit, and capable of attaining a height of some 1.8m (6ft) with their roots confined to a pot of about 18cm (7in) in diameter. However, pruning of over-vigorous growth presents no problem and can be done at almost any time of the year. Firm top sections of stems will not be difficult to root in a fresh peat and sand mixture. Feed well when they are established.

Light, airy and cool conditions suit them best, and they will be the better for spending the summer months out of doors in a sheltered position. Use a loam-based potting mixture.

Acacia armata
(Kangaroo thorn; Wattle)
- **Good light**
- **Temp: 13-18°C (55-65°F)**
- **Keep moist**

Native to Australia, *A. armata* develops into an attractive shrubby plant that does well in a conservatory, but may in time become too large for smaller rooms. However, pruning of over-vigorous growth can be undertaken in the early part of the year, which is also the best time for potting plants into larger containers. A loam-based mixture is necessary if plants are not to become too soft and lush.

New plants are made by sowing seed in spring, or by taking firm, but not old, cuttings in midsummer. Older material is too woody and less likely to succeed.

The principal attraction of this plant is the yellow flowers, which appear in spring. During the spring and summer, plants require to be fed regularly and watered freely; they need less water and no feeding during the winter months.

To encourage bloom:
Keep plants in small pots – a 13-15cm (5-6in) pot is ideal. 16♦

To encourage bloom:
Provide bright and airy conditions around the plant. 16♦

Acalypha hispida
(Chenille plant; Foxtails; Red hot cat's tail)
- **Good light**
- **Temp: 13-18°C (55-65°F)**
- **Keep moist and fed**

These striking plants, with their large leaves of mid-green colouring, grow to a height of some 1.8m (6ft) in ideal conditions. Drooping beetroot-red bracts develop from the axils of leaves to create the principal attraction of this fine plant.

The best time to purchase these plants is in the spring when the fresh young ones will get off to a better start. Keep them moist at all times, giving a little less water in winter, and feed well when they are established. When they have filled their existing containers with roots, use a loam-based potting compost to pot the plants on and help to develop them to their full potential.

Keep your acalypha in good light but avoid strong sunlight. Remove the dead bracts regularly and keep a watchful eye for pale leaf discolouration, which is a sign that troublesome red spider mites are present. Treat the undersides of leaves with insecticide promptly.

To encourage bloom:
Provide plenty of water and light. 17♦

Achimenes hybrids
(Cupid's bower; Hot water plant)
- **Good light**
- **Temp: 13-18°C (55-65°F)**
- **Keep moist and fed**

One of those cheap and cheerful plants that will go on flowering throughout the summer, and can be raised from early spring-sown seed, from cuttings, or by peeling off and planting some of the scaly rhizomes. They are fine as conventional pot plants situated in good light on a windowsill or, perhaps more splendidly, as hanging-basket plants growing overhead.

After the flowers and foliage have died down the plants should be allowed to dry out and rest throughout the winter. They can be started into growth again in the spring. At this time the rhizomes can be peeled apart so that more plants are produced. Place the rhizomes in hot water before planting, and they will generally do better.

Keep the plants moist and avoid a very dry atmosphere, which will encourage red spider mites to the detriment of the plant.

To encourage bloom:
Maintain humid, well-lit conditions during the summer. 18♦

Adenium obesum var. multiflorum
(Desert rose; Impala lily)
- **Full sun**
- **Temp: 13-30°C (55-86°F)**
- **Keep almost dry in winter**

Although it is a succulent plant in its native habitat, this adenium cannot produce the massive water-storage stem as a small specimen. It is one of the most beautiful flowering succulents, but not one of the easiest to grow, mainly because of the higher, draught-free winter temperature needed. However, given the right conditions, it will produce masses of red or pink blooms over a relatively long period during spring and summer. Plants can start to flower when only 15cm (6in) high. The thickened branching stems bear glossy bright green leaves; these normally fall during winter, when the potting mixture should be kept only slightly moist.

Grow in a good potting mixture, which can be either loam- or peat-based; to ensure the necessary free drainage it is worth mixing in about one third of sharp sand or perlite. Water can be given freely when the plant is in full growth and flower.

To encourage bloom:
Provide a winter rest. 19♦

Aechmea chantinii
(Amazonian zebra plant; Queen of the bromeliads)
- **Good light**
- **Temp: 13-18°C (55-65°F)**
- **Avoid overwatering**

Among the bromeliads this one has a reputation for being tough. It has very vicious spines along the leaf margins, which makes careful handling, and positioning, essential. The green-and-silver banded foliage itself makes a striking plant, but when the red-and-orange coloured bract appears one begins fully to appreciate the spectacle that this splendid plant displays.

Like all the more majestic plants in the bromeliad family, this will take several years to produce bracts following the purchase of a young plant. New plants can be started from offshoots that appear at the base of the parent stems of an older plant that has produced bracts. These should be planted individually in a loam-based potting mixture to which some prepared tree bark has been added. Pot as firmly as possible to prevent the plants toppling over, and keep out of direct sunlight until new growth is evident.

To encourage bloom:
Keep in bright light. 18♦

Aechmea fasciata
(Exotic brush; Silver vase; Urn plant; Vase plant)
- **Good light**
- **Temp: 13-18°C (55-65°F)**
- **Keep urn filled with water**

The silvery-grey leaves have a light grey down on them that adds much to the attraction of this most excellent of all bromeliads. Its grey leaves are broad and recurving and form a central chamber or urn, which should be filled with water. There are spines along the leaf margins, so be careful when handling. Also avoid touching the grey down on the leaves if the plants are to be seen to their best effect.

Young plants can be raised from seed, in which case bracts take some five to seven years to appear, or from basal shoots of mature plants, in which case bracts develop in two to three years.

The bract is a delightful soft pink in colour and, as if this were not enough, small but intensely blue flowers will also develop in the spiky pink bract. This is a truly fine plant that is easy to manage and will remain in 'flower' for up to nine months.

To encourage bloom:
Provide bright light and humid surroundings.

Aeschynanthus lobbianus
(Basket vine; Lipstick vine)
- **Light shade**
- **Temp: 16-21°C (60-70°F)**
- **Keep moist and fed**

These are temperamental plants that will produce exotic red flowers with seeming abandon one year, and in spite of having had identical treatment, will produce very little the next year. One of the supposed secrets of getting them to flower more reliably is to keep the plants very much on the dry side in winter and to lower the growing temperature. It is a procedure that works for many of the similar gesneriads, such as the columneas. During the warmer months, they should be kept out of bright sunlight.

The plants have glossy green leaves and have a natural pendulous habit, which adds considerably to their charm. New plants are easily started from cuttings a few centimetres in length that may be taken at any time during the spring or summer months. Arrange several cuttings to a small pot filled with peaty mixture and this will ensure that full and attractive plants develop.

To encourage bloom:
Give dry winter rest. 19♦

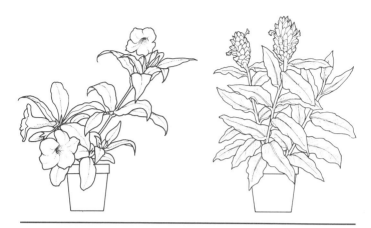

Allamanda cathartica

(Common allamanda; Golden trumpet)
- **Good light**
- **Temp: 16-21°C (60-70°F)**
- **Keep moist and fed**

The allamanda is better suited to the conservatory or sunroom than indoors. Using a loam-based potting compost this rapid grower will require ample moisture at its roots and frequent feeding while in active growth in spring and summer.

For best effect, train the active growth as it develops to a framework of some kind so that when the golden-yellow trumpet flowers appear they are set off to maximum effect. Although the flowers are sometimes sparse, there will generally be more of them if the plants are fed with a fertilizer recommended for flowering plants – something with a fairly high potash content, rather than nitrogen.

In winter, the amount of water given can be reduced and the plants can be severely pruned back to create a better shape and more manageable size.

To encourage bloom:
Keep in sunny conditions and repot each year into the next pot size.

Alpinia purpurata

(Red ginger)
- **Full sun**
- **Temp: 18-24°C (65-75°F)**
- **Water with care**

This ornamental plant from the ginger family, Zingiberaceae, provides a beautiful display of bright red bracts against a foil of glossy green leaves during the summer months. The real flowers are white and insignificant. Reaching a height of about 1.5m (5ft), this is a truly exotic subject.

To succeed, *Alpinia purpurata* needs plenty of sunshine; perhaps a sunroom or conservatory would be the ideal place in which to try this tropical plant. Use a large pot and an open potting mix of equal parts soil and humus. It is essential that this drains readily, for during the summer the plant should be watered freely but never allowed to remain waterlogged. During the winter rest it slightly, with less moisture.

Keep the temperature high, with a minimum of 18°C (65°F), and feed 'little and often' throughout the summer months. Propagate by dividing the rhizomes and replanting.

To encourage bloom:
Provide plenty of sunshine and warmth in the summer. 21♦

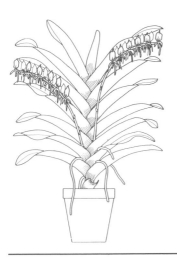

Angraecum eburneum

(Comet orchid)
- **Good light**
- **Temp: 18°C (65°F) min.**
- **Evergreen/no rest**

There are over 200 species of angraecums, although very few are seen in cultivation. They come mainly from tropical Africa.

This winter-flowering species resembles *Angraecum sesquipedale* in plant habit but the flower spikes are often longer, producing nine to 12 flowers about 10cm (4in) in diameter. The sepals, petals and spur are green and the lip pure white. Curiously, the flowers appear on the stem as if upside-down.

The plant thrives in generous conditions and should be watered throughout the year. During the summer months regular overhead spraying of the foliage and aerial roots is beneficial. The plant can also be foliar fed in the same way for nine months of the year. Although it likes a position in good light, the leaves are all too easily burnt if it is allowed to stand in bright sunlight for any length of time.

To encourage bloom:
Keep warm and humid. 21♦

Anguloa clowesii

(Cradle orchid; Tulip orchid)
- **Good light**
- **Temp: 11°C (52°F) min.**
- **Deciduous/rest in winter**

This is a small genus of about ten species, which grow naturally as epiphytes and terrestrials. They are high altitude plants from South America.

This large and beautiful species is commonly known as the 'cradle orchid' owing to the ability of the lip, which is loosely hinged, to rock back and forth when tilted. The lip is fully enclosed by the rest of the flower, which gives rise to a further popular name of 'tulip orchid'. The plant will grow well with lycastes but is considerably larger when in leaf.

Plenty of water and feed should be given during the growing season, when the plant is making up its large pseudobulbs. Water should be withheld when the leaves are shed at the end of the growing season. The flowers, 7.5cm (3in) across, appear singly from a stout stem at the same time as the new growth. They are a lovely canary yellow with a strong fragrance.

To encourage bloom:
Observe winter rest. 20♦

Anthurium andreanum

(Flamingo flower; Flamingo lily; Oilcloth flower; Painter's palette)
- **Light shade**
- **Temp: 18-24°C (65-75°F)**
- **Keep moist and fed**

One of the most spectacular of all the flowering plants grown in pots, this needs a temperature in excess of 18°C (65°F) and a high degree of humidity to give of its best. Flowers may be pink, white or red, with the latter being the colour most frequently seen.

As cut flowers *A. andreanum* has no peers. Flowers are borne on long stalks and from the time they are cut they have a full six weeks of life when placed in water, and will last much longer if left on the plant. Obtaining plants may be difficult, but they can be raised from seed and germinated in a temperature of not less than 24°C (75°F). However, it will be several years before the plants produce their exotic flowers. Leaves are large, carried on long petioles, and have an arrow-shaped appearance. Use an open leafy mix when potting on, and keep the plants well watered, misted, and away from direct sunlight.

To encourage bloom:
Provide humid conditions. 2323♦

Anthurium scherzerianum

(Flamingo flower; Pigtail plant; Tailflower)
- **Light shade**
- **Temp: 16-21°C (60-70°F)**
- **Keep moist and fed**

This is the baby brother of *A. andreanum,* but is much better suited to average room conditions, in both space requirements and care. Green leaves are produced on short petioles from soil level, and flowers are generally red in colour and produced over a long spring and summer period. The spadix in the centre of the flower has a natural whorl to it that gives rise to one of its common names, 'pigtail plant'.

All anthuriums require an open potting mixture, and one made up of equal parts of peat and well-rotted leaves will be better than an entirely peat mix, or a mix containing loam. Once established, plants need regular feeding to maintain leaf colouring and to encourage production of flowers with stouter stems – weak-stemmed flowers will require support. Like *A. andreanum* this should be kept out of direct sunlight.

To encourage bloom:
Provide humid conditions.

Aphelandra squarrosa 'Louisae'

(Saffron spike; Zebra plant)
- **Light shade**
- **Temp: 16-21°C (60-70°F)**
- **Keep moist and fed**

The aphelandra has two fairly obvious common names, 'zebra plant' and 'saffron spike', relating to different parts of the plant – one to the grey-green leaves striped with silver, and the other to the saffron-yellow spike that forms the bract produced in midsummer. It is equally attractive with or without flowers, and reaches a height of about 60cm (2ft) when grown in a 13cm (5in) diameter pot. Larger pots will produce taller plants, usually in their second year.

When in good health all aphelandras will produce a wealth of roots and, consequently, require frequent feeding and potting on as soon as they have filled their existing pots with roots. Peaty mixtures are not much use to this plant; try a proprietary brand potting soil that contains a good proportion of loam. In spring and summer established plants must be fed with every watering.

Ascocenda
- **Good light**
- **Temp: 18-24°C (65-75°F)**
- **Keep moist but do not feed**

The Ascocendas are a group of hybrids that result from the crossing of *Ascocentrum* and *Vanda* species. They flower twice yearly, in spring and early autumn, and form an attractive part of any window display. There are many varieties, most of which rarely grow above 40cm (16in) in height, making them ideally suited for people with only a limited amount of space.

The plants should be grown in a south-facing window as they require plenty of good sunlight. Plant in medium grade fir bark, preferably in a small container, and water evenly throughout the year, but do not feed. Keep plants in an area of good air circulation and ensure humidity is high (40 percent), spraying with tepid water in warm weather. The plants grow especially well under artificial light.

To encourage bloom:
Rest after flowering. 22◗

To encourage bloom:
Use a small container.

Azalea indica
(Rhododendron simsii)
(Indian azalea)
- **Good light**
- **Temp: 10-16°C (50-60°F)**
- **Keep very moist**

For a colourful display there is little that can match these plants when they are well grown. With its evergreen foliage and flowers in many colours, the azalea will be more attractive and last very much longer if given cool and light conditions indoors – hot conditions definitely shorten the life of the flowers. The most sensible way of watering is to grasp the pot in both hands and plunge it in a bucket of water and leave it submerged until every vestige of air has escaped from the soil. Depending on conditions, it may be necessary to repeat this exercise two or three times weekly during the spring and summer months, with only slightly less water being given in winter.

Remove dead flowers as they occur and place plants out in the garden for the summer, being sure to bring them in before frosts occur. Use a mix of peat and well-rotted leaves when potting on.

To encourage bloom:
Keep cool and light. 24♦

Begonia boweri
(Eyelash begonia)
- **Filtered light**
- **Temp: 13-18°C (55-65°F)**
- **Keep moist**

There are a number of evergreen, fibrous-rooted begonias worth finding space for in the home, and this is one of the best of the more compact types. Flowers are white to pale pink in colour and though small in size, plentiful in number. The principal attraction, however, is the foliage, which is a mottled pale green and almost black in colour.

Growth is low and spreading, and the rhizomatous stem becomes gnarled in time, which tends to make plants less attractive as they shed their lower leaves. Rather than continue with an older and less attractive plant it is better to start fresh plants from sections of stem with a few leaves attached, or from individual leaves. Place leaves in shallow pans of fresh, moist peat at a temperature of not less than 18°C (65°F), and preferably in a closed propagator. Use peaty soil when potting on, and the plants will need moderate feeding and watering.

To encourage bloom:
Allow to grow potbound. 24♦

33

Begonia 'Fireglow'
- Good light
- Temp: 13-18°C (55-65°F)
- Keep moist and fed

Developed on the European
Continent, this plant has provided
something of a revolution with the
improvement of growing techniques
and the appearance of more varied
flower colouring on the scene. In the
original version, there were only
single red flowers but now there are
single and double flowers in a wide
variety of attractive shades.

In good light plants flower for many
months through spring and summer,
but a constant guard must be kept
against mildew, which manifests
itself as a white powdery patch on
leaves – treat with a suitable
fungicide. To combat mildew further,
offer light and fresh air as opposed to
stuffy and hot conditions. Dead
flowers resting on lower leaves will
also cause rotting of foliage.

Use peaty soil when potting and
keep moist and feed moderately. Cut
back in autumn after flowering and
keep on the dry side over winter.

To encourage bloom:
Grow in bright light.

Begonia coccinea 'Orange Rubra'
(Angelwing begonia)
- Filtered light
- Temp: 16-21°C (60-70°F)
- Keep moist and fed

With glossy green leaves and lovely
orange-coloured flowers this is one
of the taller growing fibrous-rooted
begonias (sometimes referred to as
cane-type begonias). *Begonia*
'Orange Rubra' is only one example
of the many cane-type begonias to
be seen in florists' and nurseries,
and will offer a splendid show when
in flower.

As the plants age they will have a
natural tendency to shed their lower
leaves, which will result in less
attractive, bare stems, and this is one
very good reason for raising fresh
plants from easily rooted cuttings at
regular intervals. Cuttings with three
or four firm leaves can be taken at
almost any time if a heated
propagating case is available. Use
rooting powder on the severed end
of the cutting before inserting it in
peat with a little sand added. When
potting cuttings on it is advisable to
put several cuttings in a pot for a
fuller and more attractive display.

To encourage bloom:
Keep in a humid but not stuffy
atmosphere. 41▸

Begonia semperflorens

(Wax begonia)
- **Good light**
- **Temp: 10-16°C (50-60°F)**
- **Keep moist and fed**

Often much in evidence as a summer bedding plant, this species is also excellent for decorating windowsills indoors when grown in a pot. In fact, an interesting use for *B. semperflorens* is to grow them out of doors as bedding plants during the summer months and to dig a few up and pot them before frosts occur. The foliage can be severely cut back, and in a surprisingly short time fresh growth will develop and eventually fresh flowers will appear and last for several weeks.

Many have bronze-coloured foliage that greatly enhances the plants. All must have ample light, especially during the darker months of the year. The temperature can be quite low, providing the soil is not allowed to become excessively wet. Remember to give a weak liquid feed at every watering. For new plants, sow seed in the spring.

To encourage boom:
Give plenty of light. 41♦

Begonia x tuberhybrida

- **Filtered light**
- **Temp: 10-18°C (50-65°F)**
- **Keep moist and fed**

These popular and colourful plants are widely grown for home decoration. They also do well in pots and tubs on terraces and patios, as well as in summer-bedding schemes in gardens. They are tuberous-rooted and grow 30-60cm (12-24in) high and 30-38cm (12-15in) wide.

The large, rose-like flowers, often 7.5-15cm (3-6in) wide and in single and double forms, appear from mid to late summer. Many named forms are available, including the rich yellow 'Festiva', bright crimson 'Olympia', and rose-pink 'Rhapsody'.

During spring, start the tubers into growth by placing them hollow side uppermost in boxes of moist peat at 18°C (65°F). As soon as the tubers develop shoots, pot them up individually into loam-based compost in 12.5cm (5in) wide pots. When the plants fill their containers with roots, transfer them into 15-20cm (6-8in) wide pots

To encourage bloom:
Keep away from cold draughts.

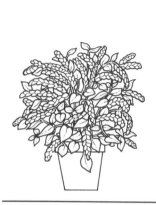 

Beloperone guttata
(Shrimp plant)
- **Light shade**
- **Temp: 16-21°C (60-70°F)**
- **Keep moist and fed**

The common name of 'shrimp plant' derives from the shrimp-like bracts that are freely produced on vigorous plants. On the more common 'shrimp plant' bracts are a dullish red in colour, but there is also *B. g. lutea,* which has interesting greenish yellow bracts.

Purchased plants should have their roots inspected immediately, and if a mass of roots is in evidence the plants must be potted without delay into a loam-based mixture. Failure to do so will mean leaf discolouration and a general decline of the plant. Regular feeding is also of the utmost importance, and avoid dank, airless conditions. Growing tips of young plants should be removed to encourage a more bushy appearance. And if one has the courage to do so it will strengthen young plants if all the early bracts that develop are removed.

To encourage bloom:
Prune rigorously each year for compact, free-flowering plants.

Billbergia pyramidalis
- **Good light**
- **Temp: 13-18°C (55-65°F)**
- **Keep on the dry side**

Belonging to the bromeliad family, billbergias are very tolerant houseplants that will thrive more on neglect than on constant, fussing care. This species has golden green leaves and produces attractive spikes of orange-pink bracts and red and blue flowers at almost any time of the year. Individual bracts last for only a week or so, but each mature plant bears several spikes.

Grow this bromeliad in loose-textured, lime-free potting mix and water only when the top layer of soil has dried out. Use soft water or rain water if possible. Normal room temperatures and bright light will keep this plant perfectly healthy.

Billbergias are generally free of pests and diseases. Propagation is also no problem; simply remove and pot up the offsets that develop around the base of the parent plant.

To encourage bloom:
Keep in bright light. 42♦

Bougainvillea
(Paper flower)
- **Sunny location**
- **Temp: 13-18°C (55-65°F)**
- **Keep dry in winter**

Few flowering plants are capable of giving a display that equals that of the paper-thin bracts of the bougainvillea, particularly when seen in its natural tropical habitat.

In pots they can be more difficult to manage if the owner is someone who is forever watering. These plants should be well watered and allowed to dry reasonably before repeating, and when the foliage turns colour and drops in the autumn it is a sign that water should be withheld until the following early spring when new growth appears and watering can begin again. Pruning – it tolerates quite severe cutting back – can be done in the autumn. Repotting can be undertaken in spring, and is best done by removing some of the old soil and potting the plant into the same container with a fresh loam-based mixture. During the summer months fresh air and full sunlight are essential.

To encourage bloom:
Provide several hours sunshine a day during summer. 43♦

Bouvardia domestica
(Jasmine plant; Trompetilla)
- **Light shade**
- **Temp: 13-18°C (55-65°F)**
- **Keep moist and fed**

These compact, shrubby plants produce flowers of many colours on the end of slightly drooping stems. They are ideal for a window location that offers good light and a modicum of fresh air, but not necessarily cold conditions. An added bonus with the bouvardia is that it is autumn flowering, so providing a display when there are fewer flowering pot plants around.

During the summer months established plants will be better for being placed out of doors in a sheltered position – in colder areas they will need the protection of an unheated greenhouse.

Plants should be watered freely and fed regularly during the summer months, less water and no feeding being required during winter. Plants are best potted in the spring, and a loam-based mixture will suit them better than an all-peat preparation. Spring is also the time to take cuttings or divide the roots.

To encourage bloom:
Pinch out growing tips in summer for autumn bloom.

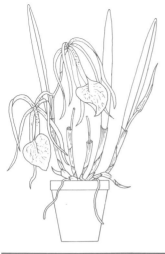

Brassavola nodosa
(Lady of the night)
- **Good light**
- **Temp: 13°C (55°F) min.**
- **Evergreen/dry rest**

Brassavolas are very popular with amateur growers, partly because they are easy to cultivate and also for the strange shapes of some of the flowers. The 15 species known are either epiphytic or lithophytic and come from Central and South America.

In this species the pseudobulbs and leaves are very slender and appear as one, both being cylindrical in shape. The plants are best grown on tree-fern fibre, with just a little compost, and suspended from the greenhouse roof. Brassavolas object to excessive moisture and should be kept quite dry during their lengthy period of rest.

Brassavola nodosa is very fragrant, especially in the cool of the evening or at night. It can be found in flower at any time of the year. The flowers, often four to five on a stem, are creamy-green and up to 7.5cm (3in) across when fully open. The lip is white with purple spots.

To encourage bloom:
Observe rest period. 42♦

Browallia speciosa
(Bush violet)
- **Good light**
- **Temp: 13-18°C (55-65°F)**
- **Keep moist and fed**

The flower colouring of *B. speciosa* ranges from blue to violet-blue, but there are white varieties available. It should be reasonably easy to raise new plants from seed on the windowsill for the person who is moderately competent with indoor plants. Sow seed in spring in peat to which a little sharp sand has been added, and after sowing just cover the seed with a fine layer of sand. Place a sheet of glass over the container holding the seed, and over the glass place a sheet of newspaper until the seed has germinated. When large enough to handle, the seedlings can be pricked off into a very peaty mixture with reasonable space for seedlings to develop. Subsequently, transfer the tiny plants to small pots filled with loam-based mixture and allow to grow on.

From then on keep them moist, fed, and in good light. Discard the plants after they have flowered.

To encourage bloom:
Keep plants cool and fed during the summer months. 44♦

Calanthe vestita

- Good light
- Temp: 18°C (65°F) min.
- Deciduous/dry rest

With tall, upright flower spikes and many long-lasting flowers, *Calanthe* is deservedly a special favourite with orchid growers. Given warm-house conditions, it grows easily and is thus a good plant for beginners. Of the 150 species known, most are terrestrials; they come from a wide area, including South Africa, Asia and Central America.

The flowers of *Calanthe vestita* range in colour from white to deep pink, the lip often being stronger in colour than the rest of the flower.

A warm greenhouse with good light suits this plant best. This deciduous species produces rather large, angular pseudobulbs with wide, ribbed leaves. During the growing season the plant should be liberally watered and fed until the leaves turn yellow and fall during the early winter months. At this stage watering should be gradually reduced. After flowering the pseudobulbs should be repotted in a well-drained compost.

To encourage bloom:
Observe rest period. 44

Calceolaria hybrids

(Pocketbook plant; Pouch flower; Slipper flower; Slipperwort)

- Good light
- Temp: 10-16°C (50-60°F)
- Keep moist and fed

These pouch-like flowers are available in a bewildering range of colours. Many different strains are available and all will give a splendid display if a few standard rules are followed. First and foremost is that these plants must have good light, a loam-based mixture in which to grow, and regular feeding once they have filled their pots with roots.

When buying a mature plant from a retailer it is important to check the roots in the pot on getting the plant home; an overcrowded root system means the plant should be potted on straight away. It is also wise to give plants a general inspection before buying, particularly on the undersides of leaves, and to reject any that have pests present.

These are temporary plants and should be discarded after flowering.

To encourage bloom:
Keep the plants cool and in bright light (but not direct sunlight). Water regularly to keep the soil moist.

Callistemon citrinus
(Bottlebrush; Crimson bottlebrush)
- **Good light**
- **Temp: 13-16°C (55-60°F)**
- **Keep moist and fed**

An Australian plant, the callistemon gets its common name of 'bottlebrush plant' from the formation of the unusual flower, which is in the shape of the brush used for cleaning out bottles.

It is a green-leaved woody shrub that will, in time, reach a height of about 150cm (5ft) if growing conditions are agreeable. Position it in a light, although not necessarily sunny, location, and it will be better if the growing temperature is around 16°C (60°F), as warmer temperatures tend to produce softer and less attractive plants.

The soil should be kept moist, but not saturated for long periods, though much will depend on the growing position; in sunnier spots it will obviously be necessary to water more often. Use free-draining loam-based mixture when potting on. When established, the plants need frequent feeding.

To encourage bloom:
Keep the plant fairly cool in airy surroundings. 45♦

Camellia japonica
(Common camellia; Tea plant)
- **Good light**
- **Temp: 10-16°C (50-60°F)**
- **Keep moist with rain water**

These make fine garden plants in sheltered areas if the soil in which they are growing is acid rather than alkaline.

Perhaps not so good for the indoor location, they are nevertheless excellent plants for porches and conservatories that offer a little shelter from the elements. Plants that are grown from seed sown in the spring, or from cuttings rooted in the autumn, can be purchased in small pots from good retailers.

With careful handling these small plants can be gradually potted on until they are in containers of 25cm (10in) in diameter – use the acid soil recommended for camellias at each potting stage, and collect rain water for watering.

In time plants of about 150cm (5ft) in height will have developed, and in early spring there can surely be nothing more appealing than camellia blooms in white, pink or red.

To encourage bloom:
Maintain cool conditions. 45♦

Right: Begonia semperflorens
*Long an outdoor favourite, the wax
begonia is small and pretty. The
flowers appear on and off for many
months making it a valuable asset in
the indoor garden.* 35♦

Below: Begonia 'Orange Rubra'
*A fine angelwing begonia with
handsome leaves spotted in white,
and cascades of orange flowers.* 34♦

41

Above: **Brassavola nodosa**
*Small but with charm, this orchid has
needlelike leaves and heavenly
scented white flowers that perfume
the whole room at night.* 38♦

Left: **Billbergia pyramidalis**
*Golden-green leaves and orange-
pink flower bracts make this easy to
grow bromeliad a favourite.* 36♦

Right: **Bougainvillea**
*This popular red or purple flowering
climbing plant is perfect for the
sunny window. With careful culture it
will bloom freely throughout the
summer. Needs support; very
tropical and pretty.* 37♦

Above: **Browallia speciosa**
This delightful plant is now available in compact hybrids that flower freely. They can be placed outdoors during the summer months. 38♦

Below: **Calanthe vestita**
Do not let the fact that this orchid is deciduous deter you; it makes up for its bareness in winter with dainty pink-purple and white blooms. 39♦

Above: **Callistemon citrinus**
*Brilliant colour makes callistemon a
popular plant, but it is large and
requires space. Blooming in summer
or autumn and rather unusual, it adds
interest to the indoor garden.* 40♦

Right: **Camellia japonica**
*Many varieties of fine flowering
evergreens for that cool location.
Flower colours range from white to
red. Outstanding.* 40♦

Above: **Cattleya Bob Betts 'Mont Millais'**
Known as the corsage flower, cattleyas are always sure to please the indoor gardener. The flowers are large and generally fragrant. C. Bob Betts 'Mont Millais' is a fine white and a parent of many cattleya hybrids. 59♦

Left: **Capsicum annuum**
This lovely decorative plant has handsome brilliant red, yellow or purple fruit in winter. 57♦

Above: **Catharanthus roseus**
*Rose red flowers in summer make
this a fine seasonal plant for indoors.*

*New plants are best started from
cuttings or seed each year. Unusual
and worth the space.* 58♦

Above: **Celosia argentea 'Pyramidalis'**
The red or yellow flowers resemble plumes. An ideal plant for the windowsill, as dwarf varieties grow to only 30cm (12in). Generally pale green, the leaves of some varieties are a beautiful bronze. 59♦

Above: **Columnea microphylla**
*With tiny leaves and bright scarlet
and yellow flowers, this trailing
gesneriad creates a sensation.
Needs warm, humid conditions.* 64▸

Below: **Citrus mitis**
*A handsome small tree, C. mitis
bears tiny oranges in winter, making it
a decorative windowsill plant. Ideal
for small places. Easy to grow.* 61▸

Above: **Coelogyne ochracea**
Pretty as a picture, this dainty harbinger of spring has yellow and white flowers. A fine orchid. 63♦

Left: **Crocus**
Yellow crocuses are usually the earliest to bloom of the large-flowered varieties. Bring them into the warm only when the buds begin to show colour. 65♦

Right: **Clivia miniata**
If you can't grow anything, this plant will make you a gardener. Easy to bloom each spring with magnificent clusters of orange flowers. Handsome straplike dark green leaves. Highly recommended. 62♦

Above: **Cymbidium hybrids**
This large group of orchids offers handsome long-lasting flowers in an array of colours. The miniature hybrid shown here is called Elmwood, an easy to grow and very elegant variety. 67♦

Left: **Cuphea ignea**
The black and white ashlike tips of the red tubular flowers give this abundantly blooming plant its common name of cigar flower. 66♦

Right: **Cyclamen persicum**
Cyclamen grow wild in Greece and along the eastern shores of the Mediterranean. Hybrids from these are highly prized indoor flowering plants. They come in beautiful pastel shades; always desirable. 66♦

Above:
Dipladenia splendens 'Rosea'
An elegant climbing plant that needs warmth and humidity to flourish. Plants will flower at 25cm (10in). 68♦

Above right:
Dendrobium Gatton Sunray
This colourful dendrobium is hard to resist. With a little extra care the plant will bloom twice a year. 67♦

Right: **Encyclia cochleata**
The cockleshell orchid is easy and superb for unusual flowers. 68♦

Above: **Episcia cupreata**
This is one of the popular episcias, with fine scarlet flowers and leaves that look sugar-coated. 71♦

Left: **Episcia dianthiflora**
From tropical Mexico, this white flowering episcia is a favourite houseplant; decorative foliage adds to its appeal. Use it in hanging containers for maximum display. 71♦

Campanula isophylla

(Bellflower; Falling stars; Italian bellflower; Star-of-Bethlehem; Trailing campanula)
- **Good light**
- **Temp: 10-16°C (50-60°F)**
- **Keep moist, but dry in winter**

This exquisite plant is available in both pale blue and white colouring. The species is quite tough, but will be happier in lower temperatures, around 10°C (50°F), than it will be if grown in hot, stuffy rooms.

The leaves are small and pale green in colour and flowers are bell-shaped and produced continuously over a very long period from spring through into autumn. To encourage the maximum number of flowers, it is advisable to remove all dead flowers as soon as they appear.

Set off to best effect when grown in hanging baskets or containers, these plants will need frequent watering and ample feeding during spring and summer.

In the autumn when they are becoming more miserable in appearance they can be severely cut back, kept on the dry side, then repotted in the spring to start life all over again.

To encourage bloom:
Pinch off flowers as they fade.

Capsicum annuum

(Ornamental chilli; Red pepper)
- **Good light**
- **Temp: 10-16°C (50-60°F)**
- **Keep moist and fed**

These bright red-fruited plants are raised from seed sown in the spring in temperatures of not less than 21°C (70°F). When large enough to handle, the tiny seedlings are transferred from their initial boxes or pans to small pots filled with loam-based mixture, and subsequently go on into 13-18cm (5-7in) pots depending on the size of the plants required.

When in their final pots, it is much better to place the plants out of doors in full sun for the summer months, plunging pots in peat to reduce the amount of watering needed.

At all times full light is essential, and this is of particular importance once the fruits have formed, as they fall alarmingly when light is poor – during fog for example. Discard these plants at the end of the growing season.

To encourage bloom:
Give ample sun and ventilation. 46♦

Catharanthus roseus
(Vinca rosea)
(Madagascar periwinkle)
- **Sunny location**
- **Temp: 13-18°C (55-65°F)**
- **Keep moist and fed**

This is a charming, trouble-free little plant that may be easily grown from seed sown in the spring or from tip cuttings taken at the same time of year. Cuttings of about 7.5cm (3in) in length should be taken from plants of the previous year and inserted in peat and sand mixture at a temperature of about 21°C (70°F).

Leaves are a bright glossy green and flowers may be either white or pink. It is really best to treat these as annuals so that fresh plants are raised in the spring each year and older plants discarded. A loam-based potting mixture will suit them best and once they have got under way it is advisable to remove the growing tips to encourage a more compact shape. They should be kept on a bright windowsill; while in active growth keep moist and feed with a weak liquid fertilizer at each watering.

Cattleya forbesii
- **Good light**
- **Temp: 13°C (55°F) min.**
- **Evergreen/semi-rest**

Discovered in Brazil in 1823, this orchid is a bifoliate of dainty growth, with pencil-thin pseudobulbs. Its yellow tan-coloured flowers, produced in summer, are 7.5-10cm (3-4in) across, and have a tubular lip with side lobes of pale pink on the outside, and a deep yellow throat marked with wavy red lines.

This is an easy plant for the beginner and is also suitable for culture in an indoor growing case. It should not be overpotted, but kept in as small a pot as possible; unlike many cattleyas it rarely becomes top heavy. It should be grown in a position of good light all the year round and during the summer months can be lightly sprayed with water, taking care to avoid the flowers while in bloom. At one time this plant was considered a rather insignificant member of the genus, but today its small, pastel flowers are welcomed as charming and delicate.

To encourage bloom:
Raise new young plants. Feed well when growing actively. 47♦

To encourage bloom:
Lightly syringe with clean water.

Cattleya hybrids

(Corsage flower)
- **Good filtered light**
- **Temp: 13°C (55°F) min.**
- **Evergreen/some rest**

The cattleya hybrids produce spectacular flowers up to 15cm (6in) across, ranging in colour from deep lavenders and pinks through to pure glistening white.

For best results grow these plants in a greenhouse and provide stable temperature conditions, with 13°C (55°F) as a winter night minimum. Maintain a humid but buoyant atmosphere. Bright filtered light is preferable to direct sun. Using medium-grade fir bark as the potting mix, they can be grown in various containers such as pots, pans and baskets. Good drainage is essential.

By choosing a selection from the many hybrids available, it is possible to enjoy a display of these stunning flowers throughout the year. Many of the hybrids need a resting period after they have flowered. The plants are not usually bothered by insect pests.

To encourage bloom:
Keep plants dry while in flower. 46♦

Celosia argentea

(Cockscomb; Plume celosia; Prince of Wales' feathers)
- **Good light**
- **Temp: 10-16°C (50-60°F)**
- **Keep moist and fed**

The variety *C. argentea* 'Cristata' is generally referred to as the 'cockscomb' because the bract it produces resembles the comb of the cockerel. The variety 'Pyramidalis' has plumed flowers in red or yellow. In any event, these are annual plants that are produced in large quantities both for indoor decoration in pots and for use as a bedding plant in the garden.

Over the years there have been many new varieties of this plant, but most have a somewhat grotesque appearance and leave much to be desired, but they clearly have attraction for some indoor-plant growers. Cheapness has some bearing on *C. argentea*'s popularity. Although it is discarded after flowering, the plant is very easily raised from seed sown in the spring. Seedlings are subsequently pricked off, and grown on in larger pots – the eventual size of pot dictating to some extent the dimensions of the mature plant.

To encourage bloom:
Keep cool and bright. 48♦

Chrysanthemum
(Florist's mum)
- **Good light**
- **Temp: 13-18°C (55-65°F)**
- **Keep moist**

This has become one of the world's most popular flowering pot plants, mainly because it can be produced at any time of the year by commercial growers with the right sort of equipment and facilities.

The natural flowering time of this plant is from late summer through the autumn when about two thirds of the day is dark. It is these conditions that cause chrysanthemum flower buds to initiate and subsequently come into flower. However, by using black polythene to cover plants over and reduce the amount of daylight, the grower can simulate autumn light conditions and induce plants to flower at an unnatural time. Additional artificial lighting can be used to extend the day length if required.

Trouble-free indoors, these plants need good light, moisture, and weak feeding. Plant in the garden after flowering; they will survive where winter conditions allow but dwarfed forms will grow tall.

To encourage bloom:
Keep plants very moist.

Cineraria
(Senecio cruentus)
- **Good light**
- **Temp: 13-18°C (55-65°F)**
- **Keep moist and fed**

The compact, coarse green leaves and bright daisy flowers of this plant make it one of the most popular pot plants among the cheaper range. Ideally, seed should be sown in early spring and plantlets pricked off and potted on as they establish themselves.

Seed should be chosen wisely, and where growing space is limited the more miniature varieties should be selected. Seed of larger-growing types will develop into plants of splendid size in time if potted on and given regular feeding. A loam-based mixture is important as these are greedy plants that thrive on ample nourishment, both from the soil in which they are growing and from the subsequent feeding that they receive.

When raised in a greenhouse the cineraria can become the host for every pest that has ever been thought of, so inspect plants regularly and treat accordingly.

To encourage bloom:
Keep cool and fed.

Citrus mitis
(Citrofortunella mitis)
(Calamondin orange)
- ● **Sunny location**
- ● **Temp: 13-18°C (55-65°F)**
- ● **Keep moist and fed**

Citrus mitis is one of the most decorative of potted plants when its branches are festooned with perfectly shaped miniature oranges. The glossy green foliage will become yellow if underfed, particularly from magnesium deficiency – to combat this deficiency treat with sequestered iron.

Full light is essential, but foliage may become scorched if plants are placed too close to window panes on very sunny days. During the summer months plants will do better if placed out of doors in full sun. While in the garden it is important not to neglect feeding and watering. Failure to keep the soil moist will result in shrivelling of leaves.

White, heavily scented flowers appear in late summer. To help with pollination draw your hands through the flowers periodically. Flowers are followed by small green fruits that will in time develop into miniature oranges – dozens of them!

To encourage bloom and fruit:
Put plants outdoors in the summer and keep them moist. 49▼

Clerodendron thomsoniae
(Bleeding heart vine; Glory bower)
- ● **Good light**
- ● **Temp: 16-21°C (60-70°F)**
- ● **Keep moist and fed**

This is a useful plant for spacious surroundings, or for training against the wall of a heated greenhouse or conservatory. It is a natural climbing plant, the stems of which will entwine themselves around any sort of climbing framework that may be provided.

New plants are started from cuttings taken from any firm shoots that are not producing flowers – a temperature of about 21°C (70°F) is needed to encourage rooting. When a reasonable amount of root is evident the young plants can be potted into small pots filled with loam-based potting soil.

In the early stages of growth a temperature minimum of 18°C (65°F) should be the aim, with a slightly lower level for plants that are established in larger containers. The plant has coarse green leaves attached to woody stems, but the red and white flowers that develop in clusters are the main attraction. Prune to shape after flowering.

To encourage bloom:
Prune after blooming is over.

Clivia miniata
(Kaffir lily)
- **Shade**
- **Temp: 16-21°C (60-70°F)**
- **Keep moist**

To encourage these plants to flower freely, keep their roots in pot-bound condition – not a very difficult task as they very quickly make sufficient root to fill existing containers. Getting these plants to produce their exotic orange bell-flowers is always a problem, but older plants will usually reward the patience expended on them in the end.

Leaves are thick, broad, and strap-like and are produced from very large bulbous stems at soil level. Clean leaves with a damp cloth to keep them looking their best. Inevitably, plants will require quite large pots as they mature, and when potting on it is advisable to use a loam-based mixture that will sustain the plant over a longer period of time.

Having outgrown their pots and perhaps their allotted space indoors, the bulbous clumps can be divided to make new plants.

To encourage bloom:
Grow slightly potbound and keep dry during winter rest. 51♦

Coelogyne cristata
- **Good light**
- **Temp: 10°C (50°F) min.**
- **Evergreen/dry rest**

Perhaps the most familiar of the genus, this species likes to grow on undisturbed into a specimen plant. The flower spike appears from the centre of the new growth and its snowy-white flowers, broken only by a blotch of golden yellow at the centre of the lip, appear in mid-winter and last for four or five weeks.

Although the genus contains well over 100 species, few coelogynes are found in collections today. This is a pity, for they are orchids of great merit. They are, in the main, easy to grow and many species thrive in cool conditions, requiring a warmer environment only during their active growing season. Rest well in winter to achieve flowering.

Many coelogynes are suitable for growing on into specimen plants. However, be warned: a specimen plant of one of the larger-growing species can take up a considerable amount of space in the greenhouse. Fortunately, it is possible to choose from a wide range of smaller-growing species.

To encourage bloom:
Observe winter rest period.

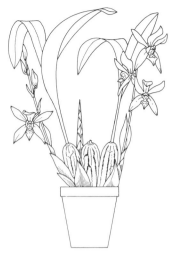

Coelogyne ochracea
- **Good light**
- **Temp: 10°C (50°F) min.**
- **Evergreen/dry rest**

This popular species from India has shiny green pseudobulbs topped by a pair of leaves. The flower spikes are produced freely from the new growth while it is very young. Like all coelogynes, it prefers to be grown on into a specimen plant with as little disturbance as possible, although this species is unlikely to become unmanageable in size. The flowers are extremely pretty and full of fragrance.

After flowering grow the plant on well into the autumn, by which time the season's growth will have matured and the plant will rest. Place in full light for the winter and withhold all water until the new growths appear in early spring. The pseudobulbs will shrivel during this time but they will quickly plump up again when normal watering is resumed.

Ideal for beginners, it is equally at home growing indoors or in a cool greenhouse.

To encourage bloom:
Keep plant dry at the roots durings its winter rest period.

Columnea banksii
(Goldfish vine)
- **Light shade**
- **Temp: 16-21°C (60-70°F)**
- **Keep moist, but drier in winter**

This much-neglected plant has many fine qualities, not least the fact that it is not at all difficult to rear and is almost totally free of pests. Evergreen, oval-shaped leaves are a dull green in colour and are attached to woody stems. Initially, the stems are supple and will hang naturally over the container in which the plant is growing, but in time they become rigid.

Besides the distinct advantage of being a natural hanging plant, this columnea will also oblige with a wealth of reddish-orange flowers in early spring when flowering houseplants are not so plentiful.

However, getting plants to produce their flowers can be a problem, but one way is to keep the soil very much on the dry side during winter and at the same time lower the growing temperature by several degrees. New plants are easily started from cuttings.

(See also Columnea banskii variegata, page 220.)

To encourage bloom:
Observe winter rest period.

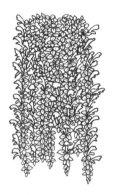

Columnea microphylla
(Goldfish vine)
- **Shade**
- **Temp: 18-21°C (65-70°F)**
- **Keep moist, drier in winter**

This is one of the more difficult columneas to grow successfully. The difficulty lies in the fact that it requires a constant temperature in the region of 18-21°C (65-70°F). Nevertheless, once the challenge is accepted, the results can be very rewarding. The small, oval-shaped, pale-green leaves are attached to wiry stems that hang perpendicularly from the container in which the plant is growing. Essentially, it is a hanging plant and can only be seen at its best when provided with a hanging pot or basket in which to grow.

Flowers, generally produced during the summer months, are rich orange and red in colour and on mature plants are produced in great abundance. Something that adds to their attraction is that mature plants in large baskets may have trails 1.8m (6ft) or more in length, and may well have flowers from top to bottom.

It is important to keep the soil moist and to feed regularly with weak liquid fertilizer.

To encourage bloom:
Keep dry during winter. 49♦

Convallaria majalis
(Lily of the valley)
- **Light shade**
- **Temp: 10-16°C (50-60°F)**
- **Keep moist**

This popular garden plant grows from a creeping horizontal rhizome and bears delicate white bell-shaped flowers. The leaves grow in pairs, and are mid-green and elliptical. Though spring-flowering out of doors, the plants can be induced to bloom in winter indoors. They take up little space, growing only 20cm (8in) tall, and, with their sweet fragrance, make an attractive addition to any indoor garden.

New plants can be grown from rhizomes planted in the autumn. The rhizomes should be put in shallow bowls of sphagnum moss and soil and kept in a cool, shaded area of the greenhouse until January. The plants must be kept cool while growing – never above 16°C (60°F) – and the soil must be evenly moist. After January, the plants can gradually be introduced to the sunlight and the warmth of the house. Flowers will open in about three weeks.

To encourage bloom:
Do not allow soil to dry out.

Crocus
- **Good light with sunshine**
- **Temp: 7-16°C (45-60°F)**
- **Keep moist while growing**

Flowering crocuses on the windowsill give a clear indication that spring is on the way, but one has to think of them in early autumn, when the corms are planted. Bold groups in shallow pans filled with houseplant soil are better than small pots with a few wispy leaves and flowers. They must be planted in early autumn and put in a dark, cool place outdoors to develop the essential roots before shoot growth begins.

A simple way of creating dark conditions is to place a black flower-pot over the pot holding the corms. Once growth begins, the corms can be exposed to the light and taken indoors, where they will quite quickly start to bloom. Flowers will last for a longer period in cool and airy conditions than in warmer, stuffy rooms. After flowering, the corms should be planted out in the garden, or stored to flower in new soil the following season.

To encourage bloom:
Keep corms dark and cool in early stages; then provide warmth and light as growth begins. 50♦

Crossandra infundibuliformis
(Firecracker flower)
- **Good light**
- **Temp: 16-21°C (60-70°F)**
- **Keep moist**

These are neat plants for the windowsill, needing light and airy conditions, with some protection from strong sunlight. The soil needs to be kept moist at all times, with less water being required in winter. In winter there will also be no need to feed plants, but while in active growth they will respond to feeding with weak liquid fertilizer. Vigorous plants will tolerate and benefit from feeding at every watering. An alternative to liquid feeding would be the use of tablet or stick-form fertilizers that are pressed into the soil and made available to the plant over a period of several weeks.

Naturally glossy green leaves are topped by bright orange flowers in the spring, with the possibility of further flowers later in the year. New plants can be started from seed or cuttings.

To encourage bloom:
Provide plants with good air circulation at all times.

65

 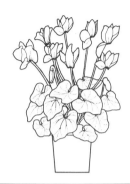

Cuphea ignea

(Cigar flower; Firecracker flower; Mexican cigar plant)
- **Good light**
- **Temp: 10-16°C (50-60°F)**
- **Keep moist and fed**

This is a straggly plant with a mass of tiny leaves pin-pointed with an abundance of red tubular flowers. The ends of the tubular flowers are lipped with blackish-grey colouring not unlike cigar ash – hence the appropriate common name of 'cigar flower'.

New plants can be raised from seed sown in the spring or from stem cuttings taken in late summer. When only one or two plants are required it is usually better to purchase established plants, so saving the bother of overwintering or raising seed plants.

Cupheas are very easy to manage on a light windowsill, needing no particular attention other than the usual watering and feeding. Once established in 13cm (5in) pots no further potting is needed, as plants will tend to become too large. Discard after flowering.

To encourage bloom:
Provide bright light. 52♦

Cyclamen persicum

(Alpine violet; Poor man's orchid; Shooting star)
- **Good light**
- **Temp: 10-16°C (50-60°F)**
- **Keep moist, but dry after flowering**

Ever popular, the cyclamen has a cool beauty that is matched by few other plants. Centrally heated rooms kept at excessively high temperature can be its worst enemy. On a cool windowsill that offers good light the life of the cyclamen indoors will be much extended.

Water well by pouring water on to the soil surface and ensuring that surplus water is seen to drain through the holes in the bottom of the pot; repeat only when the foliage feels limp to the touch. But never allow leaves and flowers to flag excessively.

Clear out dead flowers and leaves complete with their stems to prevent rotting. Following flowering, plants die back naturally and should be stored cool and dry until new growth is evident – which is also the time to pot on.

To encourage bloom:
Give plenty of water. Keep the plants cool and humid (but do not spray the flowers). Give resting period. 53♦

Cymbidium hybrids
- **Protect from strong sun**
- **Temp: 10°C (50°F) min.**
- **Evergreen/no rest**

Dendrobium Gatton Sunray
- **Good light**
- **Temp: 13°C (55°F) min.**
- **Evergreen/dry winter rest**

Cymbidium hybrids have rightly gained a reputation throughout the world. There are hundreds to choose from, both large plants and the delightful, easy-care miniatures.

The miniature hybrid cymbidiums provide an alternative for the grower with limited space. Being smaller and more easily managed plants, they can be accommodated in the home. Their more compact blooms are just as rewarding, and are often of rich colouring.

To achieve regular flowering all cymbidiums should be repotted every other year. Use a potting mix of peat moss, sand, perlite and fir bark.

Cymbidiums, particularly if grown in the drier indoor atmosphere, can be prone to attacks from red spider mite. Regular sponging and wiping of the leaves with water, particularly the undersides, will keep this at bay.

A magnificent hybrid, this is the largest of the cultivated dendrobiums, and requires plenty of growing space. It is an extremely robust plant, the canes growing to a height of 2m (6.5ft) or more. The extremely large and showy flowers, which appear in trusses during the early summer, are more than 10cm (4in) across and last in perfection for about ten days. A large plant will produce numerous trusses, each carrying several flowers. This will extend the flowering period, as not all the trusses come into flower at the same time.

The plant succeeds best in an intermediate greenhouse where it can be given good light and a decided rest during the winter months. In view of its large size, this plant should not be attempted where adequate space and light cannot be given.

To encourage bloom:
Give full light in winter, but provide shade in summer. 52♦

To encourage bloom:
Provide good light. 55♦

Dipladenia splendens 'Rosea'

(Pink allamande)
- **Good light**
- **Temp: 16-21°C (60-70°F)**
- **Keep moist and fed**

This is a natural climbing plant best suited to the heated conservatory or greenhouse, but a challenging plant that will be good for the ego of the houseplant-grower who cultivates it successfully. Indoors, it is best to confine the roots to pots of modest size so that growth is restricted. However, very small pots are often difficult to manage, so pots of 13cm (5in) diameter will be best.

For potting, use a loam-based mixture as opposed to a very peaty mix, which will tend to produce soft growth.

During the summer months healthy plants are festooned with attractive soft pink flowers, and these are the principal feature of the dipladenia. After flowering the plant can be pruned to shape, if needed.

The soil should be kept moist without being totally saturated for long periods, and regular feeding will be beneficial when growth is active.

To encourage bloom:
Keep in a sunny place. 54♦

Encyclia cochleata

(Cockleshell orchid)
- **Shade from direct sun**
- **Temp: 10°C (50°F) min.**
- **Evergreen/slight rest**

A subject for the cool house, this South American species produces flattened pear-shaped pseudobulbs about 18cm (7in) tall. The flowers resemble the shape of an octopus in water, with their thin green sepals and petals which droop down below the rounded, dark purple lip.

Several flowers are produced at a time in succession on a flowering spike which, on a large mature plant, can continue flowering for up to two years. Such is the vigour of this species that this is no way impairs its new growth, with the result that two years' flower spikes can be in flower at the same time.

It is one of the few orchids that can be repotted while in bloom. This will be necessary when the new growth has started in the spring. The old leafless pseudobulbs can be removed for propagation. When potted up singly they will readily develop new growths.

To encourage bloom:
Do not overwater. 55♦

Encyclia mariae

- **Shade from direct sun**
- **Temp: 9°C (48°F) min.**
- **Semi-deciduous/dry rest**

This species of orchid is cool-growing and blooms during the summer. One to five flowers are carried on a thin stem, each being about 5cm (2in) wide; the sepals and petals are lime green and the very broad lip, which is often the widest part of the flower, is pure white.

The flowers are extremely large for the size of the plant, and last well. The plant should not be heavily watered at any time and is intolerant of soggy conditions. Allow the plant to rest while not in active growth, and keep in a fairly shady aspect. Propagation from the oldest pseudobulbs is slow: it is better to leave them on the plant provided it is healthy. The plant should not be sprayed, as the leaves are susceptible to water marks.

This plant can also be grown on a piece of bark, where it should be allowed to remain undisturbed for a number of years. If too many leafless bulbs build up, these should be removed very carefully without disturbing the plant.

To encourage bloom:
Do not overwater.

Encyclia vitellina

- **Shade from direct light**
- **Temp: 10°C (50°F) min.**
- **Evergreen/dry rest**

The most colourful of the South American encyclias, this orchid likes to be grown under cool greenhouse conditions, and will also do well indoors, where it is more tolerant of the drier conditions. The pseudobulbs are oval and carry two blue-green leaves. The flower spike appears at the top of the bulb from between the leaves and grows to 30cm (12in) or more in length on a large plant. At least 12 star-shaped flowers of the most brilliant orange-red are produced on branching stems. The narrow lip, in balance with the rest of the flower, is orange. The blooms are long-lasting, and a colourful sight in the early autumn.

The plant can be grown in a pot or, where greenhouse culture is provided, mounted on a piece of cork bark, where it will make a fine specimen. It will prefer the slightly drier conditions afforded to this type of growing. A dry rest is required for the duration of the winter while the plant is inactive. Overhead spraying is not recommended, as the foliage easily becomes water marked.

To encourage bloom:
Do not overwater.

Epidendrum ibaguense
- **Good light**
- **Temp: 9°C (48°(F) min.**
- **Evergreen/no rest**

Epidendrums seem to divide naturally into two categories: those with oval or rounded pseudobulbs, and those that produce reed-like stems *E. ibaguense*, also known as *E. radicans*, is a reed-stem species. The stems vary from 60-150cm (2-5ft) in height according to environment and produce rounded leaves and many aerial roots over most of their length. The flowers (2.5cm; 1in) are orange-red or scarlet, the lip flat and very frilled. This is a plant for the cool greenhouse with good light. One successful specimen is known to have flowered continuously for four years.

The epidendrums form one of the largest orchid genera; over 1,000 species are known, coming mainly from Central and South America. So varied are the plants accepted within the genus, in vegetation and flower size and appearance, that some groups have been accorded a genus of their own. Those that remain within the genus are epiphytic.

To encourage bloom
Avoid high temperatures.

Epidendrum stamfordianum
- **Good light**
- **Temp: 13°C (55°F) min.**
- **Evergreen/dry rest**

This Central American orchid produces tall, club-shaped pseudobulbs that carry two or three thick leaves. The branching flower spike comes from the base of the plant, a unique feature among the epidendrums. The flower spike is many flowered; the fragrant blooms are yellow, spotted with red. The plant likes to be grown fairly warm, in a position of good light, and is therefore best suited to a reasonably warm greenhouse. It should be well watered during the summer growing season and allowed a complete winter's rest. The plant may be grown in a pot or on bark, where it will grow an extensive aerial root system. Propagation is best achieved by division of the main plant when it is large enough.

This large-growing plant is a good example of a bulb-type epidendrum as distinct from the reed type. It is also one of the most attractive epidendrums, although it is not frequently seen in collections.

To encourage bloom:
Secure mature plants.

Episcia cupreata
(Flame violet)
- **Good indirect light**
- **Temp: 16-21°C (60-70°F)**
- **Keep on the dry side**

Episcia dianthiflora
(Lace flower)
- **Light shade**
- **Temp: 13-18°C (55-65°F)**
- **Keep on the dry side**

This is an attractive plant that grows in a pendulous fashion and looks good in small hanging pots. Leaves are an attractive greyish silver and green, and flowers, though small, are of brilliant red colouring and appear for many months in the middle of the year. Where growing conditions are to their liking, these plants can be grouped in hanging baskets of reasonable size to make a splendid feature in a room.

Good light is essential, but strong, direct sunlight should be avoided. In terms of temperature there is little to worry about in the summer, but the winter temperature should not drop below 16°C (60°F). Plants need to be potted with a peaty mixture.

In winter it is important to give water sparingly and only when it is really needed by the plant. Winter feeding is not necessary, but plants will benefit from regular applications at other times.

A delightful plant, *E. dianthiflora* has small rosettes of green leaves and produces mis-shapen tubular flowers, white in colour with lace-like, ragged edges to the petals. Growth hangs perpendicularly on stems that will become firm as they age, which makes this one of the best natural trailing plants for indoors.

Avoid excessively wet conditions; aim to give the potting mixture a good watering and allow it to dry quite appreciably before repeating. If plants are growing in hanging pots with drip trays attached it is important to empty these trays an hour or so after watering to ensure that the soil does not become too saturated. Feed established plants occasionally, but do not overdo it; pot on only when the plants are very well rooted. Raise new plants from the rosettes of leaves.

To encourage bloom:
Provide adequate humidity. 56♦

To encourage bloom:
Provide adequate humidity. 56♦

Erica
(French heather; Heath)
- **Good light**
- **Temp: Below 16°C (60°F)**
- **Keep moist**

There are numerous types of ericas, or heathers as they are more commonly known, but for the most part they will develop into neat mounds of needle-like foliage with colourful flowers appearing throughout the year. Individual varieties produce their blooms over a period of weeks, but from a well-chosen collection you could get flowers throughout the year, even in winter.

Almost all the ericas that grow outside will also do very well in large shallow containers. They should be periodically clipped to retain their shape and can spend most of their time on the patio out of doors, being brought in while in flower. In the home these plants require the lightest and coolest location for a long life. Following the flowering period, transfer the plants to the patio and trim any untidy growth.

Eucharis grandiflora
(Amazon lily)
- **Good indirect light**
- **Temp: 13-18°C (55-65°F)**
- **Keep dry when resting**

Grown from bulbs placed one to a 13cm (5in) pot, these are indeed exciting plants to grow, both indoors and in a frost-protected greenhouse, where they should be placed in good light but not full sunlight. The plant's broad green leaves are pleasing enough in themselves, but it is not until the creamy white flowers appear that the full beauty of this easy-care plant is appreciated.

Following flowering and natural dying down of the foliage it is essential that the plant be kept very dry and allowed to rest in a cool, dry place until new growth is evident, when watering can begin again in the normal way. Ideally, resting plants should be placed on their sides under the greenhouse staging. If treated in this way plants will be more inclined to produce their exotic flowers. Feed occasionally with liquid fertilizer when in leaf.

To encourage bloom:
Keep cool and bright. 75♦

To encourage bloom:
Observe rest period. 73♦

Above: **Eucharis grandiflora**
Bright white glistening flowers and large dark green leaves combine to display nature at her best. Highly recommended for indoor gardens. The blooms are fragrant. 72♦

Left: **Exacum affine**
Exacum has small fragrant flowers that last into the winter months. 90◆

Above: **Erica Hyemalis**
This winter-flowering erica can be grown successfully indoors in cool conditions. 72◆

Below: **Euphorbia pulcherrima**
This popular indoor plant is tough to beat for midwinter colour with its large showy bracts in shades of red, pink or white. This photograph shows several individual plants grouped together, each one of which produces bracts of a single colour. 90◆

Above: **Fuchsia 'Snowcap'**
Lovely plants with pendent flowers in various colours, fuchsias can be difficult but worth the trouble. Highly regarded as an indoor plant where growing conditions are suitable. 91♦

Right: **Freesia**
Available in many different colours, the graceful flowers of freesias are exquisitely scented. Beautiful for indoor display as cut flowers. 91♦

Below: **Gardenia jasminoides**
Very popular but difficult to bloom, with lovely scented white flowers. 92♦

Above: **Gomeza crispa**
An attractive orchid with dainty sprays of flowers appearing in the summer. Easy to grow. 93♦

Above right:
Gloriosa rothschildiana
A fine tuberous plant with narrow leaves and showy orange, crimson and yellow flowers in summer. 92♦

Right: **Guzmania lingulata 'Minor Orange'**
A fine small bromeliad, this guzmania has a rosette of apple green leaves. A spectacular orange inforescence that lasts for several months puts this plant high on anyone's list for indoor colour. Be sure to keep the humidity high. 93♦

Above: **Heliotropium hybrid**
The fragrant purple flowers of heliotrope bloom from spring to autumn. A dependable plant for the beginner to grow with confidence. 95♦

Below: **Heliconia angustifolia**
Very tropical in appearance, with orange bracts and green-white flowers. Different, and one of the best heliconias for indoors. 95♦

Above: **Haemanthus katharinae**
Once coaxed into bloom, the
rewards are certainly worth the effort
– the bright red flower head will
certainly dazzle the eye. Needs
plenty of sun to thrive indoors. 94♦

Above: **Hibiscus rosa-sinensis**
*Many varieties grow and bloom
indoors, with large colourful flowers.
Try in tubs in a garden room.* 96♦

Left: **Hyacinthus orientalis**
*The very fragrant packed flower
spikes make hyacinths an indoor
favourite. Varieties are available in
many colours. Take your pick from
white, yellow, pink or blue.* 98♦

Above right: **Hoya bella**
*This fine plant has waxy clusters of
fragrant white-purple flowers that
perfume a room. Especially
rewarding in hanging baskets.* 97♦

Right: **Hoya australis**
*Blooming in summer or autumn, this
plant from Australia has small white
waxy flowers with a tinge of red around
the centre. Grow potbound.* 97♦

Above: **Hypocyrta glabra**
Known for their goldfish shaped
orange flowers, hypocyrtas are
compact plants; the shiny leaves of
this species make it handsome even
when not in bloom. 99♦

Left: **Impatiens wallerana**
One of the easiest houseplants to
grow, busy Lizzie produces red or
white flowers throughout the year.
Easy tc propagate from cuttings. 100♦

Right: **Hydrangea macrophylla**
Lacecap type
Shrubby plants with fine clusters of
pink, blue or white flowers; a traditional
and very successful houseplant for
cool rooms. 99♦

Above: **Ixia hybrid**
The rich crimson blooms of the corn lily provide dazzling indoor colour in late spring. Very free-flowering, but it must be kept cool all the time. 100♦

Right: **Jacobinia carnea**
A handsome Brazilian plant with dark green leaves and plumes of pink flowers. Nice amenable plant for a sunny window. Easy to grow. 101♦

Above: **Ixora coccinea**
'Peter Rapsley'
*A charming and undemanding plant
with beautiful clusters of red flowers
in early summer.* 101♦

Above: **Jasminum polyanthum**
*Grow this vigorous climber in a cool
greenhouse and provide support.
The fragrant flowers open from
midwinter until spring.* 102♦

Above: **Kohleria amabilis**
A gesneriad with lovely green leaves and beautiful pink flowers in spring and summer. Makes a fine show in a hanging basket, but needs warm and humid conditions to thrive. 102♦

Eulophia guinensis
- **Good light**
- **Temp: 18°C (65°F) min.**
- **Deciduous/dry rest**

Most of the 20 known species of the orchid genus *Eulophia* come from tropical and sub-tropical Africa, and almost all are terrestrial. The genus can be divided roughly into two groups according to vegetation and flower form.

In one group, the plants have a broad, pear-shaped pseudobulb that produces fairly long deciduous leaves that fall when the growing period is completed. The sepals and petals of the flowers are small in comparison with the lip, which is the main attraction.

E.guinensis belongs to this group and is probably the most familiar. After a cool, dry rest throughout the winter the plant should be brought into the warm house and encouraged into growth by light and watering. When growth is still in progress, the flower spike appears and grows to a height of 60-90cm (2-3ft), producing six to 15 flowers. The lip is 2.5-4cm (1-1.6in) in diameter, spade-shaped and rose-pink with darker veins.

To encourage bloom:
Keep moist and in good light.

Euphorbia fulgens
(Scarlet plume)
- **Good light**
- **Temp: 16-21°C (60-70°F)**
- **Keep on the dry side**

This is an untidy sort of plant that produces small but brilliantly coloured scarlet flowers in early spring – a good time for indoor flowering plants when there is so little colour around. Like the more common *E. pulcherrima* (poinsettia) the bright scarlet flower is in fact a bract that surrounds the smaller and insignificant central flowers.

New plants can be grown from tip cuttings about 10cm (4in) in length, which should be inserted in clean peat moss and kept at a temperature not less than 21°C (70°F). The sap of this euphorbia can cause skin irritation, so gloves must be worn when the stem of the plant is being cut. Feed occasionally. Avoid both wet and cold conditions.

Plants will grow to a height of about 120cm (4ft) in ideal conditions. Check regularly for mealy bugs which may infest this plant if it is grown in too dry an atmosphere.

To encourage bloom:
Keep plant in bright light.

Euphorbia pulcherrima
(Christmas flower; Poinsettia)
- **Good light**
- **Temp: 16-21°C (60-70°F)**
- **Keep moist and fed**

This plant with its bright red, creamy green, or pink-coloured bracts is by far the finest of all winter-flowering indoor plants. The end of autumn to early winter is their natural flowering time and, given reasonable care, they will continue in colour for many months.

Avoid temperatures below 16°C (60°F) and be careful to water plants and allow them to dry reasonably before repeating. Feeding should never be to excess – weak liquid fertilizer can be given each week, and this should be sufficient for most plants.

To get plants to flower for a second year indoors ensure that only natural daylight is made available from early autumn until early winter. When not in flower, prune to shape.

Tip cuttings can be taken from new side-shoots after the bracts have dropped. Wash the poisonous latex from the cut end and insert in an equal mix of peat and sharp sand.

To encourage bloom:
Be sure a dark period is given. 74♦

Exacum affine
(Arabian violet; German violet; Persian violet)
- **Good light**
- **Temp: 13-18°C (55-65°F)**
- **Keep moist and fed**

In small pots on the windowsill there can be few prettier plants than *E. affine,* which has glossy green foliage and scented lavender-blue flowers. An added bonus is that, if old flowerheads are removed, the plant will continue in flower for many months from midsummer onwards.

In common with almost all flowering plants this one should have a very light location in which to grow. But very strong sunlight must be avoided, particularly when it is being magnified by window panes. Besides being a good individual plant *E. affine* is an excellent subject for including in mixed plant arrangements. Keep established plants moist and fed. New plants should be raised annually from seed.

New varieties with bright blue and with white flowers are available, so extending the colour range of this delightful plant.

To encourage bloom:
Keep plants humid and brightly lit, and pick off flowers as they fade. 74♦

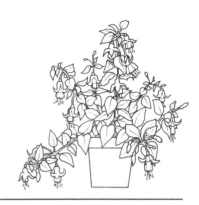

Freesia
- **Good light**
- **Temp: 10-16°C (50-60°F)**
- **Moist; dry in winter**

Among the most fragrant of all flowers the freesias are available in many wonderful colours, and will fill the entire room with their scent. The small bulbs belong to the iris family, and should be planted in loam-based houseplant soil in the autumn. Plant just below the soil surface and place bulbs almost touching in a shallow pot about 18cm (7in) in diameter. Pots are then placed in a cool, sheltered place (an unheated greenhouse, for example) in good light to establish. Once under way they can be transferred to a warmer location to develop their flowers, and placed on a light and cool windowsill indoors when blooms are present. Freesias are excellent as cut flowers, too.

Keep moist while in leaf; feeding is not normally necessary as bulbs are planted in fresh soil each autumn. Dry off and store bulbs after flowering.

To encourage bloom:
Keep cool and brightly lit. 76♦

Fuchsia
(Lady's eardrops)
- **Sunny location**
- **Temp: 13-18°C (55-65°F)**
- **Keep moist, and feed well**

Given proper care this is possibly the best of all the potted plants as far as flower production and length of season goes. They can produce blooms from spring until early autumn with a seemingly never-ending display. But they can also be extremely disappointing for the indoor plant grower, as fuchsias must have maximum light if they are to flower as well as they might. It will often mean that plants are happier and produce more flowers if grown on the windowsill outside the window rather than the sill in the room. In poor light indoors it will be impossible for plants to produce flowers.

A loam-based potting mix is essential for healthy plants. Keep them moist and well fed while in active growth, and prune back severely in the autumn when they begin to lose their summer sparkle.

To encourage bloom:
Mist spray plants regularly to maintain a high humidity. Provide as much light as possible. 76♦

Gardenia jasminoides
(Cape jasmine)
● **Light shade, no sun**
● **Temp: 18-21°C (65-70°F)**
● **Keep moist**

Gloriosa rothschildiana
(Glory lily)
● **Good light**
● **Temp: 13-18°C (55-65°F)**
● **Keep moist, but dry when dormant**

These are shrubby plants with small oval-shaped green leaves that will have a marked tendency to take on chlorotic yellow colouring if conditions are not to the liking of the plant. They are difficult plants to care for, needing a temperature of not less than 18°C (65°F), a lightly shaded location, and careful watering and feeding. Rain water is preferable to tap water and it will benefit plants if the foliage is misted over with water when the atmosphere tends to be dry. Frequent weak feeding will be better than giving occasional heavy doses. Use an acid-type fertilizer and pot the plants in an acid or peat-based mixture.

But, in spite of the problems, the gardenia is well worth trying to raise, as there are few flowers that can match its heavy, overpowering scent. Flowers are creamy white and up to 10cm (4in) across.

These showy plants have glossy leaves and upright habit. They produce a wealth of exotic flowers during the summer months in orange and yellow with a crimson edge.

Plants should be started from tubers; these should go one to an 11.5cm (4.5in) pot in peaty soil and later be transferred to pots of about 18cm (7in) in diameter when the smaller pots are well filled with roots. Use a loam-based mixture at this stage and put at least three of the contents of the smaller pots into the larger one, so that a good show comes into flower.

It is also wise to place three or four 150cm (5ft) canes around the edge of the pot to which plants can be tied as they develop. Rest tubers during winter in a cool dry place.

To encourage bloom:
Keep in constant warmth and high humidity as flower buds form. 76♦

To encourage bloom:
Keep plants moist when growing actively but be sure to provide dry dormant period. 79♦

Gomeza crispa
- **Light shade**
- **Temp: 10°C (50°F) min.**
- **Evergreen/no rest**

This epiphytic orchid is a plant for the cool greenhouse, requiring some protection from full light during the summer months. Free drainage for the root system is of great importance and for this reason it is a good subject to grow on a raft or piece of cork bark. If grown in a pot, a coarse material, such as fir bark, should be used. As the plant grows upwards, away from the pot, the roots should be allowed to grow outside, where they should gain sufficient nourishment from the atmosphere. Spraying during the summer is helpful.

The plant produces pseudobulbs and leaves similar to those of odontoglossums, only paler in colour. The flowers are carried on arching sprays, up to 23cm (9in) long, and there are often two sprays to a pseudobulb. The sweetly scented, lime-green flowers, about 1.25cm (0.5in) across, are densely clustered on the spike and appear during the summer and autumn.

To encourage bloom:
Syringe with clean water.

Guzmania lingulata
(Orange star; Scarlet star)
- **Good light**
- **Temp: 13-18°C (55-65°F)**
- **Keep on the dry side**

Belonging to the fine bromeliad family, there are a number of guzmanias that can be found in the quest for new plants to add to the houseplant collection, and all of them will be very easy to manage indoors.

The growing habit is that of most bromeliads – the plant forms a stiff rosette of leaves that protrude from a short and stout central trunk. Overlapping leaves make a natural watertight urn, which must be kept filled with water. However, it is advisable to empty the urn and refill with fresh water periodically. Rain water is preferred but try to avoid getting the soil in the pot too wet. Impressive orange-scarlet bracts develop on short stems from the centre of the urn during winter. New plants can be started from offsets.

Bromeliads should be grown in a free-draining mixture; equal parts of a loam-based medium and peat will be ideal. Alternatively, use a prepared bromeliad mix.

To encourage bloom:
Grow in bright filtered light. 79♦

Haemanthus katharinae

*(Blood flower; Blood lily;
Catharine wheel)*
- **Good light**
- **Temp: 16-21°C (60-70°F)**
- **Keep moist, dry when dormant**

Haemanthus are grown from bulbs
planted to a little over half their depth
in a free-draining, loam-based
potting mixture. To help with the
drainage incorporate a good amount
of sand and ensure that some
drainage material – pot shards, for
instance – is placed in the bottom of
the pot before adding the mixture.

Water sparingly until green
leathery leaves appear, then more
freely, but never to excess. On
stems about 30cm (12in) in length
the plant bears globes of small
orange-red flowers in late spring.
Place single bulbs in pots of 13cm
(5in) diameter and continue growing
the plants in the same potting
mixture for several years to get the
best results. When foliage naturally
colours at the end of the summer
allow the soil to dry completely and
store the bulb in a warm dry place.

To encourage bloom:
Grow in bright light when active and
repot only when roots appear on the
surface of the soil. 81♦

Hedychium gardnerianum

(Kahli ginger)
- **Good light**
- **Temp: 16-21°C (60-70°F)**
- **Keep moist, and feed well**

These plants of the ginger family
(Zingiberaceae) can be grown by
dividing the rhizomes in the spring
and planting them independently.
Once under way plants will grow
apace and in time will require
containers of about 25cm (10in)
diameter. Once established, these
plants need regular feeding. Lemon-
yellow flowers are produced in
summer on stems that may be
120cm (4ft) or more in length.
Immediately after flowering, these
stems should be cut down.

Where the climate permits, the
plants in their pots can be placed out
of doors during the summer months.
They make excellent terrace plants
when in decorative containers.
Water freely in summer, but plants
must be brought indoors before the
weather turns cold and wet.

To encourage bloom:
Provide plenty of sunshine and keep
plants moist and fed.

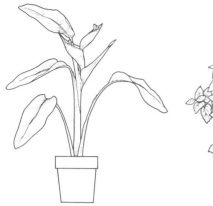

Heliconia angustifolia
- **Good light**
- **Temp: 13-18°C (55-65°F)**
- **Keep moist; dry winter rest**

Heliotropium hybrids
(Cherry pie; Heliotrope)
- **Sunny location**
- **Temp: 13-18°C (55-65°F)**
- **Keep moist and fed**

A native of Brazil and belonging to the same family of plants as the banana, *H. angustifolia* flowers during the summer months. Flowers are white and green in colour with scarlet spathes and can be quite dramatic against glossy green foliage.

New plants can be started by dividing roots in early spring and planting them in 13cm (5in) pots filled with a loam-based potting mixture. These are hungry plants and will quickly exhaust the goodness contained in an all-peat growing medium.

Plants should be freely watered during the summer months and will benefit from having the foliage misted with water at regular intervals each day. Feed well during these active months. No water is required during the winter months when the plants are resting.

To encourage bloom:
Grow in bright light and give dry winter rest. 80♦

An old-fashioned plant that is as popular as ever, being easy to care for and free-flowering both in the garden and on the windowsill indoors.

New plants may be grown from seed sown in the spring, or from stem cuttings inserted in a peaty houseplant mixture. Cuttings of non-flowering pieces about 10cm (4in) in length can be taken at any time during the summer months. Once under way it is advisable to remove the growing tips of the young plants to encourage branching. Standard plants can be grown, but this will take some time and entails growing a single stem that should be stripped of all foliage except for the topmost cluster of branches. These plants must be protected from winter cold.

The attractive flowers appear in the summer and, depending on the variety, are violet, lavender or white in colour. The plants are generally disease-free.

To encourage bloom:
Water freely while in growth. 80♦

Hibiscus rosa-sinensis

(Chinese hibiscus; Chinese rose; Rose mallow)
- **Sunny location**
- **Temp: 13-18°C (55-65°F)**
- **Keep moist and fed**

These shrubby plants are widely dispersed throughout the tropics. They make fine indoor plants for the very light window location. Special growth-depressing chemicals are used to keep the plants short and compact, and to induce abundant blooms.

Trumpet flowers in numerous colours remain open for only a single day, but they are constantly being renewed from new buds during the summer months. It is important that plants have the best possible light and that the soil does not dry out during spring and summer; less water is required in winter.

Harsh pruning is not necessary, but in the autumn plants may be trimmed back to better shape. In the spring, when new growth is evident, pot the plants on into slightly larger containers. Use a loam-based mixture for best results.

To encourage bloom:
Keep in constant temperature; sudden changes may cause buds to drop. Provide ample sunshine. 82♦

Hippeastrum hybrids

(Amaryllis)
- **Good light**
- **Temp: 13-18°C (55-65°F)**
- **Keep moist; dry winter rest**

Production of high-quality hippeastrum bulbs is one of the great skills of the more specialized commercial growers. But once matured, and in good light, these bulbs will produce their exotic trumpet flowers in a range of many colours. These are carried on stout stems 90cm (3ft) or more in height.

Bulbs can be purchased complete with their pots and growing soil and simply require the addition of water to start them growing. They should be kept moist but not excessively wet. However, problems can arise in subsequent years as not everyone can manage to get these plants to flower a second time. It helps to continue to feed the bulb and leaves after flowering until such time as the foliage dies down naturally, when the soil should be dried out and the plant stored cool and dry for the winter.

To encourage bloom:
Grow in bright light when active. Observe rest period.

Hoya australis

(Porcelain flower; Wax plant; Wax vine)
- **Good light**
- **Temp: 16-21°C (60-70°F)**
- **Keep moist and fed**

These attractive plants will climb or trail. To climb they will need a supporting frame, and to trail a hanging basket is ideal. The growing tips should be removed to encourage a bushy appearance. However, avoid unnecessary pruning as plants produce their flowers from older rather than new growth.

A loam-based, well-drained potting mixture should be used and the addition of a little charcoal when potting will prevent the mixture becoming sour. Remember to keep plants on the dry side during winter.

New plants can be raised from stem cuttings taken from the previous year's growth and inserted in peat and sand at a temperature of about 21°C (70°F). Or, more simply, trailing pieces of stem can be pegged down during the summer and then cut from the parent plant and potted individually when they have rooted.

To encourage bloom:
Grow in bright light. 83♦

Hoya bella

(Miniature wax plant)
- **Light shade**
- **Temp: 16-21°C (60-70°F)**
- **Keep on the dry side**

When well established and in full bloom there can be few more rewarding plants than *Hoya bella* growing in a hanging container. The small pale green leaves are attached to wiry stems, but it is the flowers hanging in clusters that are the main attraction. Individual flowers have the appearance of exquisitely cut jewels, white in colour flushed with a delicate shade of pink.

For best results use a loam-based potting mixture that incorporates a reasonable amount of sand to ensure good drainage. If the hanging container is provided with a built-in drip tray, then check an hour or so after watering and tip away any surplus water in the tray. Also, check regularly for signs of mealy bug on the undersides of leaves.

To encourage bloom:
Do not prune or move plants in bud. Give winter rest. 83♦

Hoya carnosa
(Wax plant)
- **Good light**
- **Temp: 13-21°C (55-70°F)**
- **Keep moist and fed**

Hyacinthus orientalis
(Hyacinth)
- **Good light**
- **Temp: 10-16°C (50-60°F)**
- **Keep moist; dry rest**

The twining stems and dark green leaves of this vigorous plant are quick to grow but the flowers that sprout from the leaf and stem joints are slow to appear. They are more likely to appear first on mature plants, but the clusters of pendulous pink jewels are well worth waiting for. As with all the hoyas, let the old flowers fall naturally and do not break off the flower stalks as these are the source of the following year's flowers.

This hoya makes a rather untidy basket plant, and is seen to best effect when trained to a framework of some kind. In this respect the plant is well suited to a heated conservatory, where growth can be trained overhead so that the flowers can be admired to full advantage when they appear. Well-draining, loam-based potting mixture is essential. Give frequent checks for mealy bugs in branches.

During the winter there can be few more pleasing sights than a bowl of colourful and fragrant hyacinth flowers. It is essential to purchase bulbs that have been specially prepared to flower at this time, as ordinary bulbs will not succeed. Plant three or more bulbs in a peaty, fibrous mixture during the autumn and then plunge the pot to a depth of about 13cm (5in) out of doors in peat or sand. In these cool conditions the bulbs will develop a sound root system, and plants can be taken indoors when growth is evident. Alternatively, keep the pot indoors in a cool, dark place for several weeks.

In warm rooms flowers will go through their cycle more rapidly, so it is advisable to provide a cool room and, perhaps, bring the plants into the sitting room for special occasions! After flowering, plant in the garden.

To encourage bloom:
Maintain good light as buds form.

To encourage bloom:
Bring into warmth gradually.

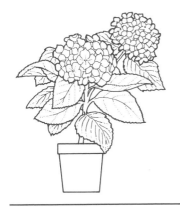

Hydrangea macrophylla
Common hydrangea; House hydrangea; Snowball flower)
- **Good light**
- **Temp: 10-16°C (50-60°F)**
- **Keep wet; rest in winter**

The quality of hydrangeas offered for sale as potted plants, like every other potted plant, varies enormously. So, when purchasing hydrangeas ensure that they have fresh green leaves and are not simply a few leaves at the top of a leafless stem with a few ragged flowers attached. Quality plants in many varieties are available, so choose well.

Hydrangeas in pots are offered in the spring and from the moment of acquisition they must be thoroughly watered until the autumn, when plants die back and should be rested overwinter.

Good light and cool conditions are also essential, and when plants have finished flowering indoors they may be placed on the terrace in tubs, or planted in the garden where they should be protected against spring frost. Take stem cuttings in the summer for new plants.

To encourage bloom:
Keep cool and bright. 85♦

Hypocyrta glabra
(Goldfish plant)
- **Light shade**
- **Temp: 16-21°C (60-70°F)**
- **Keep just moist; drier in winter**

With so many plants to choose from, the glossy green succulent foliage and curiously shaped orange flowers make the hypocyrta an excellent plant for rooms offering limited space. Plants can be grown conventionally in pots on the windowsill, or they may be placed in smaller hanging containers. As hanging plants the generally drier conditions that prevail will suit hypocyrtas as they are capable of storing a considerable amount of water in their attractive puffy leaves.

Temperatures in the range 16-21°C (60-70°F) will suit them fine, as will a watering programme that errs on the side of dry rather than wet. These are hungry plants, but an occasional feed will keep them in good trim and help to retain their bright green colouring. New plants can be raised from stem cuttings.

To encourage bloom:
Do not overwater. 84♦

Impatiens wallerana

(Busy Lizzie; Patience plant; Patient Lucy; Snap weed; Sultana; Touch-me-not)
- **Good light**
- **Temp: 10-16°C (50-60°F)**
- **Keep wet and fed**

Capable of attracting a wide assortment of destructive pests, impatiens is, nevertheless, one of the most appealing of all our less costly potted plants.

Good light is essential, and the feeding of established plants is a must. Purchased plants that appear too large for their pots – and this is often the case – should be potted into larger containers without delay. The potting mixture should be loam-based, and the new pot should be only slightly larger than the existing one. In fact, impatiens is one of those odd plants that will tolerate potting more than once in a season. They can develop into splendid plants in time and are also very good in hanging baskets. Remember, though, to inspect frequently for pests and use appropriate remedies without delay.

To encourage bloom:
Allow soil to dry between waterings. Young plants produce flowers most readily – keep taking cuttings. 84♦

Ixia hybrids

(Corn lily; Grass lily)
- **Good light**
- **Temp: 10-16°C (50-60°F)**
- **Keep moist; give winter rest**

The hybrids of *Ixia* come in many delightful colours that will brighten any windowsill. Flowers are fragrant and carried on slender stems.

For a full and pleasing effect try planting five bulbs in a well-draining, loam-based mixture in 13cm (5in) diameter pots in late autumn. Plant the bulbs 7.5cm (3in) deep and place the pots in a dark, cool place until growth is evident. The pots can then be transferred to a cool windowsill indoors. Feeding is not necessary, but the soil must be kept moist, with care being taken to avoid saturation over long periods.

When the foliage begins to die back naturally, cease watering and store the bulbs in a dry, frost-free place until the next season. Do not try planting in the garden: ixias are not hardy out of doors in most temperate climates.

To encourage bloom:
Grow cool and bright once these plants are active. 86♦

Ixora coccinea
(Flame of the woods; Indian jasmine)
- **Good light**
- **Temp: 16-21°C (60-70°F)**
- **Keep moist; drier in winter**

Jacobinia carnea
(Brazilian plume; King's crown)
- **Good light**
- **Temp: 16-21°C (60-70°F)**
- **Keep moist and fed**

As the name suggests, *I. coccinea* has brilliant red flowers, but there are also many other colours. All are robust plants growing to a height of about 90cm (3ft).

While in active growth these plants will need regular feeding, but none in winter. The same with watering – ample when plants are in growth, but very little over the winter period. In common with most flowering pot plants these will need a light location in order to obtain the maximum numbers of flowers.

New plants can be grown from cuttings 7.5-10cm (3-4in) long taken in spring and placed in fresh peat at a temperature of about 18°C (65°F). At all stages of potting a proprietary potting mixture is important. It is also essential to ensure that the soil is well drained. Pruning to shape can be done in early spring.

This attractive plant has pink flowers that bloom in late summer but there are other varieties occasionally available. Take cuttings of young shoots about 10cm (4in) in length in the spring, using fresh peat and a heated propagator to encourage rooting. Older plants should be cut down to the base after flowering and will flower in subsequent years, but it is often better, if space is limited, to produce new plants from cuttings and to discard the older plant.

While in active growth this vigorous plant will need regular feeding to retain leaf colouring, and ample watering. If an old plant is kept for the following year it will require no feed and little water during the winter. *Jacobinia carnea* is an ideal garden-room plant.

For mature plants use a loam-based potting mixture and repot regularly as the plant grows. Give a winter rest at about 13°C (55°F).

To encourage bloom:
Grow in warm, moist conditions without sudden changes. 87♦

To encourage bloom:
Provide ample light. Take cuttings for vigorous young plants. 87♦

Jasminum polyanthum
(Pink jasmine)
- **Good light, some sunshine**
- **Temp: 10-16°C (50-60°F)**
- **Keep moist and fed**

This climbing plant produces rampant growth in ideal conditions and must have some sort of framework for the spiralling growth to wind around. In winter, plants must be kept in the coolest possible place and will tolerate being out of doors if frosts are not expected.

New plants can be raised very easily from summer-struck cuttings, several cuttings going into a 13cm (5in) pot after they have been rooted in pans or boxes of peat. Use loam-based potting mix, putting the more robust plants in time into 18cm (7in) pots. Provide a fan-shaped framework in the pot so that foliage is well spread, which will in turn display the flowers to best effect when they appear.

The flowers are more white than pink in colour, but the unopened buds are a delicate shade of pink. Feed and water well while active.

Kohleria amabilis
(Tree gloxinia)
- **Good light**
- **Temp: 16-21°C (60-70°F)**
- **Keep moist and fed**

Plant *Kohleria amabilis* in hanging containers suspended at head level to appreciate fully the attractive bright green foliage and to enjoy the flowers to the full when they appear in late spring and early summer.

However, encouraging plants to produce their attractive pink blooms is not easy. Moist soil, a humid atmosphere and a light position will all help flowering. A further encouragement would be the use of a houseplant food specifically recommended for flowering plants – one that has a fairly high potash content, as opposed to nitrogen. If special fertilizers are unobtainable, try one of the many fertilizers recommended for tomato plants.

Raise new plants by taking cuttings of young shoots in late spring, or by dividing the rhizomes in early spring. Use a peaty soil for potting.

To encourage bloom:
Grow cool and bright. 87♦

To encourage bloom:
Grow warm and humid. 88♦

Laelia anceps
- **Good light**
- **Temp: 10°C (50°F) min.**
- **Evergreen/dry winter rest**

Some 75 species of *Laelia* have been recorded, almost all from Mexico and the northern parts of South America. Though in appearance both plant and flower are similar to the cattleyas, with which many intergeneric hybrids have been made, it is a delightful genus in its own right, and is favoured by many growers. As with cattleyas, its flower spikes are produced from the apex of the pseudobulbs. The flower spike grows erect to 60cm (2ft) or more and produces two to five flowers, each about 10cm (4in) across. They are pale or deep rose-pink in colour, the lip being a darker hue.

This is an excellent species for the beginner. It can be grown easily in a cool greenhouse or indoors, where it enjoys light conditions. If preferred, it can be grown on a block of wood or cork bark, when an extensive aerial root system will develop.

Propagation is a simple matter of separating the back bulbs and potting them up singly.

To encourage bloom:
Grow cool and bright. 97♦

Laelia gouldiana
- **Good light**
- **Temp: 13°C (55°F) min.**
- **Evergreen/dry winter rest**

One of the most popular of the epiphytic Mexican laelias. The club-shaped pseudobulbs are topped with one or – more often – two stiff, dark green leaves that are pointed at their tips. The flower spike appears from the apex of the partially completed bulb during the autumn and grows to 45cm (18in) in height carrying three to five brightly coloured cattleya-like flowers. Their colouring is a rich rose-purple, the lip similarly coloured. They last for several weeks during the early half of the winter.

This orchid is suitable for the warmest end of the cool greenhouse in a position of good light. Light is very important for successful flowering and for this reason the plant does not always flower well as a houseplant. Plants are at their best when grown into large specimens; continued division can cause them to miss a flowering season. The spring growth is often slow to start and it may be summer before the plants really get going.

To encourage bloom:
Avoid shady positions.

Laelia purpurata
- Moderate light
- Temp: 13°C (55°F) min.
- Evergreen/dry winter rest

This orchid is the national flower of Brazil and deserves the honour. Growing to a height of 45-60cm (1.5-2ft) including the leaf, the plant produces a short spike of two to six flowers, each 13-18cm (5-7in) in diameter. Very variable in colour, the narrow sepals and petals range from white to pale purple, with a frilled deep purple lip.

Moderate light is required and a well-drained compost is important; no laelia does well if there is an excess of water at the root. The plant requires a definite period of rest, when little or no water should be given.

This species has always been extremely popular with collectors but it is now becoming increasingly difficult to obtain. Many commercial nurseries are now raising it from seed using selected clones. Therefore, it should not die out in cultivation in the foreseeable future.

To encourage bloom:
Give a definite rest period.

Lantana camara
(Common lantana; Shrub verbena; Yellow sage)
- Good light
- Temp: 10-18°C (50-65°F)
- Water and feed well

For indoor use it is better to prune lantanas to shape annually in autumn so that a neat and compact shape is maintained. Stems are twiggy and leaves mid-green in colour. The plant will not be difficult to care for if given good light and cool conditions.

Healthy plants in the right surroundings will produce masses of globular flowers throughout the summer months; in poor light, flowers will be less plentiful. Flowers themselves are something of an enigma, as one may see flowers of varying colour on the same plant.

While they are growing more actively in summer, keep plants well watered and fed, but give less water and no feed in winter. Keep a careful check for white on the undersides of leaves, and treat as soon as noticed. This will mean the plant is infested with whitefly.

To encourage bloom:
Provide ample sunshine 106♦

Above: **Laelia anceps**
A large orchid but well worth its space; bears 10cm (4in) pink flowers that last for two months or more on the plant. Very showy in bloom. Needs plenty of sun to thrive. 103♦

Above: **Lilium auratum**
What could be nicer than these fine large white lilies in the home? In pots they add a colourful note to the window garden in summer. 122♦

Below: **Lantana camara**
Lantanas make fine indoor plants, with their yellow and orange flowers and rather odd wrinkled leaves. Good for your brightest window. 104♦

Above: **Lapageria rosea**
The beautiful flowers of this vining plant – here the red with the white-flowered variety – make a stunning show in summer and autumn. Excellent if you have room. 121♦

Above: **Manettia bicolor**
This vining plant will grow well indoors and produce tubular flowers about 2cm (0.8in) long in summer. Prune severely in spring to prevent the plant becoming straggly, and feed and water generously during the growing period. 124♦

Above right: **Lycaste aromatica**
This popular small orchid is ideal for those new to orchid growing. 123♦

Right: **Leptospermum scoparium**
Providing it receives plenty of light, this plant is easily grown indoors. 121♦

Above: **Masdevallia coccinea**
Beautiful flowers shaped like kites make this plant look very unlike the orchid it is. Handsome foliage; worth space in cool situations. Provides welcome winter colour. 124♦

110

Above: **Medinilla magnifica**
And magnificent it is in bloom, with pendulous panicles of carmine flowers in pink bracts. 125♦

Below: **Miltonia Peach Blossom**
A fine small orchid with flat-faced pink flowers, large for the size of the plant. A popular variety. 125♦

Above: **Nerine bowdenii**
This bulbous plant produces a welcome display of attractive pink flowers in autumn. 127♦

Above left: **Miltonia roezlii**
An easy orchid to grow in most situations, this miltonia has white flowers tinged with purple, which last many weeks on the plant. 126♦

Left: **Nerium oleander**
Bushy and big but colourful, with pink, white or red flowers at intervals throughout the summer. 127♦

Right: **Narcissus tazetta 'Paper White'**
Even the novice gardener can bring this lovely white-flowering plant into bloom indoors. Fragrant. 126♦

Above: **Oncidium papilio**
The famous 'butterfly orchid' grows well in warm houses and flowers at various times. It does, however, need special care. 130♦

Right: **Odontioda Jumbo 'Mont Millais'**
One of the brilliantly coloured hybrids of Odontoglossum and Cochlioda. A stunning indoor plant. 128♦

Above: **Passiflora caerulea**
Known for its spectacular 7.5cm (3in) flowers of white, blue, and purple, here is nature at her best. A large vine that needs space. 132♦

Left: **Pachystachys lutea**
A shrubby plant with lance shaped leaves and clearly marked veins; overlapping yellow bracts protect the white tubular flowers. 131♦

Right: **Odontoglossum grande**
A most dependable orchid, with large yellow and brown flowers that last for weeks. Sure to bloom. 129♦

Above: **Pelargonium zonale**
Compact clusters of single or double blooms above ring-marked leaves signify these classic geraniums. Ideal for beginners. 133♦

Below: **Pelargonium peltatum 'Rouletti'**
A new bicoloured hybrid. Trailing geraniums, ideal for hanging baskets, prefer a little shade. 133♦

Above: **Pelargonium grandiflorum 'Fanny Eden'**
Large, multicoloured flowers make these hybrids a particular favourite. Like most pelargoniums, they thrive in bright but cool conditions. 133♦

Above: **Pentas lanceolata**
*Showy umbels of pink flowers make
Pentas a great beauty. A compact
and amenable houseplant.* 134♦

Left: **Pleione formosana
'Snow White'**
*Can't grow anything? Try this
exquisite white flowering orchid from
China. Sure to please – with lovely
10cm (4in) blooms in spring.* 135♦

Lapageria rosea
(Chilean bellflower; Copihue)
- Good light
- Temp: 10-18°C (50-65°F)
- Keep moist; drier in winter

L. rosea can be a most rewarding plant to grow, providing all the right conditions can be met. In an ideal situation the plant will produce elegant funnel-shaped flowers that hang in the most graceful fashion. There are a number of colours available but many people feel that the original crimson form and the white-flowered variety make a stunning combination when grown together.

Grow in a lime-free potting mixture and use rain water when watering. Provide a framework either in the pot or against the wall for the foliage to climb through. Plants flower mainly in the summer and attain a height of about 4.5m (15ft). Provide good drainage and water with care, avoiding hot and dry conditions.

Prune lightly after flowering to take out weak growths. Propagate by seed sown in early spring or by layering strong shoots. Spray against aphids on young shoots.

To encourage bloom:
Maintain lime-free conditions. 107♦

Leptospermum scoparium
(Manuka; tea tree)
- Good light
- Temp: 13-18°C (55-65°F)
- Keep moist and fed

This small-leaved evergreen shrub bears a profusion of rich pink, five-petalled flowers in the summer, though cultivars also exist with white or red blossom. Growing to a height of 1m (40in), the species originates from New Zealand and there are many different varieties.

Grow the shrub in equal parts soil and humus, and keep the mixture moist, being careful that it is neither too soggy nor too dry. Positioning the plant in a south-facing window is best as it requires plenty of sunlight, though it can tolerate a cool atmosphere of 7°C (45°F). The plant should be fed regularly with plant food.

Repot every third year and take cuttings from ripe wood in August. Seeds can be grown in March in a good seed compost.

To encourage bloom:
Only mature plants bear flowers so buy a specimen that is a few years old. 108♦

Lilium auratum

(Golden-rayed lily)
- **Good light, some sunshine**
- **Temp: 10-16°C (50-60°F)**
- **Keep moist; dry rest period**

These are not the easiest of plants to manage indoors if they are used as permanent subjects, but they are excellent as temporary plants brought indoors when in bloom.

Bulbs are ready for planting in the autumn and should be planted about half way down a 20cm (8in) pot filled with lime-free peaty mixture. After potting, place the plants in a sheltered spot outside (a cold frame, for example) and cover the pots with a 10-13cm (4-5in) layer of peat. When growth shows through, the plants can be taken into a cool room. Water moderately until the growth becomes more vigorous, then water more freely, using rain water for preference. Stems will require staking. These plants need repotting annually in fresh mixture.

Lilium longiflorum

(Easter Lily)
- **Good but diffused sunlight**
- **Temp: 10-16°C (50-60°F)**
- **Keep moist, but allow dry rest period**

This beautiful bulbous plant, up to 90cm (3ft) high, creates a dazzling display of white, heavily fragrant, trumpet-shaped flowers, 12.5-18cm (5-7in) long, during mid-summer. During autumn, pot up the bulbs 15cm (6in) deep in rich compost – they tolerate lime – and keep cool at 10-16°C (50-60°F) to encourage the development of root growth. When the shoots are 10cm (4in) high, move the pots to a bright and slightly warmer position. Keep the compost moist from flowering time to when the leaves start to yellow.

When flowering is over, reduce the temperature and keep the compost only slightly moist until autumn.

Repot with fresh bulbs in autumn, planting the old ones into a naturalized setting in the garden.

To encourage bloom:
Start in shade and coolness, then grow cool and bright. 106♦

To encourage bloom:
Start in shade and coolness, then grow in light shade.

Lilium speciosum
- **Good but diffused sunlight**
- **Temp: 10-16°C (50-60°F)**
- **Keep moist, but allow dry rest period**

This spectacular lily grows 1.2-1.8m (4-6ft) high and is superb for growing in a pot, where its late-summer white flowers create great interest. The flowers are fragrant, bowl-shaped and 7.5-13cm (3-5in) long, nodding and heavily shaded with crimson.

The bulbs should be potted up in autumn, in lime-free compost, and kept cool at 10-16°C (50-60°F). This cool period encourages the development of strong roots. When the shoots are about 4in (10cm) high, move the pots into a bright and slightly warmer position.

After flowering, keep the compost only slightly moist and move the pots to a cooler position. In autumn, plant out the bulbs into a naturalized part of the garden. Use fresh bulbs for forcing into flower the following year.

To encourage bloom:
Start in shade and coolness, then grow in light shade.

Lycaste aromatica
- **Good light**
- **Temp: 10-13°C (50-55°F) min**
- **Deciduous/dry winter rest**

As the name suggests, this species is heavily scented. The bright yellow flowers, 5cm (2in) across, often appear at the same time as the new growth, and are carried singly on a stem about 15cm (6in) long. There may be as many as ten flowers to each pseudobulb.

The plant needs moisture and warmth when in full growth, but take care not to get water on the large, broad leaves, as they tend to develop brown spots if this occurs. Cooler and drier conditions are essential when the plant is at rest and in flower.

Propagation is by removal of the older pseudobulbs, which should not remain on the plant for too many years. It is better to restrict the size of the plant to five or six bulbs, provided they remain about the same size; should the bulbs become smaller, remove all but three or four.

Between 30 and 40 *Lycaste* species are known, including both terrestrial and epiphytic plants.

To encourage bloom:
Keep cool and dry. 109♦

Manettia bicolor

(Candy corn plant; Firecracker plant; Firecracker vine)
- **Good light**
- **Temp: 16-21°C (60-70°F)**
- **Keep moist and fed**

To keep this plant under control requires a framework of some kind through which its twining growth can be trained. Depending on the shape wanted, taller supports can be provided for plants to climb.

New plants can be raised from spring-sown seed, or from cuttings of young growth taken in midsummer and kept warm. When potting, ensure that a liberal amount of sand and charcoal is incorporated in the mixture, which should be loam-based.

Water freely and feed frequently during the growing season, and moderately when growth slows up. Delightful tubular flowers – red with a yellow tip – appear throughout the summer months. Plants can be moderately pruned after they have flowered. During the summer *Manettia* will need protection from strong sunlight.

To encourage bloom:
Provide bright light all year round and keep plants moist and fed when growing actively. 108♦

Masdevallia coccinea
- **Shady conditions**
- **Temp: 10°C (50°F) min.**
- **Evergreen/no rest**

This is one of the most fascinating orchid genera, as remarkable for the uniformity of its vegetation as for the diversity of form and colour of its flowers. Three hundred species are recorded, growing mainly in the higher-altitude areas of Mexico, Brazil and Colombia. The structure of the flowers is in contrast to that of many orchids, as the sepals are very large in comparison with the other segments of the flower.

This species produces leaves 30cm (12in) in length, and the flower spikes are often much taller. These bear a single flower of 7.5-10cm (3-4in), with sepals that taper sharply towards the tips. The colour varies from lilac to deep crimson.

Because of the high-altitude conditions of its natural habitat, the cool house with plenty of shade and fresh air during the summer months provides the ideal environment. Masdevallias do not produce pseudobulbs – the thick leaves spring directly from a rhizome.

To encourage bloom:
Keep plants continually moist. 110♦

Medinilla magnifica
(Love plant; Rose grape)
- **Light shade**
- **Temp: 18-24°C (65-75°F)**
- **Keep moist and fed**

Native to the Philippines, this plant will be a test for all who are interested in houseplants, but the reward of seeing pink flower clusters suspended from healthy plants will make all the effort worthwhile. Warm conditions, around 21°C (70°F), and a lightly shaded location are essential. Plants must be watered well throughout the year, with slightly less needed in winter.

Pendulous flowers may appear throughout the year, with summer being the most prolific time. The plants have square-shaped stems from which the flowers sprout and develop in the most amazing fashion. Use a loam-based potting mixture to which some peat and leaf mould have been added. Feed when in active growth. To get the full effect of the pendulous flowers place the plant on a pedestal.

To encourage bloom:
Keep in humid conditions. Only mature plants will bloom. 111♦

Miltonia Peach Blossom
(Pansy orchid)
- **Medium light**
- **Temp: 13°C (55°F) min.**
- **Evergreen/no rest**

This is a typical *Miltonia* hybrid produced from the soft-leaved Colombian species commonly known as the 'pansy orchids'. These hybrids come in a wide variety of colours — white, yellow, pink and red. Peach Blossom is one of the most popular varieties with large, plum red flowers, the colour shading to white towards the edges.

This orchid and other similar hybrids should be grown in an intermediate greenhouse or a warm room. Their dislike of cold, damp conditions makes them ideally suited to the drier atmosphere in the home. Watering should be on a continuous basis; never allow the plants to dry out completely. The foliage should not be sprayed and feeding should be applied to the pot when watering. One weak feed every three weeks during the spring and summer should be sufficient.

Repotting should be done when the new growth is showing, which may be spring or autumn.

To encourage bloom:
Maintain stable conditions. 111♦

Miltonia roezlii

(Pansy orchid)
- **Medium light**
- **Temp: 13°C (55°F) min.**
- **Evergreen/no rest**

This extremely pretty plant is one of the soft-leaved Colombian species. It produces the typical neat oval pseudobulbs of the type and these are partially covered by soft, silver-green leaves. The flower spike appears from inside the first or second leaf on the newly completed bulb and carries two to four white flowers. The two lateral petals are painted purple at their bases and the lip has a yellow blotch that spreads out from the centre, or 'mask'. Although this plant is quite rare, supplies should be available from nursery-raised stock.

Although this species likes fairly warm conditions, it should not be allowed to suffer from too high temperatures. The intermediate section of the cool house will suit it. A beginner would find the many superb hybrids that have been raised from this species tolerant and easy to grow in suitable conditions.

To encourage bloom:
Maintain humid conditions. 112♦

Narcissus tazetta 'Paper White'

- **Sunny location**
- **Temp: 10-16°C (50-60°F)**
- **Keep moist; dry rest period**

This is just one example of the many fine bulbs that can be made to flower in pots indoors in early spring, so giving a feeling of spring before its arrival. To succeed, these bulbs have to be thought of in the autumn when they are being sold by retailers. Plant them in shallow pans filled with bulb fibre so that the tips of the bulbs are just poking through the surface of the mixture. After potting, place the planted bulbs in a corner out of doors and cover the pots with about 13cm (5in) of peat or sand, then forget about them!

When the growing tips are showing through the peat or sand surface, move the pots and put them in a cool place indoors. The warmer the place the quicker the bulbs will come into flower, and the shorter will be their life once they have flowered. Avoid excesses of temperature.

To encourage bloom:
Start in coolness and in the dark. Keep fairly cool in light conditions for long flowering period. 113♦

Nerine bowdenii
- **Sunny location**
- **Temp: 10-16°C (50-60°F)**
- **Keep moist; dry in summer**

These bulbous plants are native to South Africa, and most attractive when grown as pot plants indoors or as hardy plants in the garden. Good light and cool conditions are essential needs.

The bulbs are about the same size as those of small daffodils and should be planted five to a 13cm (5in) pot during late summer. Place drainage material in the bottom of the pot then half fill it with loam-based potting mixture. Place the bulbs on this mixture then fill in the remainder of the space with more soil, firming it around the bulbs and leaving the neck of the bulbs exposed. Keep the potting mixture moist. Oddly, these bulbs rest in bone dry condition from early to late summer, when they are best placed on a sunny shelf in the greenhouse. Potting on is seldom necessary. Beautiful pink flowers appear in the autumn before the leaves.

To encourage bloom:
Provide dry rest in summer. Grow in full sun. 113♦

Nerium oleander
(Oleander; Rose bay)
- **Sunny location**
- **Temp: 13-21°C (55-70°F)**
- **Keep moist and fed**

Another fine plant frequently seen in the tropics, and yet equally at home in agreeable conditions indoors. A light and sunny location is essential, and plants should be well watered in summer when in active growth — less is required in winter. The same rule applies with feeding, none in winter, but once or twice each week when producing new leaves.

The semi-double rose-coloured flowers are slightly pendulous, fragrant, and a joy to have about the house. Cuttings of non-flowering shoots can be taken at any time during the summer months. Prepare the cuttings about 13cm (5in) in length and insert them in peaty mixture in modest heat. Be sure to wear gloves when taking cuttings to prevent the sap getting on to your skin. This plant is extremely poisonous if any part of it is eaten. When potting use a loam-based mixture.

To encourage bloom:
Provide plants with as much sunlight as possible all year. 112♦

Odontioda
- **Good light**
- **Temp: 10°C (50°F) min.**
- **Evergreen/no rest**

Odontiodas result from crossing an *Odontoglossum* with a *Cochlioda*. The most often used cochlioda is *C. noezliana*, which brings its brilliant scarlet colouration to the resulting hybrids. There is a wide range to choose from; new varieties are being raised all the time, and these quickly supersede the older ones. The best way to make a selection is probably to visit a nursery, see the plants in flower, and take advice from the experts.

Odontiodas require cool growing conditions in a position of good light. These plants do not divide or propagate very easily and should be grown on into as large a specimen as possible. Leafless pseudobulbs should not be allowed to outnumber those in leaf and are always better removed when this stage is reached. Regular repotting is essential to ensure the compost remains fresh.

Odontoglossum bictoniense
- **Light shade**
- **Temp: 10°C (50°F) min.**
- **Evergreen/semi-rest**

Native to Guatemala, this orchid is a vigorous grower and will quickly grow into a specimen plant. Erect flower spikes appear at the end of the summer, growing quickly in warm weather to reach heights up to 120cm (48in) and bearing 20 long-lasting flowers on each spike. The flowers open in succession so that there are usually eight or nine out at once over a period of several weeks. The flowers are about 3-4cm (1.25-1.6in) across, yellowy green with brown spots and a striking white or pink lip.

O. bictoniense, which can be grown successfully as a houseplant, requires cool conditions with medium shade and does not need a total rest in winter, though water should be reduced when flowering has finished, until new growth appears in the spring.

This species is very variable. The plant is easily propagated from the leafless pseudobulbs.

To encourage bloom:
Grow cool and airy. 115♦

To encourage bloom:
Keep moist when in flower.

Odontoglossum grande

(Clown orchid; Tiger orchid)
● **Light shade**
● **Temp: 10°C (50°F) min.**
● **Evergreen/dry winter rest**

Known widely as the 'clown orchid' due to the clown-like figure represented by the column in the centre of the flower, this is certainly one of the most widely grown in this genus, and popular as a houseplant. The flowers are very large, up to 15cm (6in) across, yellow with bright chestnut-brown markings.

It has hard dark leaves and very tough pseudobulbs, and needs a decided rest during the winter months. During the growing season it needs plenty of moisture at the roots. As the new growth starts to make a pseudobulb towards the end of the summer the flower spike develops. Once flowering is finished and the pseudobulbs have fully matured, water should be withheld until spring, when the new growth appears. The plants need light shade and should be grown in a medium-grade bark compost. They should receive full light in winter.

To encourage bloom:
Observe winter rest period. 117♦

Odontoglossum pulchellum

(Lily of the valley orchid)
● **Light shade**
● **Temp: 10°C (50°F) min.**
● **Evergreen/slight rest**

An extremely popular and vigorous Guatemalan orchid. The waxy, white flowers, though small – 1-2cm (0.4-0.8in) across – bloom in masses and have a lovely scent, which explains why the plant is known as the 'lily of the valley orchid'. It flowers in spring and produces more than one shoot from each pseudobulb, making it ideal for growing into a specimen. The plants are thin-rooted and need cool conditions, a fine-grade bark mix, and medium shade in the summer.

If left unsupported the slender flower spikes will often assume a pendent position by the time they are in bloom. If an upright position is preferred, the spikes should be lightly tied to thin supporting canes, when the flowers will stand well clear of the foliage.

It can be easily propagated by the removal of back bulbs.

To encourage bloom:
Keep moist when in flower.

Oncidium ornithorhynchum
(Dancing doll orchid)
- **Good light**
- **Temp: 10°C (50°F) min.**
- **Evergreen/semi-rest**

An extremely showy species from Mexico and Guatemala, this plant has a compact habit and light green pseudobulbs each topped with several thin leaves. The short, slender and arching flower spikes are produced very freely in the autumn and carry the individual flowers on side branches. The colour is a soft rose-lilac with a yellow crest on the lip. They are long-lasting and beautifully fragrant.

Propagation is by division and removal of back bulbs, although the plant is at its best when grown on into a specimen. A very fine rooting system is produced, indicating that a well-drained compost is important. The plant dislikes cold and damp and should therefore not be sprayed overhead or kept too wet at any time. Otherwise, normal cool house conditions will suit it. It is a delightful beginner's orchid of great charm that will do equally well indoors.

To encourage bloom:
Grow cool and bright.

Oncidium papilio
(Butterfly orchid)
- **Good light**
- **Temp: 18°C (65°F) min.**
- **Evergreen/semi-dry rest**

Often referred to as the 'butterfly orchid' because of its resemblance to that insect, this species has flowers that open on the end of a long slender stem and sway in the slightest air movement. Only one per stem opens at any one time, but in succession, so that the plant is in flower for many months. The flowers, which can be up to 13cm (5in) across, are a mixture of chestnut brown and yellow.

The plant has squat pseudobulbs each of which supports a solitary, rigid, reddish-green leaf. The plant grows best on a raft suspended from the roof of the warm house, where it will get that little extra bit of light. It should never be kept too wet at the roots, and does best when kept continually on the dry side, relying upon the humidity in the greenhouse for most of its moisture. It should not be overhead sprayed.

To encourage bloom:
Keep warm and bright. 114♦

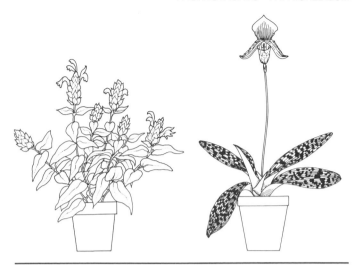

Pachystachys lutea
- Good light
- **Temp: 16-21°C (60-70°F)**
- Keep moist and fed

This is a relative of the more familiar aphelandra, but has less vividly marked foliage – the pachystachys having simple mid-green, roughly lance-shaped leaves. However, where the pachystachys scores is in its much longer flowering period and in the fact that healthy plants will produce a far greater number of flowers. Flowers are erect in habit and a rich yellow in colour – or more correctly the bracts are rich yellow, the flowers produced from the bracts being white and tubular in appearance.

Success lies with light, water, and feeding. Avoid direct sun, but keep in the light, and water and feed well. No feeding and less water in winter. Repot annually in a loam-based potting mixture.

Take tip cuttings from the lower branches in spring, dipping the cut end in hormone rooting powder before placing the cuttings in a peat moss and sand mix.

To encourage bloom:
Feed a high-potassium fertilizer. 116♦

Paphiopedilum Maudiae
(Lady's slipper; Slipper orchid)
- **Diffuse light**
- **Temp: 13°C (55°F) min.**
- **Evergreen/no rest**

This is probably the most consistently popular *Paphiopedilum* hybrid in the world. The plant has the grace and beauty found among a few of the species, which have been overshadowed by the heavier, rounded type of hybrids.

The plant is a strong, vigorous grower that can be continually divided without harm to produce further plants. The foliage is beautifully mottled in light and dark green, the leaves are short and rounded. The tall, slender stem carries a single large bloom, distinctively marked in white and deep apple green. Its coloured variety, *Paph.* Maudiae 'Coloratum', shows the same markings on a rich purple ground.

Its ease of culture and long-lasting, long-stemmed blooms, which can be produced twice in one year, have made this hybrid popular for the cut flower trade.

To encourage bloom:
Maintain humidity and warmth but with good ventilation.

Paphiopedilum parishii
- **Good light**
- **Temp: 13°C (55°F) min.**
- **Evergreen/no rest**

A very striking orchid from Burma and Thailand that often grows epiphytically. The long narrow leaves are smooth and bright glossy green. The erect flower stem, which can grow to 60cm (24in) in height, bears four to seven flowers, each about 7.5cm (3in) across, from autumn to spring. The twisted petals are long and pendulous, purplish-brown in overall colour, and spotted towards the flower centre.

This species does not require a great deal of light to flower, but will only bloom when mature. For this reason it should be grown without division. It is one of the very few paphiopedilums which produce a spray of flowers that open all at the same time on the stem. To keep the foliage clean and unmarked avoid allowing water to remain on the surface of the leaves, and be careful not to give too much light. This applies particularly to bright spring sunshine.

To encourage bloom:
Protect from cold draughts.

Passiflora caerulea
(Passion flower)
- **Sunny location**
- **Temp: 10-16°C (50-60°F)**
- **Keep moist and fed**

This plant is a rampant grower that will need some form of support for the twining growth to attach itself to. Hardy out of doors in agreeable climates, but out or in the plant will give a better show of flowers if the roots are confined to a small space. If allowed a free root run it will tend to produce masses of foliage at the expense of flowers.

Sriking 7.5cm (3in) flowers intricately patterned in blue, white and purple appear in late summer and are followed by colourful orange-yellow fruits.

To do well this plant needs good light, ample watering while in active growth, and feeding with a fertilizer containing a high percentage of potash – a tomato food, for example. When potting is essential, use a loam-based mixture.

New plants can be raised from seed or cuttings in spring.

To encourage bloom:
Provide ample light. Do not use pots larger than 20cm (8in) across, otherwise stems and leaves develop at the expense of flowers.

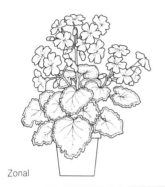

Zonal

Regal

Pelargonium
(Geranium)
- **Sunny location**
- **Temp: 10-18°C (50-65°F)**
- **Keep moist; drier in winter**

Great favourites throughout the world, the pelargoniums come in three principal types: zonals (*P. hortorum* – mainly derived from *P. zonale*); regals (*P. domesticum* – derived from *P. cucullatum, P. fulgidum* and *P. grandiflorum*); and the ivy-leaved forms (*P. peltatum*).

Zontal pelargoniums take their name from the zonal marking of bronze or maroon around the centre of each leaf. The flowers appear over a long period and the plants can grow into shrubs up to 1.8m (6ft) tall.

Regals grow to a maximum height of about 60cm (2ft) and produce impressive, funnel-shaped flowers in many shades from pink to purple. They appear mainly from early spring to midsummer.

Ivy-leaved pelargoniums, with their trailing stems up to 90cm (3ft) long, are ideal for growing in hanging baskets. The compact flowers appear mainly in spring.

There are pelargoniums from these groups that will suit almost any indoor situation, provided it offers ample light and the atmosphere is cool and airy. Use a loam-based potting mixture and water moderately during the warm months. Keep the soil just moist in winter.

Raise new plants from cuttings that have been removed from the parent plant for about twenty four hours before being inserted in a peat-and-sand mixture. Today, however, there is a great emphasis on raising plants from seed, and these do amazingly well.

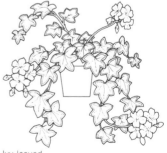

Ivy-leaved

To encourage bloom:
Feed actively growing plants with a high-potassium fertilizer every two weeks. Grow slightly potbound for profuse flowers. 118–119▸

133

Pentas lanceolata
(Egyptian star cluster; Egyptian star flower)
- **Good light**
- **Temp: 16-21°C (60-70°F)**
- **Keep moist and fed**

Though not often supplied by growers, this is a fine plant that can be seen in better plant collections. Plants can be started from new shoots about 10cm (4in) in length taken in the spring and placed in a peaty mixture – a warm propagating case will encourage rooting. Once rooted well, the small pots of cuttings should be transferred to slightly larger pots. Place drainage material in the bottom of the new pot before adding loam-based mixture and some grit for improved drainage.

As they develop, remove the growing tips of the young plants. This will encourage a compact habit and prevent the plants growing too tall. Keep the plants in good light and feed regularly and water well while actively growing.

These plants normally flower from early autumn until midwinter, but blooms can appear during the summer months as well.

To encourage bloom:
Maintain bright light throughout the year and allow plants to become slightly potbound. 120♦

Phalaenopsis Hennessy
(Moth orchid)
- **Light shade**
- **Temp: 18-21°C (65-70°F) min.**
- **Evergreen/no rest**

This hybrid is an example of a peppermint-striped phalaenopsis. The plant is very free-flowering, blooming throughout the year, and the branched spikes may bear up to 30 flowers at a time. The individual flowers are 9-12cm (3.5-4.75in) across, white to light pink in basic colour, with red or pink stripes or, in some forms, spots. This hybrid is of fairly recent breeding. From a particular cross, only a percentage of the seedlings will carry the elusive candy-striped markings that are highly valued to increase the variety within the genus.

Phalaenopsis are highly susceptible to damp conditions, when premature spotting of the flowers will occur. A movement of air from an electric fan combined with a drier atmosphere while the plants are in bloom will help to prevent this common problem. The plants will also suffer if given poor light during the winter.

To encourage bloom:
Keep warm and shaded. 137♦

Pleione formosana
- **Good light**
- **Temp: 4.5°C (40°F) min.**
- **Deciduous/dry rest**

About 20 species of pleiones are known and these are found growing close to the snowline of the Himalayas, and also in parts of China and Formosa. The Himalayan species are probably better suited to the conditions of an alpine house, but others do well in the cool section of an orchid house.

The plant consists of a single, squat, roundish pseudobulb, which lasts for only one year. New growth springs from the base of the pseudobulb, and in its early stages produces a flower spike from its centre. This spike bears one or two flowers, up to 10cm (4in) across. The common species has flowers ranging from pure white to pale pinky-mauve. In all variations the broad lip is frilled, and in the coloured forms it is spotted with red-purple.

In the early spring the plants should be taken from their pot, and reset about half-buried in a fine but well-draining compost.

To encourage bloom:
Grow cool and bright. 120♦

Primula malacoides
(Baby primrose; Fairy primrose)
- **Good light**
- **Temp: 10-16°C (50-60°F)**
- **Keep moist and fed**

This is one of the most charming of all the annual flowering houseplants. *Primula malacoides* presents its lovely flowers, in many colour shades, during the winter and spring months of the year and is almost indispensable for that added touch of colour on the sunny windowsill.

Keep the plants in a cool and light place to do well, and at no time expose them to hot and dry conditions. In such conditions there is a much greater chance of the plants being attacked by red spider mites. These can be detected by careful inspection on the undersides of leaves, and should be treated with the appropriate insecticide as soon as they are noticed. Feed regularly to retain leaf colour.

Grow primulas in a loam-based potting mix and keep them moist while they are actively growing and flowering. Discard *Primula malacoides* plants after flowering and raise new plants from seed.

To encourage bloom:
Pick off faded flowers regularly. Give liquid fertilizer when flowering. 137♦

Primula obconica
● **Good light**
● **Temp: 10-16°C (50-60°F)**
● **Keep moist and fed**

These are marvellous plants that seem to flower from one year's end to the next and are very little trouble when it comes to care and attention. Flowers in a variety of colours are more plentiful in winter and spring, but they are likely to be present at almost any time on vigorous plants. Cool, light, and airy conditions are essential. Plants must be kept moist and regularly fed.

The principal drawback with this plant is that it can cause a most irritating rash. Anyone suffering any form of skin problem following the introduction of this plant to the room should immediately suspect and should not actually touch the plant.

To prolong the flowering period give a weak solution of liquid fertilizer every two weeks and pick off fading flowers. This primula can be kept for a second season provided it is kept cool and dry during the summer. In the autumn remove dead leaves and topdress with fresh soil.

To encourage bloom:
Pick off flowers as they fade. Give liquid fertilizer regularly during the flowering period.

Primula vulgaris
● **Good light**
● **Temp: 10-16°C (50-60°F)**
● **Keep moist and fed**

This is now one of the most popular small plants during the winter period. Easily grown from seed sown in the spring, the plants bloom during the winter months. The leaves are pale green and rough in texture, and flowers of many colours are now available; the flowers are infinitely larger than those of a few years ago.

Excellent planted in bowls with other foliage and flowering plants, they will also provide a fine show when a number of plants of different colour are grouped together in a small container.

After flowering indoors, the plants can be put in the garden in a shaded spot to flower the following year.

Keep pot-grown plants in a humid atmosphere while indoors; hot, dry conditions may cause foliage to turn yellow and will cut down the flowering period. Use a loam-based potting mixture and feed every two weeks while the plants are in bloom.

To encourage bloom:
Keep cool with good ventilation. 139♦

Above: **Phalaenopsis hybrids**
Now available in yellow, pink, white or 'peppermint' stripes like this P. Hennessy, these are the beauties of the orchid group. 134♦

Right: **Primula malacoides**
Whorls of rose-purple flowers make this an attractive indoor plant. Handsome wavy edged leaves. 135♦

Above: **Punica granatum 'Nana'**-
Scarlet red flowers always create a
sensation when you grow this
miniature pomegranate. 153♦

Left: **Rechsteineria cardinalis**
An overlooked gesneriad, this fine
plant has brilliant red 5cm (2in)
flowers for many weeks in summer.
Ideal size for windowsills. 153♦

Right: **Primula vulgaris**
This is essentially a garden plant that
can be easily raised indoors for
winter flowers. The beautiful colours
of the blooms are most effective
when several plants are grouped
together. 136♦

Above left: **Reinwardtia trigyna**
*Sometimes called the yellow
petunia, this plant has yellow flowers
in spring. Not often seen but worth
the search.* 154♦

Left: **Schizocentron elegans**
*Blooming at intervals through spring
into early summer, this is an easy and
colourful pot plant.* 156♦

Above and right: **Saintpaulia**
*A huge group of favourite plants with
varieties in many colours. Also
available as miniatures.* 156♦

Above: **Smithiantha cinnabarina**
Lush green leaves and handsome
bell shaped orange-red flowers
make this plant welcome.157♦

Above: **Sinningia**
Many fine hybrids are now available, *all with brilliantly coloured flowers for* *a superb indoor display.* 157♦

Above: **Stanhopea wardii**
*An unusual orchid with large leaves
and waxy flowers borne from the
bottom of the plant. Heavily scented
with a pleasing fragrance.* 159♦

Left: **Solanum capsicastrum**
*Prized mainly for its orange fruits
rather than its small white flowers,
this compact plant brings colour to
the windowsill in winter.* 158♦

Right: **Spathiphyllum
'Mauna Loa'**
*Striking flowers, compact growth
and ability to endure neglect make
this recommended.* 158♦

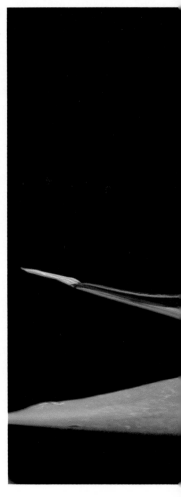

Right: **Streptocarpus hybrid**
If you want dazzling flowers look to the fine streptocarpus hybrids. Blooms come in wonderful shades of violet, pink or white. 161♦

Below: **Strelitzia reginae**
A stunning plant with 15crn (6in) blooms. Needs warmth and space. Spectacular but temperamental. 160♦

Above: **Thunbergia alata**
A colourful tropical vining plant that grows well in warm airy conditions. Easy and worthwhile. 161♦

Above: **Vallota speciosa**
A bulbous plant from South Africa, this beauty is easy to grow and quite spectacular in bloom. 163♦

Left: **Tulipa (Triumph type)**
These fine flowers can be forced during the winter to provide welcome colour in the home. 163♦

Above right: **Trichopilia tortilis**
A fine indoor orchid that really does grow and bloom indoors. Unusual flowers with corkscrew petals. 162♦

Right: **Stephanotis floribunda**
It is hard to beat the fragrance of Madagascar jasmine. White star shaped 2.5cm (1in) flowers appear in clusters in summer. 160♦

Above: **Vriesea splendens**
This superb bromeliad offers not only striking foliage but also a long-lasting 'sword' of red bracts. 165♦

Below: **Vanda suavis**
This beautiful orchid from Java and Bali produces fragrant waxy flowers during the autumn. 164♦

Above: **Zephyranthes candida**
Zephyr flowers are pretty and bear graceful blooms during the summer and into the autumn. Flower colour is usually white, but orange and pink varieties are also seen. 166♦

Above:
Zygopetalum intermedium
Another popular orchid, this one
bears lovely fragrant green and
purple flowers in midwinter. A
welcome addition indoors. 166♦

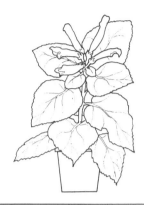

Punica granatum 'Nana'
(Dwarf pomegranate)
- **Good light**
- **Temp: 10-18°C (50-65°F)**
- **Keep moist and fed**

The dwarf pomegranate is a compact and shrubby plant with masses of small green leaves, and it will not be difficult to care for if given good light and cool conditions. Besides the evergreen foliage, the reddish scarlet flowers are also a feature; these are suspended from the plant in similar fashion to those of the fuchsia, but are not quite so plentiful.

If flowers are pollinated with a soft brush when pollen is present there is every chance that small pomegranate fruits will develop; these are not edible, but will be of considerable interest. To preserve a neat appearance it is advisable to periodically prune back any growth that is tending to get out of hand. Keep the soil moist, and feed occasionally, but not in winter.

To encourage bloom:
Provide plenty of sunshine while the plant is actively growing. Provide a rest period during the winter. 138♦

Rechsteineria cardinalis
(Cardinal flower)
- **Light shade**
- **Temp: 18-21°C (65-70°F)**
- **Keep moist and fed**

This is a gesneriad with green velvety leaves that produces flowers of bright red colouring in the autumn. For a neat and colourful plant that is not too difficult to care for, *Rechsteineria cardinalis* (also known as *Sinningia cardinalis*) can be thoroughly recommended.

A temperature of not less than 18°C (65°F) is needed and water must be tepid rather than straight from a cold tap. Exposure to bright light will leach the colouring from foliage and mar the appearance of the plant, so place in light shade. Keep the plant out of draughts.

Water well and feed occasionally during spring and summer when plants are in leaf, but when the foliage dies back naturally withhold water and keep the rhizome bone dry and warm until fresh growth appears.

For new plants take leaf or stem cuttings, grow from seed, or plant pieces of rhizomes.

To encourage bloom:
Give a definite winter rest. 138♦

Reinwardtia trigyna
(Yellow flax)
- **Good light**
- **Temp: 13-18°C (55-65°F)**
- **Keep moist during summer**

This untidy, twining shrub bears a profusion of bright golden flowers in spring and makes an unusual addition to any indoor garden. It grows to a height of 75cm (30in) and should be pinched back occasionally to prevent it becoming too straggly.

R. trigyna grows well in the shade, where it should be positioned during spring and early summer, but, for best results, the plant should be put in a sunny place for the remainder of the year. Pot it in a light soil that drains easily and mist the leaves in summer to provide humidity. During periods of growth, water the plant freely and feed moderately.

New plants can be propagated from cuttings taken in the spring.

Rivina humilis
(Baby pepper; Bloodberry; Rouge plant)
- **Good light**
- **Temp: 16-21°C (60-70°F)**
- **Keep moist; drier in winter**

Although an evergreen, these plants will give much better results if fresh material is raised each year. This can be done by sowing seed in the spring for young and vigorous plants to be ready in the summer, or by propagating cuttings. If using the cuttings method, at least one plant must be retained from the previous year so that cuttings can be taken from it for rooting in a heated propagator in the spring.

These neat plants have thin leaves and whitish flowers in the summer to be followed by the further bonus of decorative berries of a bright red colour in the autumn. Keep moist and fed while in active growth, giving less water and no feed to plants retained over the winter period. Check plants regularly for red spider mites and treat promptly.

To encourage bloom:
Place in a sunny position in late summer and autumn. 140●

To encourage bloom:
Raise new plants each year.

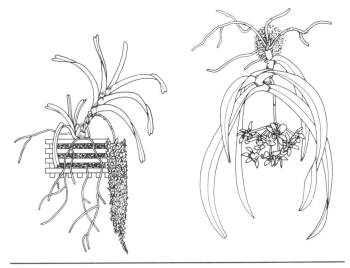

Rhynchostylis retusa

(Foxtail orchid)
- **Slight shade**
- **Temp: 13°C (55°F) min.**
- **Evergreen/no rest**

Four species make up this well-known and popular epiphytic genus. Their natural habitat is Malaysia and Indonesia and, consequently, they enjoy reasonably warm conditions. Because the flowers grow densely in cylindrical fashion on a pendent raceme or spike, they are commonly known as 'foxtail orchids', although this name is also given to other orchids that produce their flowers in similar fashion (eg *Aerides fieldingii*).

This species produces a plant up to 60cm (2ft) in height with a pendulous spike of 38-50cm (15-20in) which carries many thick, waxy and highly fragrant flowers, each up to 2cm (0.8in) in diameter. These are basically white but may be lightly or heavily spotted with magenta-purple. The hook-shaped lip is solid magenta. The flowers appear from winter to spring and last for only two or three weeks, but if well grown the plant will flower more often.

To encourage bloom:
Lightly syringe with clean water.

Saccolabium acutifolium

- **Fairly heavy shade**
- **Temp: 13°C (55°F) min.**
- **Evergreen/no rest**

This orchid belongs to a small epiphytic group of about 20 species. It originates from India and is now more correctly *Gastrochilus acutifolius*, although the older name persists in horticulture. The plant produces upward growing (monopodial) stems from which grow the narrow, pointed leaves. The fragrant flowers come from between the leaves and are carried on a short, pendent stem in the form of a rosette. These are highly variable and can be pure yellow-green, shaded with brown to an almost solid red colouring. The lip is of curious shape, basically white, occasionally spotted in red with a central yellow stain, and frilled around the edge.

The plant will grow happily on a piece of bark in a pendent position, when it will produce a number of dangling aerial roots. It should be kept permanently moist and prefers to be grown in fairly heavy shade. During the summer months it can be sprayed generously.

To encourage bloom:
Keep moist.

Saintpaulia ionantha
(African violet)
- **Good light**
- **Temp: 16-21°C (60-70°F)**
- **Keep moist and fed**

This is by far the most popular flowering plant. There is no particular flowering time, but bloom will be much improved if plants are grown in good light, and this means a light window – no draughts – during the day and under an artificial light in the evening.

Use tepid water and apply it to the surface of the potting mixture ensuring that it drains right through the pot – any surplus accumulating in the drip dish should be removed as it is fatal to allow plants to stand in water for any length of time. Use a standard loam-based potting mixture with some extra peat added. Feed with fertilizer every two weeks.

New plants can be grown from firm leaves taken at any time and placed in a heated propagator or a plastic bag to conserve warmth and moisture. After 6 to 10 weeks tiny plantlets appear at the base of the leaf; these can be separated and grown into mature plants.

To encourage bloom:
Grow slightly potbound. 141♦

Schizocentron elegans (Heterocentron)
(Spanish shawl)
- **Good light**
- **Temp: 16-21°C (60-70°F)**
- **Keep moist and fed**

This compact windowsill plant is ideal for the beginner wishing to have something easy to keep in flower. Neat mounds of green foliage are topped by purplish flowers that are in evidence through the spring and into early summer.

It is best kept in a smaller pot using a loam-based potting mixture, but a keen eye must be maintained for watering and feeding, as smaller pots tend to dry out more rapidly. While actively growing, plants should be fed at every watering with a weak liquid fertilizer. Alternatively, feeding tablets may be placed in the soil as directed by the manufacturer.

New plants can be produced in the autumn by cutting back the foliage of older plants to little more than stumps, then dividing the roots. Alternatively, tip cuttings about 7.5cm (3in) long can be taken at any time and rooted in a mixture of peat and sand.

To encourage bloom:
Provide bright light all year. 140♦

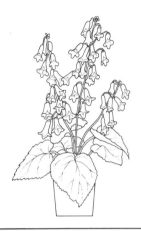

Sinningia speciosa
(Gloxinia)
- **Good light**
- **Temp: 13-18°C (55-65°F)**
- **Keep moist; dry rest**

These plants may be acquired as tubers to be grown on, as seed to be sown and reared, or as finished plants from the retailer. Whatever the choice, splendid plants can be owned and admired; they have large, soft green leaves and their trumpet flowers up to 7.5cm (3in) across are produced throughout the summer months. A rosette of leaves develops from the tuber to be topped by almost stemless flowers.

While in leaf plants must be fed only with a high nitrogen fertilizer, but change to a high potash one when flower buds appear. Good light is maybe the most important need of this plant when in flower. Remove dead flowers to encourage new ones. When foliage dies down naturally in early autumn, allow the standard potting mixture to dry completely and store the tuber in a dry and warm place during the winter months.

To encourage bloom:
Give high-potassium feed when buds form. Pick off faded flowers. 143♦

Smithiantha cinnabarina
(Temple bells)
- **Light shade**
- **Temp: 16-21°C (60-70°F)**
- **Keep moist and fed**

These interesting and colourful plants of the Gesneriaceae family can be kept in flower for many months of the year with a planned approach. Initially plants can be raised from seed or cuttings taken in the spring – keep the temperature at around 21°C (70°F) for both. Plants will grow and produce rhizomes and these can be planted at different times: spring planting for flowers in summer; early summer planting for flowers in the autumn; and mid-summer planting for flowers in winter. If a heated greenhouse is available plants can be induced to flower over this extended season to much enhance the indoor plant scene. Once indoors avoid draughts and cold.

Lush green leaves are topped by bell-shaped flowers that are available in many colours. From a packet of seed one would expect to get a good selection of colours.

To encourage bloom:
Feed regularly when active. Observe dormant period. 142♦

Solanum capsicastrum

(Jerusalem cherry; Winter cherry)
- **Sunny location**
- **Temp: 10-16°C (50-60°F)**
- **Keep moist and fed**

These are cheap and cheerful shrubby plants with thin green leaves; they are normally available during the winter. Raised from seed the young plants are established in their pots then placed out of doors in full light and fresh air where they will make sturdy plants. Following the insignificant white flowers plants begin to develop green berries which will eventually turn red and become the plants' most interesting characteristic.

The orange-red berries remain colourful for many months if plants receive adequate light, but will fall at an alarming rate if the light is poor, and this need be for only a very short time. Keep plants moist and regularly fed. It is best to discard the plants after the berries have fallen.

Take care to keep these plants away from children – the attractive berries are poisonous if eaten.

To encourage bloom and fruit:
Mist spray the flowers to encourage the fruits to set. Maintain plants in bright light. 144♦

Spathiphyllum 'Mauna Loa'

(Peace lily; Spathe flower; White flag; White sails)
- **Light shade**
- **Temp: 18-21°C (65-70°F)**
- **Keep moist and fed**

Originally from the Hawaiian Islands, this is truly a very fine plant when grown in conditions that are in tune with its modest demands. The right temperature is one of its most important needs, never less than 18°C (65°F). The roots and the atmosphere surrounding the foliage should be moist, so misting will be beneficial in dry air conditions. Don't overwater, though.

In ideal conditions, plants will grow throughout the year and may produce elegant white spathe flowers at any time. Older plants can be divided to produce new ones and these should be potted into a loam-based mixture containing about 50 per cent peat. Place a layer of broken flower pot in the bottom of the container to improve drainage.

Check the undersides of leaves regularly for red spider mites which may infest the plant in too dry conditions.

To encourage bloom:
Keep warm and humid. 145♦

Sprekelia formosissima
(Aztec lily; Jacobean lily)
- **Sunny location**
- **Temp: 10-16°C (50-60°F)**
- **Keep moist; dry in winter**

These are bulbous indoor plants with orchid-like scarlet flowers borne on stems about 50cm (20in) tall in the spring.

    The bulbs, which are usually both expensive and in short supply, should be planted with their tips showing in a loam-based mixture that will sustain the plant in the same pot for several years. Following planting, keep in a light and warm place and water freely from the time growth is evident until the foliage dies naturally in the autumn. Then, the soil must remain bone dry until the following year. When flowers appear it will be a signal that feeding with weak liquid fertilizer should begin.

    Although frequent potting on is not needed it will benefit the plants to topdress them with new mixture every year. Every four years the bulbs should be repotted and can be divided at the same time to produce new plants.

To encourage bloom:
Observe winter rest period.

Stanhopea wardii
- **Moderate shade**
- **Temp: 10-13°C (50-55°F) min.**
- **Evergreen/dry rest**

In common with the other species, *Stanhopea wardii* produces a 30-38cm (12-15in) broad, leathery leaf from the top of an oval pseudobulb. The flower spike, when it has emerged from the plant container, carries three to nine flowers in late summer. The buds develop very quickly and the flowers, up to 10cm (4in) across when fully open, vary from pale lemon to orange, dotted with brownish-purple, with a large blotch of the same colour on each side of the lip.

    Stanhopeas are among the easiest orchids to grow, requiring the conditions of the cool to intermediate house with moderate shade and moisture at the roots at all times. They should be grown in baskets or in purpose-made pots that have holes in the walls and base to prevent the flowers being trapped within the container. A large plant will bloom freely; the spikes open in succession.

To encourage bloom:
Keep moist while active. 144♦

Stephanotis floribunda

(Madagascar jasmine)
- **Good light**
- **Temp: 13-21°C (55-70°F)**
- **Keep moist; dry in winter**

Stephanotis will quickly fill its allotted space if given a free root run. Indoors, it requires a framework around which growth can be trained. Keep on the dry side in winter, and in the lightest possible location at all times, although avoiding direct summer sunshine.

The green, leathery leaves are evergreen and the flowers appear during the summer months. The white tubular flowers are produced in clusters of five or more and have the most overpowering scent.

Grow stephanotis in a loam-based mixture and repot into a slightly larger container every year. Feed with a standard liquid fertilizer every two weeks during the spring and summer and keep the soil and surroundings moist.

Pollinated flowers will occasionally result in large seedpods forming – these should be allowed to burst open before seed is removed and sown. New plants can also be grown from tip cuttings taken in spring.

To encourage bloom:
Keep in stable conditions. 149♦

Strelitzia reginae

(Bird of paradise flower)
- **Sunny location**
- **Temp: 13-24°C (55-75°F)**
- **Keep moist; dry in winter**

This spectacular plant is suitable only where space is adequate; it grows to about 90-120cm (3-4ft) tall when confined to a pot and needs a 30cm (12in) pot when mature. It can be grown from seed but development is painfully slow; from sowing the seed to the production of flowers can be a period of five to ten years. But, if one is patient, the blue and orange flowers are quite a spectacle when they do appear, and have a very long life.

Full sunlight is essential, and plants need potting on when they have filled their existing pots with roots; use loam-based potting mixture at all stages of potting. Feeding is not desperately important and plants will tolerate long periods of draught without appearing to suffer undue harm.

Old clumps can be divided and the sections potted separately. These should flower after two to three years.

To encourage bloom:
Do not disturb mature flowering plants. Grow in sun. 147♦

Streptocarpus hybrids
(Cape primrose; Cape cowslip)
- **Good light**
- **Temp: 16-21°C (60-70°F)**
- **Do not overwater**

In recent years, as with many other more common indoor plants, we have seen considerable improvement in the types of streptocarpus that are being offered for sale. Besides the more usual blue colouring of the variety 'Constant Nymph', there are now white, pink, red and purple shades available.

In culture they are all very similar, and require a light airy location at moderate temperatures to succeed. Place in good light with some protection from direct sunlight, and temperatures in the range 16-21°C (60-70°F). Feed every two weeks during the growing season with a high-phosphate fertilizer. Excessive watering can be damaging, so it is best to water the plant well and allow it to dry before repeating, bearing in mind that plants need much less water and no feed in winter.

New plants are raised by cutting leaves into 10cm (4in) sections and placing them in fresh peat at not less than 18°C (65°F).

To encourage bloom:
Remove seedpods as they form. 147♦

Thunbergia alata
(Black-eyed Susan vine; Clock vine)
- **Sunny location**
- **Temp: 13-18°C (55-65°F)**
- **Keep moist; dry in winter**

The triangular green leaves of this plant sprout from wiry stems that twine around any form of support within reach. Throughout the summer this rather plain foliage backdrop is adorned with striking bright orange flowers each with a jet black centre – hence its apt common name of Black-eyed Susan vine.

Offer a light window location and modest temperature, and feed regularly once the plants have started to grow. For the vigorous twining growth it is essential to provide a framework to which new growth can be attached or allowed to twine naturally around. When potting on use a loam-based potting mixture.

It is best to treat this plant as an annual and raise new plants from seed sown in spring.

To encourage bloom:
Provide plants with plenty of light and sunshine. Pick off flowers as they fade to promote further bloom. 146♦

Tillandsia cyanea
(Pink quill)
- **Good light**
- **Temp: 16-21°C (60-70°F)**
- **Water moderately**

From a compact rosette of thin green leaves, *T. cyanea* will in time produce one of the most spectacular of flowering bracts, similar in shape to the cuttle fish. The bract emerges from among the leaves and eventually attains a size of about 15 by 7.5cm (6 by 3in). An added bonus is the appearance of brilliant violet-blue flowers along the margin of the bract over a period of several weeks. As one flower dies so another takes its place.

Avoid getting the soil too wet, and never be tempted to pot plants into large containers, as they will be very much happier in smaller pots in free-draining potting mixture. Use a conventional houseplant mix to which chopped pine needles have been added – the latter will keep the mixture open and prevent sodden conditions. Feeding is not important.

To encourage bloom:
Keep warm and humid.

Trichopilia tortilis
(Corkscrew orchid)
- **Shade during summer**
- **Temp: 10-13°C (50-55°F) min.**
- **Evergreen/semi-rest**

About 30 species of *Trichopilia* are known, although only a few of these are available to growers today. Despite this, they remain very popular, partly because they are not difficult to cultivate and also because of their very showy flowers, which are large in comparison with the size of the plant. The plants are epiphytic and are found mainly in S. America.

The plants, which never grow very tall, develop flattened pseudobulbs that may be rounded or elongated, and a solitary leathery leaf. Intermediate house conditions suit them well, with good shade during the summer months. The plants benefit from generous moisture at the root in full growth. After flowering, these orchids should be allowed a period of semi-rest.

This plant carries a single flower, up to 13cm (5in) across, on a pendent spike. The sepals and petals, which are narrow and twisted throughout their length, are brown, bordered by yellow-green.

To encourage bloom:
Keep moist at roots while active. 149♦

Tulipa
(Tulip)
- **Good light**
- **Temp: 10-16°C (50-60°F)**
- **Keep moist**

Possibly the most colourful of all the spring bulbs, tulips can also be grown successfully indoors for that winter splash of colour. When selecting, choose only the finest quality bulbs if you wish to obtain the best results. Also, it is wise to choose the varieties that are normally recommended for rockeries, as these will be shorter and more appropriate for indoor decoration. Among the rockery varieties there are many fascinating colours, some with the added benefit of attractive foliage.

Plant the bulbs in shallow pans in a fibrous mixture in the autumn and keep them in a cool dark place. Just the tips of the bulbs should be visible above the moistened bulb fibre. When the developing leaves are about 7.5cm (3in) tall transfer the container to a cool light place. When flower buds are just evident, the plants can be transferred to a slightly warmer place, but high temperatures must be avoided.

To encourage bloom:
Grow cool and dark at first. 148♦

Vallota speciosa
(Scarborough lily)
- **Sunny location**
- **Temp: 13-18°C (55-65°F)**
- **Keep moist**

Given reasonable light, moderate temperature, and care to prevent the potting mixture becoming excessively wet, these attractive plants will go on for years with few problems. The bulbous plants have green strap-shaped leaves and attractive scarlet flowers borne on stems about 60cm (2ft) in height.

New plants can be raised from seed or, perhaps more easily, from offsets that form around the base of the parent bulb. The offsets, which are very small, should be removed in the autumn for planting in a group in a shallow pan of peaty mixture. They do not need frequent repotting.

Unlike many bulbs, a resting period is not required, so the mixture – a rich, loam-based one is best – should be kept moist throughout the year. However, at no time should it become excessively wet.

To encourage bloom:
Provide plenty of sunshine. 148♦

Vanda suavis
- Sunny conditions
- Temp: 18°C (65°F) min.
- Evergreen/semi-rest

Veltheimia viridifolia
(Forest lily)
- Good light
- Temp: 16-21°C (60-70°F)
- Keep moist and fed

Coming from Java and Bali, this free-flowering strap-leaved epiphyte bears colourful flowers in autumn and early winter. The stems are densely leafy with curving leaves about 25cm (10in) long and 2.5cm (1in) wide. Flower spikes are horizontal, shorter than the leaves and carry five to ten flowers that vary in shape and colour. Typically they have whitish-yellow sepals and petals barred or spotted with red-brown, usually flushed with pale magenta near the base. The fragrant waxy flowers are about 7.5cm (3in) across. This vanda is moderately easy to coax into bloom in warm sunny conditions, although it should not be attempted by beginners. A well-grown plant can reach to a considerable height and in full leaf is a grand sight. It is also found under the name of *Vanda tricolor*.

New plants, complete with roots, are occasionally formed around the base of the parent.

This bulbous plant from South Africa deserves to be more popular than it is at present. Leaves are large and soft green in colour. Its flowers – pink tinged with yellow – appear during the winter months.

Bulbs of *V. viridifolia* should be planted in early autumn to flower in winter. Place the bulbs in a loam-based mixture to which a liberal amount of peat has been added; just cover the bulbs with the mixture, ensuring that the potting is done with some firmness. Keep the soil on the dry side until new growth is under way, then water more liberally. Feed with a standard liquid fertilizer every month when in active growth.

They make good centrepiece plants provided they are given cool and light indoor conditions. During the summer place the plants in an unheated greenhouse until required again in the autumn.

To encourage bloom:
Grow in full sunlight. 150♦

To encourage bloom:
Observe summer rest period.

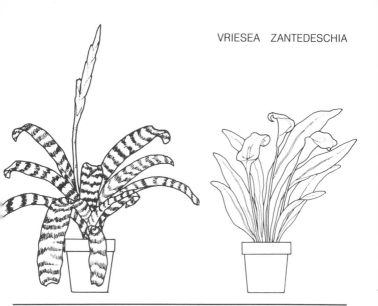

Vriesea splendens
(Flaming sword)
- **Good light; some sunshine**
- **Temp: 16-21°C (60-70°F)**
- **Keep moist; drier in winter**

This plant is a member of the splendid bromeliad family with a typical rosette of overlapping leaves that form a natural urn for holding water. The urn must be kept topped up at all times but needs to be cleaned out and freshly watered.

The broad recurving leaves of *Vriesea splendens* are grey-green in colour with darker bands of brownish purple across the leaf. The flower spike usually develops in the summer and may last for many weeks. The bright red bracts enclosing the short-lived yellow flowers provide the main display.

Grow this plant in a mixture of equal parts of loam-based growing medium and fir bark chips, or use a commercially prepared bromeliad mix. The main rosette flowers only once then dies, but as the plant deteriorates offsets form at the base of the trunk and, once rooted these can be detached and potted separately to provide new plants.

To encourage bloom:
Grow in bright light. 150♦

Zantedeschia rehmannii
(Calla lily; Pink arum; Pink calla; Trumpet lily)
- **Good light**
- **Temp: 10-16°C (50-60°F)**
- **Keep moist; dry in winter**

Frequently seen in flower borders out of doors, this compact arum with attractive leaves and pinkish flowers is also a fine plant for summer flowering indoors. It grows to a height of about 60cm (2ft). Ample water and frequent feeding are essential when plants are in leaf and flower.

In the autumn, when foliage begins to die down naturally, watering should be gradually discontinued until the soil is quite dry. Leave it in this condition until the following early spring. At this time the rhizomes should be repotted into fresh soil with reasonable body to it. A loam-based mixture would be suitable for potting, but a liberal amount of peat should be added.

New plants can be started either from the small offshoots or by dividing the rhizomes when repotting.

To encourage bloom:
Grow in cool conditions when active. Observe rest period from midsummer until late autumn.

Zephyranthes candida
(Swamp lily; Zephyr flower)
● **Good light**
● **Temp: 16-21°C (60-70°F)**
● **Keep moist; dry in winter**

These bulbs are usually planted as
outdoor subjects, where they thrive
in well-drained loam in full sun. With
care, they can be raised indoors, too.
This species produces shining
white, crocus-like flowers during late
summer; pink and orange varieties
are also available.

Place 4 or 5 bulbs in a 15cm (6in)
pot in spring and cover them with a
free-draining potting mix made up of
equal parts of loam and peat. Keep
the pot in a sunny window and water
generously, allowing the soil to dry
out between waterings. Feeding is
not necessary.

When flowering is over, gradually
reduce watering until the leaves die
down completely. Store the dry
bulbs in a cool, shaded place during
the winter months, ready for planting
up again the following spring.

Propagate *Zephyranthes* by
detaching the offset bulbs that
develop beside the main bulb.

Zygopetalum intermedium
● **Good light**
● **Temp: 13°C (55°F) min.**
● **Evergreen/dry rest**

This genus comprises 20 species,
most of which come from Brazil.
They are mainly terrestrial,
producing rounded pseudobulbs
with long but fairly narrow leaves.

These are plants for the
intermediate house and require
good light, with plenty of moisture at
the root when in full growth. Air
movement around the plant in
conditions of high humidity is very
important, otherwise the leaves soon
become badly spotted; they should
never be sprayed.

This plant produces an upright
flower spike, 45-60cm (18-24in) in
height, from inside the first leaves of
a new growth. The spike bears four
to eight flowers, each 7.5cm (3in)
across. The sepals and petals are of
equal size, and bright green blotched
with brown. The lip, in contrast, is
broad, flat and heavily lined with
purple. These heavily scented
flowers last for four or five weeks
during the winter months.

To encourage bloom:
Provide bright conditions: 151♦

To encourage bloom:
Keep moist at root. 152♦

Part Two
FOLIAGE HOUSEPLANTS

Pilea cadierei nana

Author

William Davidson is involved with all aspects of houseplants, and has been employed by Rochfords, Europe's leading growers, for most of his working life. His interests encompass growing, exhibiting, writing, consultancy and lecturing, as well as radio and television programmes. He is the author of many successful books on houseplants.

Cryptanthus bromelioides 'It'

Index of Scientific Names

The plants are arranged in alphabetical order of Latin name.
Page numbers in **bold** refer to text entries; those in *italics* refer to photographs.

Index of Common Names

Introduction to Foliage Houseplants

Over the past three decades, houseplants in all shapes and sizes have shown an astonishing increase in popularity. The previous most popular time for indoor plants was at the turn of the century, when many foliage and flowering plants were brought in from tropical regions. Most were kept in heated glasshouses and conservatories, to be removed and put to use as indoor subjects for limited periods, as few homes were warm enough or light enough to sustain plants for more than a limited period. However, some – such as palms, ferns and the indestructible aspidistra – were able to cope with the spartan conditions.

Central heating, better light and generally more agreeable modern living conditions have done much to popularize houseplants, and an incredible range of decorative foliage plants is now well within the scope of the more adventurous grower.

Selection

There are all sorts of aids that one can use in order to improve the well-being of plants; but getting the right plant at the outset can often prove to be the best approach. It is essential that plants for sale are stored in heated premises which are reasonably light and able to offer agreeable conditions while the plants are awaiting a purchaser; low temperatures can soon prove fatal to delicate plants. When selecting, look for plants that are fresh and free of blemishes. It may also help if the plant has a care card with some directions on plant care attached.

Early care

Any plant purchased during the winter should be carefully wrapped by the retailer and protected from cold on the way home. Place the plant inside a heated car if the journey home is of any length, and at all costs avoid putting tender plants in the unheated boot of a car.

Winter-purchased plants will be the most difficult to establish indoors and should be carefully unwrapped, watered if necessary, and placed in a temperature of around 18°C (65°F) in reasonable light to give them the best possible chance of adjusting to an entirely new set of conditions. Almost all plants will have been grown in heated greenhouses and will take unkindly to a sudden lowering of temperature.

Winter feeding should not be necessary, but plants bought at other times should be fed soon after they are brought indoors, and feeding should continue on a regular basis while they are in active growth. Plants bought in summer that are obviously too large for their growing pots can to advantage be potted into slightly larger containers without too much delay.

Temperature and location

One should check the care tag that comes with the plant and endeavour to match as nearly as possible the recommended temperature. Some plants need cooler conditions than others, and only a few of those that are generally available will need a very high temperature that exceeds 21°C (70°F). Avoid cold conditions and draughts, as these can have very ill effects.

Brightly coloured and variegated plants will generally require to be grown in lighter conditions than those that have entirely green foliage, such as *Rhoicissus rhomboidea*. For poor light locations select green-foliaged subjects. Avoid placing plants in the hot stream of air ascending from heating appliances, and keep them out of very strong, direct sunlight.

Watering and feeding

Just about the most important requirement of all indoor potted plants is correct watering. Some, such as philodendrons, need moist soil, but most will be better for a good watering and a period of reasonable drying out before further water is given. Tepid water will be more suitable than cold water, and rain water will suit some plants better than hard tap water. Less water is generally needed in winter, and a combination of cold and wetness can be particularly damaging for many plants. Ailing plants should be given a minimal amount of water and no food, and should be kept in warm conditions out of direct sunlight.

Never overfeed, and never feed plants that are ailing or have been freshly potted. Winter feeding is seldom necessary, and when feeding while plants are growing one should ensure that the directions on the fertilizer being used are followed, bearing in mind that too much food may be more harmful than too little.

Potting

The fine root system of most potted plants will require an open and peaty potting mixture which the roots can easily penetrate and grow into, so garden soil is seldom suitable. Use a properly prepared mixture that contains a lot of peat and incorporates a balanced fertilizer that will sustain the plant. The new pot should be only a little larger than the old one. Following potting, the soil should be well watered, then watered sparingly, so that roots will seek moisture and establish more readily in the new container.

Grouping

Large and stately plants make an impressive feature in a room, but it will often be found that smaller plants have much more appeal if they are placed in small groups. Plants in groups create their own humidity and will grow better, especially in a dry atmosphere.

Propagation

Plants with large leaves are difficult to propagate indoors, but there is a wide range of subjects with smaller leaves which are reasonably easy to manage. Clean peat should be used, and a small heated propagator will be an asset, as will a rooting powder or liquid. Temperatures in the region of 21°C (70°F) and a close atmosphere will encourage cuttings to root more rapidly. Provide reasonable light for cuttings, but avoid direct sunlight.

Above: **Acorus gramineus**
An easy-care, grassy-foliaged plant that does well in low temperatures if kept moist and in reasonable light. 185♦

Right: **Abutilon sevitzia**
A colourful, free-growing plant that thrives in moderate temperatures. Prune to shape at any time. 185♦

Below right:
Aglaonema 'Silver Queen'
A member of the Araceae family, this plant thrives in warm conditions. 186♦

Below: **Adiantum**
These come in many varieties, mostly with delicate foliage that is a perfect foil for other plants. 186♦

Above:
Aglaonema pseudobracteatum
*An interesting subject for adding
height and colour to collections.* 187♦

Below: **Alocasia indica**
*For the skilled plant person; needs
high humidity and constant warmth.
Veined leaves are a big plus.* 187♦

Above: **Alpinia sanderae**
Narrow, green-and-white variegated leaves are carried on tall, slender stems. *Careful cultivation is necessary to retain colouring and to prevent loss of leaves.* 188♦

179

Above: **Aralia elegantissima**
A striking plant with very dark green, almost black, foliage that is delicate on young plants but becomes coarse with age. Needs warmth. 189♦

Left: **Ananas bracteatus striatus**
An extremely ornamental member of the bromeliad family that will develop dazzling colour in good light. 188♦

Right: **Anthurium crystallinum**
The large, boldly veined leaves of this plant are impressive and best supported. A subject for very warm, humid conditions. 189♦

Left: **Aralia sieboldii variegata**
A truly splendid plant with broad, palmate leaves radiating from a stout central stem. Splendidly coloured in pale green and cream. 190♦

Below left: **Araucaria excelsa**
Composed of a multitude of fresh green, pine-needle leaves attached to tiered layers of spreading stems that themselves are arranged on a stout central stem. 190♦

Right: **Ardisia crispa (crenulata)**
Firm, shrubby plants with oval-shaped leaves of very dark green colouring that are waved along their margins. Because of their slow rate of growth, these are excellent where space is limited. 191♦

Below: **Asparagus meyerii**
A distinctive plant, producing long, cylindrical pale green growths. Growth emanates from soil level in the centre of the pot and sprays out in all directions. 192♦

Above: **Asplenium nidus avis**
Smooth, pale green leaves radiate from the centre in an attractive arrangement. Needs moist conditions. 193♦

Below:
Aucuba japonica variegata
The spotted laurel has pleasingly variegated foliage and is a very tough plant for cooler conditions. 194♦

Abutilon sevitzia
- Good light
- Temp: 13-18°C (55-65°F)
- Frequent feeding

Vigorous growing plant for cooler conditions that offer good light, but not full sun when close to glass. Has attractively variegated maple-type leaves and pendulous orange-coloured flowers not unlike a small single hollyhock.

A loam-based mixture is essential when potting plants on – a task that must not be neglected if plants are to do as well as they can. While in active growth feed at every watering, to keep colour. Firm cuttings about 10cm (4in) in length will root readily in peaty mixture if placed in a heated propagator; when growth begins, remove the growing tip of the cutting. When well cared for, individual stems will put on 90cm (3ft) of growth in one season, but pruning can be undertaken at any time to limit growth. Never allow plants to stand in water for long periods, but water copiously while fresh leaves appear.

Soft growth attracts many pests, so a careful and frequent check is advised, especially under the leaves.

Take care
Whitefly can be a nuisance. 177♦

Acorus gramineus variegata
(Sweet flag)
- Grows anywhere
- Temp: 7-13°C (45-55°F)
- Keep moist

Not particularly attractive as an individual, but a fine plant for grouping with others. Well suited for inclusion in a bottle garden or converted fishtank, the acorus has a distinctive shape and is not invasive. Grassy foliage is green and gold in colour and produces neat clumps that may be divided at almost any time in order to produce new plants.

Very much the average indoor plant, it will respond well to a modicum of attention, but abhors hot and dry conditions and too much fussing over. A light location with protection from strong sun is best, and it will not object to some fresh air from open windows on warmer days.

Few pests seem to bother this plant, but in hot and dry conditions red spider may make an appearance and should be treated with one of the many available insecticides as soon as detected. When potting on, a loam-based mixture is best, but one should avoid putting plants into very large pots.

Take care
Divide every second year. 176♦

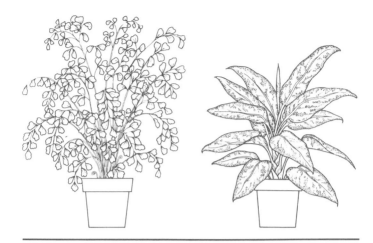

Adiantum
(Maidenhair fern)
- **Light shade**
- **Temp: 18-21°C (65-70°F)**
- **Moist surroundings**

Numerous varieties are available of these most delicate and beautiful foliage plants, whose pale green foliage contrasts with their black stems.

Bright, direct sunlight and dry atmospheric conditions will prove fatal. Offer maidenhair ferns lightly shaded positions in a warm room: place plants in a larger container and surround their pots with a moisture-retaining material such as peat. Misting of foliage is often recommended, but this exercise can have undesirable effects if the surrounding air temperature is inadequate. It is therefore better to use the mister to wet the soil surface.

Avoid use of chemicals on foliage. When potting on, a peaty mixture is needed, and once plants have established in their pots weak liquid feeding will be needed every time the plant is watered. During winter, feeding is not important and watering should be only sufficient to keep the soil moist.

Take care
Slugs find this foliage desirable. 176♦

Aglaonema crispum 'Silver Queen'
(Silver spear)
- **Light shade**
- **Temp:18-21°C (65-70°F)**
- **Keep moist**

There are numerous aglaonemas that form central clumps that increase in size as plants mature, but the variety A. 'Silver Queen' is superior in all respects. Individual spear-shaped leaves are produced at soil level and have a grey-green background colouring liberally spotted with silver.

New plants are made by separating the clumps at any time of year and potting them individually in a peaty mixture in small pots. As plants mature they can be potted on into slightly larger containers, and will in time produce offsets of their own. For the second and subsequent potting operations, use a potting mix that contains some loam, but it should still be very much on the peaty side. Warm, moist and shaded conditions are essential if leaves are to retain their texture and brightness. Watering requires some care; plants must be moist at all times, but not saturated, especially in winter.

Take care
Mealy bug can weaken growth. 177♦

Aglaonema pseudobracteatum
(Golden evergreen)
- **Light shade**
- **Temp: 18-21°C (65-70°F)**
- **Keep moist**

A demanding plant, best suited to the experienced grower; the principal difficulty is the high temperature, which must be maintained. A height of 1m (39in) is not unusual in mature specimens. Leaf perimeter is green with a centre of whitish yellow.

New plants are propagated from top sections of stems with three sound leaves attached. Severed ends are allowed to dry for a few hours before being treated with rooting powder; plant in peaty mixture in small pots, and plunge in moist peat in a heated propagating case; to ensure success the temperature should be around 21°C (70°F). When potting cuttings for growing on, put three cuttings in a 13cm (5in) pot, using a potting mixture with a percentage of loam.

These plants are not much troubled by pests, but mealy bugs are sometimes found where the leaf stalks curl round the main stem. In this situation, thorough saturation with liquid insecticide will be needed.

Take care
Ensure adequate temperature. 178♦

Alocasia indica
- **Light shade**
- **Temp: 18-24°C (65-75°F)**
- **Keep moist**

One of the more exotic and temperamental members of the Araceae family. There are numerous cultivars, all with exotic velvety appearance and arrow-shaped leaves.

Their most important needs are for a temperature of around 24°C (75°F) and for a humid atmosphere. The soil in the pot must be kept moist at all times, and it is essential that the surrounding atmosphere is also moist; this will mean placing the plant on a large tray filled with gravel, which should be kept permanently wet. The tray can contain water, but the level should never be up to the surface of the pebbles so that the plant pot is actually standing in water. Plants allowed to stand in water become waterlogged, and will rot and die. Feeding is not important, but it will do no harm if liquid fertilizer is given periodically.

Take care
Keep plants out of draughts and away from hot radiators. 178♦

Alpinia sanderae
(Silver ginger)
- **Light shade**
- **Temp: 18-24°C (65-75°F)**
- **Avoid overwatering in winter**

One of the many ornamental members of the ginger family, Zingiberaceae, but at present they are generally in short supply. The ginger plant discussed here has highly coloured, upright stems of silver and green foliage, but is made very limited use of as a houseplant.

One of the problems is that it is slow to propagate, as one has to wait for plants to mature and then to divide up the clumps into smaller sections in order to produce additional plants; this is too slow for the commercial grower, who, on account of high energy costs, must have plants that can be put through his greenhouses in the shortest possible time.

To do well indoors, *A. sanderae* will need a minimum temperature of 18°C (65°F). It will also need careful watering and must never remain saturated for long, especially in winter. Feed in frequent weak doses rather than occasional heavy ones, and not in winter.

Take care
Avoid cold and wetness in winter. 179♦

Ananas bracteatus striatus
(Ivory pineapple)
- **Good light**
- **Temp: 13-18°C (55-65°F)**
- **Keep on dry side**

The best of the South American bromeliads, the green form of which, *A. comosus*, is the pineapple of commerce. There is also a white variegated form, also known as the ivory pineapple.

In good light the natural cream colouring of the foliage will be a much better colour, but one should avoid very strong sunlight that is magnified by clear glass. Wet root conditions that offer little drying out will also be harmful. Feed occasionally but avoid overdoing it. New plants can be produced by pulling offsets from mature plants and potting them individually in a mixture containing leaf mould and peat. In reasonable conditions plants can be expected to develop small pineapples in about three years; although highly decorative, these tend to be woody and inedible. However, as pineapples are developing, the central part of the plant around the base of the leaves will change to a brilliant reddish pink.

Take care
Avoid the spined leaf margins. 180♦

Anthurium crystallinum

- **Light shade**
- **Temp: 18-24°C (65-75°F)**
- **Moist atmosphere**

This plant is among the more temperamental foliage plants. It does produce a flower, but this is in fact a thin rat's tail. However, the rat's tail has the important function of producing seed, from which new plants can be raised relatively easily in a high temperature. The patterned, heart-shaped leaves are very large and spectacular and usually have to be supported if they are to show to their best advantage.

High temperature, lightly shaded location and humid atmosphere are their principal needs. Roots should at no time dry out. Regular feeding will maintain foliage in brighter colour and better condition. Potting mixture containing a percentage of loam should be used and the pot should be provided with drainage material. Although plants must not dry at their roots, it is essential that water should drain away freely.

Pests are not a problem. Avoid handling, or cleaning the leaves with chemical concoctions.

Take care
Maintain high humidity. 181♦

Aralia elegantissima
(False aralia)
- **Light shade**
- **Temp: 18-21°C (65-70°F)**
- **Keep moist**

Also known as *Dizygotheca elegantissima*, this is one of the most attractive of the purely foliage plants, having dark green, almost black, colouring to its leaves. Graceful leaves radiate from stiff, upright stems that will attain a height of about 3m (10ft). As the plant ages it loses its delicate foliage and produces leaves that are much larger and coarser in appearance. One can remove the upper section of stem, and new growth will revert to the original delicate appearance.

Warm conditions with no drop in temperature are important; water thoroughly, soaking the soil, and allow it to dry reasonably before repeating. Feed in spring and summer, less in winter.

Mealy bug can be treated with a liquid insecticide; affected areas should be thoroughly saturated with the spray. Root mealy bugs can be seen as a whitish powder around the roots; to clear these, liquid insecticide should be watered in.

Take care
Avoid fluctuating temperatures. 181♦

Aralia sieboldii
(Castor oil plant)
- **Light shade**
- **Temp: 7-13°C (45-55°F)**
- **Water and feed well**

Also known as *Fatsia japonica*.
Besides being an excellent indoor
plant it is hardy out of doors, and will
develop into a large shrub.

The large fingered leaves have a
deceptively tough appearance, as
this plant can very easily be
damaged by chemicals for the
cleaning of foliage plants. They will
also be scorched by the sun if placed
too close to clear glass. In the first
two or three years plants will require
annual potting on until they are in 20
or 25cm (8 or 10in) pots. It then
becomes impractical in the average
home to advance them to larger
containers, and it is important to
ensure that they are regularly and
adequately fed. New plants can be
raised from seed sown in peaty
mixture in a warm propagator in the
spring.

Red spider can be troublesome in
hot, dry conditions; a sign of their
presence is pale brown patches on
leaves. Use insecticide to treat
reverse side of leaves thoroughly.

Take care
Avoid hot and dry conditions. 182♦

Araucaria excelsa
(Norfolk Island pine)
- **Light shade**
- **Temp: 13-18°C (55-65°F)**
- **Provide ample space**

A majestic tropical tree that
originates from New Zealand. It is a
marvellous foliage plant when
carefully treated and not subjected to
very high temperatures, which can
be debilitating. Hot conditions cause
normally turgid foliage to droop and
become very thin. These elegant
plants are best suited to important
and spacious locations that will allow
full development.

During early development plants
should be allowed to fill their pots
with roots before being potted on
into slightly larger containers, using a
loam-based potting mixture. When
going into their final pots of 20-25cm
(8-10in) diameter, the amount of
loam should be increased to
encourage slower but firmer growth.
New plants can be raised from seed,
but it is better to purchase small
plants and grow them on.

Few pests trouble these pines, but
excessive watering, especially in
poor light, will cause browning and
eventual loss of needles.

Take care
Avoid overpotting of young plants. 182♦

Ardisia crispa (A. crenulata)
(Coral berry)
- **Light shade**
- **Temp: 16-21°C (60-70°F)**
- **Keep moist and fed**

Although flowers are produced, the main attractions of the coral berry are the glossy green crenellated leaves and the long-lasting berries. It grows very slowly, and plants take several years to attain the maximum height of around 90cm (3ft). A stiff, upright central stem carries the woody branches, which will always be neat.

Offer a lightly shaded location for best results, and at no time be tempted to water excessively. Slow-growing plants of this kind are best kept on the dry side, particularly in winter. It is also important not to be too heavy-handed when feeding, and it should be discontinued altogether in winter. Plants with a slow growth rate are better grown in pots that are on the small side, and soil with a good percentage of loam must be used, as plants will quickly deteriorate in peat mixtures. Cuttings of firm young shoots can be taken in spring and rooted in peat at a temperature of not less than 21°C (70°F) to produce new plants.

Take care
Never overwater in winter. 183♦

Arundinaria
(Bamboo)
- **Good light**
- **Temp: 10-18°C (50-65°F)**
- **Keep moist and fed**

There are numerous varieties, some very vigorous, such as *A. gigantea* (common name, cane reed), others, such as *A. vagans*, neat and compact. These are ideal for cooler locations where there is reasonable light. In time the plants will form into bold groups of congested stems that completely fill the pots in which they are growing.

As plants increase in size they will generally require a greater amount of water, and feeding will have to be stepped up. The time will also come when plants have to be put into larger containers, and one should use a mixture containing a good amount of loam. As an alternative to potting on the complete clump one can use a fork and spade to chop the clump up into smaller sections, which in turn can be potted up as individual plants. At all stages of growth plants will need ample watering and feeding, with winter being the only time when one should ease up on both.

Take care
Divide older plants periodically.

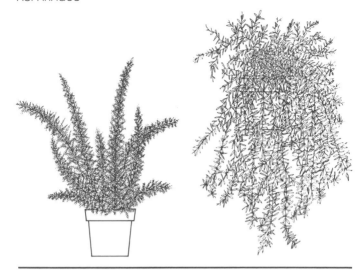

Asparagus meyerii
(Plume asparagus)
- ● **Good light, no sun**
- ● **Temp: 13-18°C (55-65°F)**
- ● **Keep moist, less in winter**

Although frequently referred to as ferns, these belong to the lily family. Not a common houseplant, *A. meyerii* is among the most elegant of indoor plants. As the common name suggests, the foliage forms pale green cylindrical plumes on stiff stems that may attain a length of 60cm (2ft). Growth forms in stout clumps and springs from soil level.

It is important when potting that the plants should be placed centrally in the new container. A loam-based potting mixture should be used to keep plants in good fettle. Once established in their pots a regular feeding schedule must be followed, especially during the spring and summer months. Plants fare better if rain water is used in preference to tap water. And when watering the soil do it thoroughly, with surplus water being clearly seen to drain through the holes in the bottom of the pot. It is then important to allow a reasonable drying-out period before further water is given. Less water is required in winter.

Take care
Never use very peaty soil. 183♦

Asparagus sprengeri
(Asparagus fern)
- ● **Good light, no sun**
- ● **Temp: 13-18°C (55-65°F)**
- ● **Water and feed well**

Though the common name suggests a fern, this is a member of the lily family. One of the most vigorous and useful of all the many fine foliage plants, it is especially effective when grown in a hanging basket.

New plants can be raised from seed sown in spring, or one can divide mature plants at almost any time of year. Before division, ensure that the soil is thoroughly wetted. As with potting on, divided pieces should be planted in pots that give the roots space, and the potting mixture must contain a reasonable amount of loam. In order to keep the lush green colouring it is important that well-rooted plants should be fed regularly. Feeding with weak liquid fertilizer at every watering is often more satisfactory than giving plants occasional heavy doses. Although plants will appreciate good light it is important to protect them from direct sun. Also, in hot, dry conditions it will help if foliage is periodically sprayed over with water.

Take care
Avoid cold winter locations.

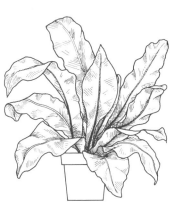

Aspidistra elatior
(Cast iron plant)
- **Light shade**
- **Temp: 13-18°C (55-65°F)**
- **Keep moist**

Popular since Victorian times, when it acquired its common name on account of its ability to withstand trying conditions. The aspidistra has been around for a very long time and there are plants alive today with a known history that goes back for over a century. A tough plant, but – like almost all such plants – the aspidistra will be much better if reasonably agreeable conditions are provided, rather than a very spartan environment that will result in the plant surviving and little else.

Reasonable light, evenly moist conditions that avoid extremes, with occasional feeding once established, will usually produce plants that are fresh and lush and much more attractive. When potting on, use a properly prepared mixture of soil that contains a good percentage of loam. Any good fertilizer will suit well-rooted plants.

The apparently tough leaves are very sensitive to the use of cleaning chemicals, and to household cleaning chemicals in general.

Take care
Never use chemicals on the foliage.

Asplenium nidus avis
(Bird's nest fern)
- **Shade**
- **Temp: 18-24°C (65-75°F)**
- **Moist roots and surroundings**

As small plants these are not very exciting, but once they have been advanced to pot sizes of around 18cm (7in) they have few equals. But the growing of these plants to perfection is one of the more difficult exercises in horticulture.
Surrounding objects touching tender leaves will almost certainly cause irreparable damage, as will spraying foliage with unsuitable chemicals, or the presence of slugs.

Leaves can be kept in good order if a temperature of around 21°C (70°F) is maintained and plants enjoy good light but not direct sun. Open, peaty mixture is needed when potting, and water applied to the top of the soil should immediately flow through. Frequent feeding of established plants with weak fertilizer is preferred to infrequent heavier doses. Keep soil moist.

Scale insects can be seen as dark brown or flesh-coloured spots adhering to the area around the midrib of the leaf. These can be sponged off with malathion.

Take care
Never handle young foliage. 184▶

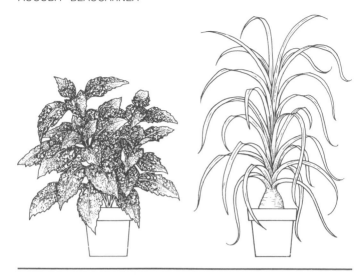

Aucuba japonica variegata
(Spotted laurel)
- **Good light**
- **Temp: 7-13°C (45-55°F)**
- **Avoid summer drying out**

An old-established plant that will tolerate varied conditions, but prefers to grow in cool conditions. This is one of the few plants that do well in a draughty hallway. And it has the bonus of fairly colourful foliage.

New plants are little trouble to propagate, and one should remove the top section of the stem with about four sound leaves attached, and insert in a peaty mixture. Putting the pot with its cutting in a heated propagator will stimulate rooting, as will the use of rooting powder or liquid. Once rooted, transfer the young plant to a slightly larger pot, using a loam-based potting soil.

While plants are in active growth they should be watered freely and fed regularly; during the winter months water sparingly and discontinue feeding. Older plants that are losing their appearance can be pruned to shape in spring. During the summer, aucubas make excellent plants for the patio.

Take care
Avoid wet winter conditions. 184♦

Beaucarnea recurvata
(Ponytail plant)
- **Light shade**
- **Temp: 10-21°C (50-70°F)**
- **Water well in summer**

A peculiar plant that people either love or hate. Leaves are narrow, green and recurving. Small plants produce neat, firm bulbs at the base of their stems, the bulbs changing into more grotesque shapes as the plant ages. Because of its odd spreading habit of growth it is used more as an individual plant than as one of a group of plants.

New plants can be raised from seed sown in peat in warm conditions at almost any time of the year. Pot the resultant seedlings into small pots of peat initially, and into loam-based compost when they are of sufficient size. As an alternative to seed, new plants can be grown from the small bulbils that develop around the base of the parent.

The plant puts up with much ill-treatment provided the soil in its pot is not allowed to remain permanently saturated. Once established, plants respond to regular feeding while in active growth; none in winter.

Take care
Avoid cold and wetness in winter.

Begonia masoniana
(Iron cross begonia)
- **Light shade**
- **Temp: 16-21°C (60-70°F)**
- **Keep dry in winter**

This fine plant grows to splendid size if given reasonable care. The rough-surfaced leaves are a brownish green in colour and have a very distinctive cross that covers the greater part of the centre of the leaf and radiates from the area where the petiole is joined. This marking resembles the German Iron Cross.

During the spring and summer months it will be found that plants grow at reasonable pace if given a warm room, moist root conditions, and weak liquid fertilizer with each watering. Plants that have filled their existing pots with roots can be potted on at any time during the summer, using a loam-based potting mixture and shallow pots. Over the winter months loss of some lower leaves will be almost inevitable, but provided the soil is kept on the dry side during this time the plant will remain in better condition and will grow away with fresh leaves in the spring.

Take care
Inspect for winter rot. 201♦

Begonia rex
(Fan plant)
- **Light shade**
- **Temp: 16-21°C (60-70°F)**
- **Keep on the dry side in winter**

These rank among the finest foliage plants, with all shades of colouring and intricate leaf patterns. Those with smaller leaves are generally easier to care for indoors.

To propagate, firm, mature leaves are removed from the plant and most of the leaf stalk is removed before a series of cuts are made through the thick veins on the underside of the leaf. The leaf is then placed underside down on moist peat (in either boxes or shallow pans) and a few pebbles are placed on top of the leaf, to keep it in contact with the moist peat. Temperatures in the region of 21°C (70°F) are required, and a propagating case. Alternatively, the leaf can be cut into squares of about 5cm (2in), and the pieces placed on moist peat.

When purchased these plants are often in pots that are much too small; repot the plant into a larger container without delay, using peaty compost.

Take care
In close conditions look out for signs of mildew developing. 201♦

Caladium candidum
(Angels' wings)
- **Light shade**
- **Temp: 18-24°C (65-75°F)**
- **Wet in summer, dry in winter**

This is possibly the most delicately beautiful of all the purely foliage plants. The leaves are heart-shaped, almost as broad as they are long, and have a kind of translucent whiteness. Across the white surface there are attractive heavy green veins.

Care is required when handling, but the very delicate appearance is deceptive, as they have a rubbery quality. When watering it is essential that the soil is soaked, and never allowed to dry out at any time during the growing season. Growth will be active from early spring to the autumn, when foliage will take on a tired appearance, and this is a sign that watering should be gradually reduced until the soil is bone dry. In this condition the tuber in its pot is stored until the following spring, when new growth appears; provide a storage temperature of around 16°C (60°F). In the early spring the soil should be moistened and the plant placed in a temperature of around 24°C (75°F) to stimulate new growth.

Take care
Provide adequate storage warmth.

Caladium hybrids
(Angels' wings)
- **Light shade**
- **Temp: 18-24°C (65-75°F)**
- **Keep moist when in leaf**

There is a wide variety of these hybrids, all in need of some cosseting if they are to succeed. Adequate temperature is essential, and they are sensitive to the effects of bright sun through clear glass.

When potting it is important to use a high proportion of peat that will drain freely. Repot over-wintered tubers soon after they have produced their first new growth. Old soil should be teased gently away, care being taken not to damage any new roots that may be forming. Rather than transfer plants to very large pots it is better, having removed much of the old soil, to repot the plant into the same container using fresh mixture.

Leaves of these plants will not tolerate any cleaning. When buying plants, get them from a reliable retailer with heated premises, as cold conditions for only a short time can be fatal. Although arum-type flowers are produced, these are unattractive and should be removed.

Take care
Provide adequate storage warmth. 202▶

Calathea makoyana
(Peacock plant)
- Shade
- Temp: 18-24°C (65-75°F)
- Keep moist and fed

Oval-shaped, paper-thin leaves are carried on petioles that may be as much as 60cm (2ft) long, and are intricately patterned. The peacock plant is of a delicate nature; it will rapidly succumb if the temperature is not to its liking. And it must at no time be exposed to direct sunlight, or shrivelling of leaves will occur.

Small plants are seldom offered for sale. It is usual for the specialist grower to raise plants in very warm beds of peat in the greenhouse; when plants are well established they are potted up into 18cm (7in) pots. For all potting operations a very peaty and open mixture containing some coarse leaf mould will be essential. And following potting it will be necessary to ensure that the soil remains just moist, but never becomes saturated for long periods.

Pests are seldom a problem, but established plants have to be fed with weak liquid fertilizer weekly from spring to autumn.

Take care
Protect from direct sunlight. 202♦

Calathea oppenheimiana tricolor
- Light shade
- Temp: 16-21°C (60-70°F)
- Water/feed mainly in summer

This is much easier to manage than almost any of the other calatheas. The leaves, on long petioles, are produced at soil level and radiate from the centre of the pot, forming compact and low-growing plants. Background colouring is a very dark green with streaks of white and pink attractively dispersed around the centre of the leaves.

Plants have to be divided in order to be increased. Although the commercial grower may find it slow to build up large stocks of these plants, they are very simple for the average indoor plantsman to cope with. Water the soil well and remove the plant from its pot before proceeding to split the clump of roots as one would divide a clump of herbaceous plants in the garden. At all potting stages use a proprietary houseplant potting mixture with a little loam added. Offer plants reasonable light and protection from direct sunlight, and always avoid excessive watering.

Take care
Avoid frequent use of chemicals. 203♦

Calathea ornata
- Shade
- Temp: 18-24°C (65-75°F)
- Needs moist soil and atmosphere

The calatheas almost all present a challenge. Adequate temperature, shade and moist surroundings are their principal needs, but moist surroundings should not be confused with totally saturated soil. In fact, the roots should not remain excessively wet for long periods, but it is important to mist the foliage and the area surrounding the plant at regular intervals.

In its junior stages of growth, *C. ornata* produces oval-shaped leaves attractively marked with very fine pink lines on a green background. As the plant ages the lines become whiter, and in older plants are not always present. The leaves are paper-thin, and deep purple underneath. Feeding should be done at each watering, giving very weak dosage, with none in winter. Tepid rain water is better than cold tap water. Place plants on gravel or similar moisture-retaining surface, or put pots into a larger container filled with damp peat.

Take care
Never expose to bright sun.

Calathea picturata
- Shade
- Temp: 18-24°C (65-75°F)
- Keep moist

Oval-shaped leaves some 15cm (6in) long are carried on short petioles that are closely grouped at soil level, producing a plant of neat and compact appearance. The margin of each leaf is green and the centre is a striking silver-grey in colour; the reverse is maroon. As with all calatheas, bright direct sunlight will quickly kill them as leaves begin to shrivel up. Calatheas are happier growing in the shade of bolder plants such as the more spreading types of philodendron, such as *P. bipinnatifidum.*

Cold draughts – and cold conditions generally – must be avoided, and if possible one should provide a moist atmosphere around the plant; this is often best achieved by placing plants in a container that includes a selection of other plants. Large containers are now freely available for making plant arrangements in. Fill a container with moist peat into which the plant pot is plunged to its rim.

Take care
Keep moist and warm.

Calathea zebrina
(Zebra plant)
- Shade
- Temp: 18-24°C (65-75°F)
- Keep moist and fed

This incredibly beautiful foliage plant will test the skills of anyone. The bold leaves are a deep velvety green with prominent patches of deeper colouring. Maximum height of around 90cm (3ft) may be attained in a well-heated greenhouse where plants are tended with professional care.

It will be fatal to allow this plant to stand in a position exposed to full sunlight for even the shortest space of time. It is remarkable that this plant with its highly coloured exotic appearance should produce such beautiful leaves while growing in shaded locations. But *C. zebrina* always does very much better when placed under and in the shade of taller plants such as ficus and philodendrons, which offer a dark canopy of leaves. When watering, use tepid water and be sure that the soil is thoroughly soaked each time; but allow a drying-out period between waterings. Feed while new leaves are growing.

Take care
Avoid draughts and direct sun. 203♦

Carex morrowii variegata
(Japanese sedge)
- Light shade
- Temp: 7-18°C (45-65°F)
- Keep moist and fed

One of the most durable potted plants of them all, putting up with a wide variation of temperatures. It will also adapt reasonably well to erratic watering and feeding neglect, but in extreme conditions there is a likelihood of leaf turning brown. The narrow, arching grassy leaves are white-striped and about 30cm (12in) long, and form neat clusters.

To do well, this plant should be well watered and allowed to dry a little before repeating. Feeding should be done during spring and summer, not at other times. When bushy clumps of leaves have formed, pot plants on into slightly larger containers using a mixture containing some loam.

Propagation is very simple: water the pot, remove the plant, then divide the clump into smaller sections and pot the pieces individually into small pots to begin with, repotting them as they become large enough. Very hot conditions will be detrimental; cool and light are best.

Take care
Divide older clumps periodically.

Ceropegia woodii
(Hearts entangled)
- **Suspend in good light**
- **Temp: 13-18°C (55-65°F)**
- **Moist, but dry in winter**

With the current fashion for hanging plants of all kinds this is the ideal plant to try, as it is so different from almost all other potted plants. Small, fleshy heart-shaped leaves are attached to wiry stems that hang perpendicularly from the plant. *C. woodii* is a hanging plant with no desire whatsoever to climb or do anything different. The leaves are mottled and grey-green in colour and the flowers are pink and tubular.

The common name of 'hearts entangled' comes from the manner in which the foliage twines around itself when the plants are growing actively. There is also the additional fascination of the gnarled bulbous growths that appear at soil level and along the stems of the plant, from which new growth sprouts. Indeed, the bulbils with growth attached can be used to propagate fresh plants, or they can be raised from cuttings.

When planting hanging containers it is advisable to propagate a batch of plants and to put five or so into each.

Take care
Avoid overwet winter conditions. 205♦

Chlorophytum comosum variegatum
(Spider plant; St. Bernard's lily)
- **Airy, good light**
- **Temp: 10-16°C (50-60°F)**
- **Frequent feeding**

Like privet hedges in the garden the chlorophytums of the houseplant world appear to be everywhere. Yet they are not always as bright and healthy as their ease of culture would suggest they should be – in fact, many are extremely poor specimens. This may be due to the fact that owners feel that they are so easy to grow that they don't have to bother at all.

Give the chlorophytum good light to prevent it becoming thin and straggly, and keep it moist at all times, especially during summer.

The most important need of all, and the one most neglected, is that of feeding, and feeding the spider plant means giving it very much more than the average indoor plant. Frequent potting on is also essential, and this could be necessary twice a year for vigorous plants. Spider plants produce large fleshy roots and quickly become starved if not supplied with sufficient nourishment. Use a loam-based potting mixture.

Take care
Aphids cause blotched leaves. 204♦

Above: **Begonia masoniana**
Distinctive brown markings in the centre of the leaf give this plant the apt common name of iron cross begonia. Plants develop into a neat, rounded shape as they age. Rough textured foliage makes cleaning impossible other than by dusting with a soft brush. 195♦

Right: **Begonia rex**
Wealth of colour in the foliage and intricate leaf patterns place these plants among the elite of houseplants. Plants vary in their ease of culture, with smaller-leaved, more compact types being generally easier to raise. Leaves are borne on rhizomatous stems. 195♦

Above: **Caladium hybrid**
Supreme foliage plants that have leaves thin enough to be translucent in some varieties. Growth dies down in the autumn. 196♦

Left: **Calathea makoyana**
The peacock plant has large, oval-shaped leaves that are intricately patterned and paper thin. Stout leaf stalks spring from soil level. 197♦

Top right: **Calathea zebrina**
The leaves of this plant have a velvety texture, and are among the most beautiful of all foliage plants. Warmth and shade essential. 199♦

Right: **Calathea oppenheimiana tricolor**
Perhaps the easiest of the calatheas to care for. Colouring varies; better examples have more pink. 197♦

Above: **Chlorophytum comosum variegatum**
The familiar spider plant develops natural plantlets that can be used for propagating new plants. 200♦

Right: **Ceropegia woodii**
Natural trailing plants with grey-coloured heart-shaped leaves that have a succulent, puffed up appearance. 200♦

Below: **Cissus discolor**
The aristocrat of the decorative pot-grown vines. It has a natural climbing habit and does best in warm, shaded and moist conditions. 217♦

Above:
Codiaeum 'Eugene Drapps'
*By far the best yellow-coloured of
the commonly named Joseph's coat
plants. Grow in good light.* 219♦

Left: **Cocos weddelliana**
*The best of the finer foliaged palms,
and a slow growing plant that will
seldom outgrow its allotted space.
With age a basal trunk will form.* 218♦

Right: **Codiaeum hybrids**
*Codiaeums in general are among the
most highly coloured of all foliage
plants, but must have ample light if
they are not to revert to green.* 218♦

Above: **Coleus**
Easily cared for and in many brilliant colours that are seen at their best when grown in good light. 219♦

Top right: **Cryptanthus bromelioides tricolor**
This earth star has an extended growth habit and beautiful colour. 221♦

Right: **Cryptanthus 'Foster's Favourite'**
The stiff, unbending leaves of this fine bromeliad form a star shape. 221♦

Below:
Columnea banksii variegata
A fine trailing plant with small, plump, green-and-white leaves. 220♦

Above: **Cyperus alternifolius**
*Insignificant green leaves occur at
the base of stately stems 1.5-2.1m
(5-7ft) tall, from which sprout
umbrella-like canopies of growth.
Much water needed.* 222♦

Left: **Cryptanthius bromelioides 'It'**
*Small, star-shaped radiating growth
is neat and compact, making plants
ideal for small plant gardens in
bottles. Fascinating pink colour.* 220♦

Below: **Cyrtomium falcatum**
*With dark green, holly-like foliage
(but with no spines), the holly fern is
a long-established favourite. A
robust plant for shady places.* 223♦

Above:
Dichorisandra albo-lineata
*Tall-growing plants of the
tradescantia tribe with green-and-
white variegation that need good
light to thrive.* 224♦

Left: **Dieffenbachia amoena**
*One of the most majestic of the
dumb canes, growing to a height of
150cm (5ft) and 120cm (4ft) across.
Bold green leaves have tracery of
white in their central areas.* 225♦

Right: **Dieffenbachia camilla**
*Introduced in the late 1970s and one
of the finest of all the many
dieffenbachias. The green-margined
leaf is almost entirely cream.* 225♦

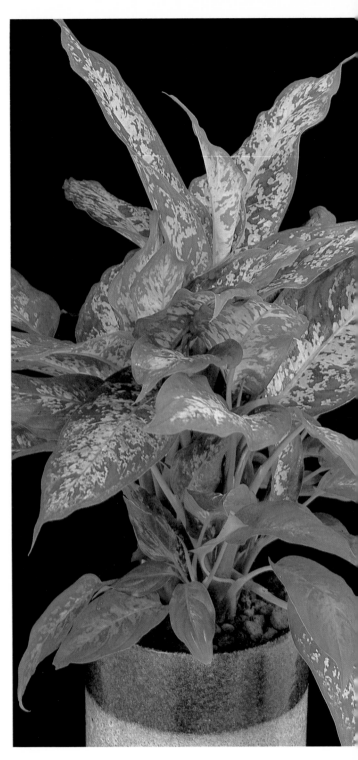

Above: **Dieffenbachia picta**
A well-established plant of graceful appearance with attractive pale green speckled foliage. 226♦

Left: **Dieffenbachia exotica**
The forerunner of the more compact dumb canes. It produces young growth at the base of the parent stem to give the plant a much fuller appearance. 226♦

Right:
Dieffenbachia 'Tropic Snow'
Bold foliage plants with stout green-and-white leaves. Needs warm, moist, shady conditions. 227♦

215

Above: **Dionaea muscipula**
The well-known Venus's fly trap is very difficult to care for, but has the fascinating ability of being able to catch flies in its sensitive leaves. 227♦

Below: **Dracaena deremensis 'Warneckii'**
A stately plant with grey-green and white striped foliage that grows to a height of 2.4-3m (8-10ft). 228♦

Cissus antarctica
(Kangaroo vine)
- **Light shade**
- **Temp: 13-18°C (55-65°F)**
- **Keep moist**

As the common name suggests, these plants originate from Australia. The mid-green leaves have toothed margins and are seen at their best when plants are allowed to climb against a framework or wall. In favourable conditions stems will add yards of growth, but trimming back to shape can be undertaken at any time of year, so there is no possibility of them out-growing their welcome. These are useful plants for the more difficult and possibly darker location indoors.

Cuttings consisting of two firm leaves with a piece of main stem attached will root at any time if a temperature of around 18-21°C (65-70°F) can be maintained; treat cuttings with a rooting powder. It is advisable to put several cuttings in one pot when they are removed from the propagator.

Peat compost will suit them fine, but it is essential that feeding is not neglected when plants are growing in this sort of mixture.

Take care
Dry soil will cause leaf-loss.

Cissus discolor
(Begonia vine)
- **Light shade**
- **Temp: 18-24°C (65-75°F)**
- **Keep moist and fed**

This most beautiful climbing foliage plant has maroon undersides, and an upper leaf surface with a mixture of silver, red, green and other colours. Plants climb by means of clinging tendrils if given some support; to prevent gaps appearing as plants extend, pin some of the straying shoots down the stem.

A dry atmosphere can result in shrivelling of the leaves, as will exposure to bright sun; and very dry soil conditions also cause leaf problems. It seems necessary to renew older plants periodically rather than allow them to become straggly. Cuttings prepared from mature, firm leaves with stem attached will root in a temperature of 21°C (70°F) if put into small pots filled with moist peat. A closed propagating case and treating cuttings with rooting powder will also speed the process. Once rooted, cuttings should be potted into slightly larger pots using peaty mixture, and the soil thereafter kept moist but not waterlogged.

Take care
Avoid bright sun. 204♦

Cocos weddelliana
(Weddell palm)
- **Light shade**
- **Temp: 16-21°C (60-70°F)**
- **Keep moist and fed**

Possibly the most beautiful and delicate of all the many palms offered for sale. However, being slow growing it is seen less often these days, as the commercial grower concentrates his efforts on palms that attain saleable size in a shorter time. One choice specimen of *C. weddelliana* is over 60 years old, with many fine stems reaching a height of some 3m (10ft).

A position out of direct sunlight is advised but one should not put the plant in the darkest corner, as reasonable light is essential to its well-being. Established plants can be fed at every watering with weak liquid fertilizer, with less being given – perhaps none at all – in winter. Some chemicals are harmful, so one should check suitability with the supplier before applying.

Its principal enemy is red spider mite. These mites cause pale discolouration of the foliage and are mostly found on the undersides of leaves.

Take care
Check regularly for red spider. 206♦

Codiaeum hybrids
(Joseph's coat)
- **Good light**
- **Temp: 16-21°C (60-70°F)**
- **Feed and water well**

Also known as crotons, these plants are among the most colourful of all foliage plants, as the common name suggests.

Full light, with protection from the strongest sunlight, is essential if plants are to retain their bright colouring. In poor light, new growth becomes thin and poor, and colouring is less brilliant. Besides light there is a need for reasonable temperature, without which shedding of lower leaves will be inevitable. Healthy plants that are producing new leaves will require to be kept moist with regular watering, but it is important that the soil should be well drained. Frequent feeding is necessary, though less is needed in winter. On account of vigorous top growth, there will be a mass of roots in the pots of healthy plants. Large plants that seem out of proportion to their pots should be inspected in spring and summer. If well rooted they should be potted into larger pots using loam-based compost.

Take care
Check regularly for red spider. 207♦

Codiaeum 'Eugene Drapps'
(Joseph's coat)
- **Good light**
- **Temp: 16-21°C (60-70°F)**
- **Feed and water well**

One of the queens of potted plants. The leaves are lance-shaped and almost entirely yellow in colour; only on closer inspection is it seen that there is also some green present.

New plants are grown from cuttings taken from the top section of the stem. Cuttings will have four or five leaves, and will be 15cm (6in) or more in length. A temperature in excess of 21°C (70°F) is needed to encourage rooting, and conditions should be close and moist. Once rooted in their peat propagating mixture, plants must be potted into loam-based compost as soon as they have made a reasonable amount of root. Once plants have got under way the top of the stem should be pinched out, to encourage the plant to branch.

In common with all codiaeums, this one will almost certainly attract red spider mites. These are difficult to detect on yellow foliage and a magnifying glass is usually necessary.

Take care
Keep moist, warm and light. 206♦

Coleus
(Flame nettle)
- **Good light**
- **Temp: 10-16°C (50-60°F)**
- **Keep moist and fed**

For little outlay the coleus offers more foliage colour than almost any other potted plant. Small plants can be purchased almost anywhere during the spring.

On getting plants home, if they are growing in small pots, advance them to pots a little larger in size. All the coleuses are hungry plants and any neglect with potting – or subsequently with feeding – will result in plants of much poorer quality. Full sun streaming through unprotected glass will usually be harmful, but these plants need plenty of light if they are to retain their colouring. Due to their light position it will be necessary to water plants frequently (every day, in some instances), and to ensure that the soil is thoroughly soaked each time. Better coloured plants can be retained from one year to the next; but it is better to take cuttings from these in late summer and to dispose of the often overgrown larger plant.

Take care
Provide good light for fine colour. 208♦

Columnea banksii variegata
(Variegated goldfish plant)
- **Light shade**
- **Temp: 16-21°C (60-70°F)**
- **Keep moist in summer**

The columneas are generally free-flowering plants, but the variegated form of *C. banksii* can be included among foliage plants, as it rarely produces flowers. The foliage is highly variegated, slow growing, and pendulous. The leaves are plump and fleshy, and attached to slender dropping stems; plants are seen at their best when suspended in a basket or hanging pot.

Cuttings are more difficult to root than the green forms of columnea. Short sections of stem with the lower leaves removed are best for propagating; treat with rooting powder before the cuttings, five to seven in small pots, are inserted in a peat and sand mixture. A temperature of at least 21°C (70°F) is necessary and a propagator will be a great advantage. Due to the very slow rate of growth, it is necessary to allow the soil to dry reasonably between waterings. Feed with weak fertilizer, but never overdo it.

Take care
Keep reasonably warm. 208♦

Cryptanthus bromelioides 'It'
(Earth star)
- **Light shade**
- **Temp: 16-21°C (60-70°F)**
- **Keep on dry side**

A comparatively recent introduction that resembles *C. tricolor,* but is of much bolder pink and is more attractive, although individual plants vary in brightness of colour. The new variety also grows closer to the pot. The leaves are stiffer in appearance, begin with a thick base attached to a short main stem, and taper to a point.

Cryptanthuses, like all bromeliads, require to be potted into a very open, free-draining mixture. One suggestion is to prepare a mixture of coarse leaf mould and a peaty houseplant potting mixture and to pot the plants in this, using small containers. Treated tree bark that is not too coarse may be used as a substitute for leaf mould. Place a few pieces of broken pot in the bottom of the container before introducing the soil. When watering these plants it is important that they have a thorough soak and then be allowed to dry reasonably before more is given. Clean rain water will be ideal.

Take care
Avoid sodden root conditions. 210♦

Cryptanthus bromelioides tricolor

(Earth star)
- **Light shade**
- **Temp: 16-21°C (60-70°F)**
- **Keep on dry side**

The pink, green and white colouring of this plant can be spectacular in well-grown specimens, but they are not easy plants to care for. Although grouped with the other flatter-growing cryptanthuses under the same common name of earth star, these have a slightly different habit of growth. The centre of the plant tends to extend upwards, and new plant growth sprouts from the side of the parent rosette. If these side growths are left attached to the parent a full and handsome plant will in time develop; or they can be removed when of reasonable size by pulling them sideways; it is then simple to press the pieces into peaty mixture for them to produce roots.

Almost all cryptanthuses are terrestrial and are seen at their best when nestled in the crevices of an old tree stump, or surrounded by a few stones. *C. tricolor,* with its more open habit of growing, can also be effective in a hanging pot or basket.

Take care
Avoid wet and cold conditions. 209♦

Cryptanthus 'Foster's Favourite'

(Earth star)
- **Light shade**
- **Temp: 16-21°C (60-70°F)**
- **Avoid excessive watering**

Another splendid example from the fine bromeliad family from tropical South America. Named after a famous American nurseryman, this tends to be much larger than most cryptanthus plants and produces long leaves with a pheasant-feather pattern. The thick, fleshy leaves have the shape of a dagger blade and radiate from a short central stem.

In their natural habitat these plants grow on the floor of the forest among old tree stumps and boulders, so they are capable of withstanding rough treatment. But remember the old maxim – which applies to almost all indoor plants – that when low temperatures prevail or plants are likely to be exposed to trying conditions they will fare much better if kept on the dry side. In fact, no bromeliads will prosper if roots are confined to pots that are permanently saturated. An open potting mixture is essential so that water can drain through very freely.

Take care
Never overwater. 209♦

Cussonia spictata
- **Light shade**
- **Temp: 13-21°C (55-70°F)**
- **Keep moist and fed**

If obtainable, it will not be difficult to raise new plants from seed. Given moist peat in which to germinate and a temperature in the region of 21°C (70°F), seed will soon get under way. From the seedling stage a loam-based potting mixture will be best, and in the first year potting on of vigorous plants should not be neglected. By the end of their first year, have plants in 13cm (5in) pots; in the spring of the second year, pot them on into 18cm (7in) pots. In their third year, pot on into 25cm (10in) pots if plants are obviously vigorous.

At all stages of potting on of these very vigorous plants it is advisable to use loam-based potting mixture. Also, when plants are established in their pots it is essential that they should be fed with a balanced liquid fertilizer at least once each week except during the winter months. Less water is also needed during the winter, although it may be necessary to continue watering plants that are clearly growing and able to take up moisture.

Take care
Keep well nourished.

Cyperus alternifolius
(Umbrella plant)
- **Light shade**
- **Temp: 13-18°C (55-65°F)**
- **Wet conditions**

Of the two cyperus species occasionally offered for sale this one is the less suitable for indoor conditions on account of its height and its need for very high humidity. The narrow green leaves have little attraction, but green flowers produced on stems that may attain 1.8-2.4m (6-8ft) have a certain fascination. The tall stems of *C. alternifolius* provide an interesting feature at higher level when planting indoor water gardens.

When grown indoors these water-loving plants must be given all the water they require. Although it would be death to most houseplants, place the pot in a large saucer capable of holding a reasonable amount of water, and ensure that the water level is regularly topped up.

Established plants benefit from regular feeding in liquid or tablet form. Tablets pressed into the soil at the frequency recommended by the manufacturer will provide a continual source of nutrient and is one of the best methods of feeding.

Take care
Keep permanently wet. 211▶

Cyperus diffusus
(Umbrella plant)
- **Light shade**
- **Temp: 13-18°C (55-65°F)**
- **Wet conditions**

Flower stalks with their umbrella-like tops are produced in large numbers and attain around 60cm (2ft). The green leaves are not attractive, but the combination of leaves and flower stalks presents an attractive plant that will thrive in wet conditions.

Ideally, *C. diffusus* should stand in a large saucer that is kept permanently filled with water. The simplest way to raise new plants is to split up the clump of small plants into sections that can be easily accommodated in a 13cm (5in) pot. Use a compost that contains a good proportion of loam, and pot firmly so that the roots will hold together in the very wet conditions.

Few pests trouble these plants, but there may be the occasional mealy bug. These are mostly to be found around the flowers, and one should use a small firm paint brush that has been soaked in methylated spirits to remove them. Mealy bugs are white and powdery and enclose their young in a protective covering that resembles cotton wool.

Take care
Keep permanently wet.

Cyrtomium falcatum
(Holly fern)
- **Shade**
- **Temp: 16-21°C (60-70°F)**
- **Keep moist**

As the common name suggests, this fern's foliage has the appearance of holly, and is dark, glossy green in colour. Individual fronds will grow to some 60cm (2ft) in length when mature.

Suitable conditions are necessary for maximum success in fern propagation. But reasonable results can be obtained in the home if a heated propagator and moist, not saturated, conditions are available. Older leaves develop spores on the back; these have the appearance of a brownish rust that could well be mistaken for disease. When spores can be seen to fall like a fine dust when the leaf is tapped, the leaf can be removed and put in a paper bag in a warm place and left for a few days. The spores can then be sown on the surface of moist peat and placed in a propagator to germinate. They should be sown sparingly, as a dense mass of young plants will appear if conditions are right. When large enough to handle, these should be potted in peaty mixture.

Take care
Avoid direct sunlight. 211♦

223

Davallia canariensis
(Hare's foot fern)
- Light shade
- Temp: 10-16°C (50-60°F)
- Moist in summer, drier in winter

Besides being useful on the windowsill, these toughish ferns also make fine hanging plants. The fans of foliage are pale green and stiff, and are carried on firm stems.

New plants can be raised from ripe spores sown at any time in a temperature of not less than 21°C (70°F); the peat on which spores are sown should be kept moist. A simpler method is to divide the rhizomes of mature plants in spring, and to pot the small sections in pots filled with houseplant potting mixture containing a high proportion of peat.

While they are in active growth, keep plants moist; and during the less active months ensure that watering is not overdone. Established plants can be fed during spring and summer, but winter feeding should be avoided.

Be careful when contemplating the use of chemicals on these plants, as they can be very easily damaged: try the chemical on a small part of the plant first as a trial.

Take care
Avoid winter wetness.

Dichorisandra albo-lineata
- Light shade
- Temp: 16-21°C (60-70°F)
- Keep moist and fed

This member of the tradescantia family is also known as *Campelia zanonia albo-marginata*. Growing to a height of some 120cm (4ft) when confined to a pot, it produces lance-shaped leaves that are green and white in colour, edged with red. Stems are woody and plants are attractive enough, but they shed their lower leaves as they increase in height, which produces leafless stalks with rosettes of foliage at the top. Put them with other plants, so that they occupy the rear position with shorter plants in front.

Alternatively, the top section can be removed and rooted in warm conditions; when growing well it can be planted at the base of the parent plant to grow up and partly cover the bare stem. New growth will appear below where the cuttings were removed. Plants should be kept moist and warm, and when potting, loam-based mixture should be used. Plants can be fed while growing new leaves, but not in winter.

Take care
Avoid wetness and cold in winter. 212►

Dieffenbachia amoena
(Dumb cane)
- **Light shade**
- **Temp: 18-24°C (65-75°F)**
- **Keep moist and fed**

This is possibly the largest of the dieffenbachias. The large, striking grey-green leaves with central colouring of speckled white and green will add much to any collection of indoor plants, but mature plants attain a height of 1.2-1.5m (4-5ft) with equal spread. However, stout stems can be cut out with a small saw. When carrying out any sort of work on dieffenbachias, though, gloves should be worn to prevent any sap getting onto one's skin. Even moving plants that have wet foliage may result in skin disorders. Also keep plants out of reach of children and pets. The common name of dumb cane derives from the fact that if the sap of the plant gets into one's mouth it will have unpleasant effects. Fortunately, such an occurrence is unlikely, as the sap has a very nasty odour.

Dieffenbachias belong to the same family of plants as the philodendrons, and respond to the same sort of conditions.

Take care
Never get sap onto your skin.

Dieffenbachia camilla
(Dumb cane)
- **Light shade**
- **Temp: 16-21°C (60-70°F)**
- **Keep moist and fed**

The beauty of this plant lies in the incredible colouring of the leaves, which have a green margin and a central area that is almost entirely creamy white. And anyone who knows their plants will be aware that areas of white in any leaf constitute a weakness that renders the plant vulnerable to leaf rot. But the thin marginal band of green seems to offer some form of protection, and this is in fact a reasonably easy plant.

With a maximum height around 60cm (2ft), it is much better suited to indoor conditions of today than most of the dieffenbachias available. Even as a small plant this one will have a natural tendency to produce basal shoots around the main plant stem, which gives a fuller and more attractive appearance. This plant is one of the indispensables when it comes to arranging plant displays. In groups indoors many moisture-loving plants will do much better if they are placed together in arrangements.

Take care
Never get sap onto your skin. 213♦

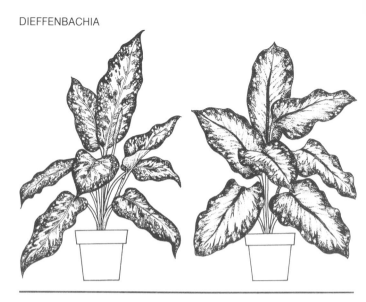

Dieffenbachia exotica
(Dumb cane)
- **Light shade**
- **Temp: 16-21°C (60-70°F)**
- **Keep moist and fed**

The introduction of *D. exotica* within the past decade was something of a revolution as far as dieffenbachias were concerned. Previous plants of this kind were decidedly difficult subjects to grow at the nurseries, to transport, and to keep once they arrived at the home of the purchaser; they were also inclined to be too large for the average room of today.

D. exotica is a neat plant growing to a maximum of 60cm (2ft) – much more suitable for indoors – and with a much tougher constitution. It tolerates lower temperatures, and if not too wet does not seem to suffer. It produces clusters of young plants at the base of the parent stem, and can be propagated easily by removing the basal shoots and planting them separately in small pots filled with peat. Once rooted they should be potted in a peaty houseplant compost. Shoots can often be removed with roots attached, but gloves should be worn.

Take care
Never get sap onto your skin. 214♦

Dieffenbachia picta
(Dumb cane)
- **Light shade**
- **Temp: 18-24°C (65-75°F)**
- **Keep moist and fed**

This is one of the traditional warm greenhouse plants that may have been found in many a Victorian conservatory at the turn of the century when exotic plants were all the rage. Not seen so frequently today, *D. picta* has speckled yellowish-green colouring and grows to a height of 90cm (3ft) when given proper care. If the top of the plant is removed when young, the plant will produce numerous side growths that will make it a more attractive shape. An effective display plant when carefully grown.

In common with all the many fine dieffenbachias these plants require warm and humid conditions. Permanently saturated soil must be avoided, but it is important that the pot is well watered with each application, and surplus water is seen to drain through the bottom of the pot. It is equally important that the soil should dry reasonably before further water is given.

Take care
Avoid low temperatures. 215♦

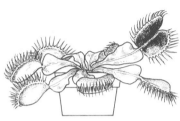

Dieffenbachia 'Tropic Snow'
(Dumb cane)
- **Light shade**
- **Temp: 18-24°C (65-75°F)**
- **Keep moist and fed**

This is a close relative of *D. amoena*, the difference being that the leaves of this plant are stiffer in appearance and have a greater area of white.

New plants are raised from cuttings, and these may be prepared either from the top section of the stem with two or more leaves attached, or from sections of thick stem that have no leaves whatsoever. Top sections are put into pots of peat at a temperature of 21°C (70°F). The stems are cut into sections 10cm (4in) long and laid on their sides in boxes of peat; it is important that the stem cutting should have a growth bud from which growth may in time develop.

Leaves of this plant are inclined to be brittle and are easily damaged if carelessly handled. There is also need for care when plant leaves are being cleaned: a supporting hand should be placed underneath the leaf as the upper area is wiped clean with a soft cloth or sponge. Do not use chemical cleaners too often.

Take care
Never get sap onto your skin. 215♦

Dionaea muscipula
(Venus's fly trap)
- **Light shade**
- **Temp: 18-27°C (65-80°F)**
- **Moist atmosphere**

The Venus's fly trap is one of the most difficult of potted plants to care for indoors, but the appealing common name will ensure that it retains continued popularity.

Plants may be bought in pots in dormant stage or be acquired in leaf and growing in small pots covered by a plastic dome. The dome offers the plant some protection and helps to retain essential humidity around the plant while it is in transit, so making the dome-covered plant a much better buy. When caring for these plants adequate warmth and high humidity are essential.

When the leaves are touched, a mechanism within the plant induces the oval-shaped leaves to fold together. There are also long stiff hairs along the margins of the leaves; a fly, alighting on the leaf, will activate the mechanism and become trapped. The plant can digest the fly, and feeding flies and minute pieces of meat to the leaves is one way of nourishing the plant.

Take care
Humidity and warmth are essential. 216♦

227

*Dracaena
deremensis* 'Bausei'

Dioscorea discolor
(Variegated yam)
- Light shade
- Temp: 18-24°C (65-75°F)
- Keep moist when in leaf

The heart-shaped leaves are maroon on the reverse; the upper surface is in many shades of dark and light green fusing together with silver-grey. The stems are thin and the species has a tendency to climb.

These plants are grown from potato-like tubers that are placed in 13cm (5in) pots filled with loam-based soil; peat would be quite unable to sustain them.

A temperature in the region of 21°C (70°F) is required to force the yams into growth, but once they start you can almost stand and watch them grow. These natural climbers will need a tall trellis for support.

The plant will die down in autumn, when tubers should be stored in their pots in a warm place. The following spring, all the old soil should be removed from around the tubers, and they should then be potted in a fresh mixture.

Ample watering and feeding will be needed while plants are growing, and they cannot abide low temperatures or bright sunlight.

Take care
Keep stored tubers warm and dry.

Dracaena deremensis
(Striped dracaena)
- Light
- Temp: 16-21°C (60-70°F)
- Keep on the dry side

There are numerous improved forms of this dracaena, all erect with broad, pointed leaves up to 60cm (2ft) long. The variations are mostly in leaf colour: *D. deremensis* Bausei has a dark green margin and glistening white centre; in *D. deremensis* Souvenir de Schriever the top-most rosette of leaves is bright yellow, but the leaves revert to the grey-green with white stripes of the parent plant as they age.

An unfortunate aspect of this type of dracaena is that they shed lower leaves as they increase in height, so that they take on a palm-like appearance with tufts of leaves at the top of otherwise bare stems. Although loss of lower leaves is a natural process, the incidence of dying and falling leaves will be aggravated by excessive watering. Water thoroughly, and then allow the soil to dry reasonably before repeating. These are hungry plants and will be in need of regular feeding, with loam-based soil recommended for potting on.

Take care
Never allow to become too wet. 216♦

Dracaena fragrans 'Massangeana'

Dracaena fragrans
(Corn palm)
- **Light shade**
- **Temp: 18-24°C (65-75°F)**
- **Keep moist and fed**

The green-foliaged type is seldom offered for sale, but there are two important cultivars. The easiest to care for is *D. fragrans* 'Massangeana', which has broad mustard-coloured leaves attached to stout central stems; and presenting a little more difficulty there is *D. fragrans* 'Victoria' with brighter creamy-gold colouring.

As with most dracaenas there will be loss of lower leaves as plants increase in height, but plants eventually take on a stately, palm-like appearance.

Fortunately, few pests trouble these plants, but there is the occasional possibility of mealy bugs finding their way into the less accessible parts that lie between the base of the leaf and the stem of the plant. Prepare malathion solution and with the aid of a hand sprayer inject the insecticide down among the base of the leaves. As with all activities involving insecticides, wear rubber gloves and take all recommended precautions.

Take care
Feed established plants well. 235♦

Dracaena godseffiana
(Gold dust dracaena)
- **Good light**
- **Temp: 16-21°C (60-70°F)**
- **Keep moist and fed**

Unlike most dracaenas, this one has rounded leaves attached to wiry stems that rarely attain a height of more than 90cm (3ft). The green form is not so attractive, but the cultivar *D. godseffiana* 'Florida Beauty' is a fine plant with yellow foliage interspersed with green.

As with all dracaenas, use a well-drained loam-based compost when potting on into larger containers. The comparatively low, spreading growth will be more suited to shallow containers. Put some drainage material in the bottom of the pot before the soil is introduced. Broken pieces of clay pot are ideal.

It is seldom necessary to use containers more than 18cm (7in) in diameter; but once plants are established in pots of this size, ensure that they get regular feeding. This usually means feeding about once a week while plants are in active growth, but in the winter only if fresh leaves are appearing and the plant is growing in very agreeable conditions.

Take care
Avoid excessive watering.

Dracaena marginata
(Silhouette plant)
- **Light shade**
- **Temp: 13-21°C (55-70°F)**
- **Keep on dry side**

D. marginata's dagger-shaped leaves have a reddish margin and are attached to firm upright whitish-grey stems. Among the easiest of indoor plants to care for, its only major objection is to excessive watering. Water plants well and allow them to dry out before repeating, and they will present few problems. Similar in habit is *D. marginata tricolor,* which has an attractive pink colouring but is a little more difficult to care for. See separate article for more details.

Both plants can grow to some 1.8-2.4m (6-8ft), but by pinching out the growing tip at a height of 90cm (3ft) it will be found that a plant with multiheads will result. This provides a more compact and neater plant for the average living room. Top sections root readily in a mixture of peat and sand if placed in a propagator at a temperature around 21°C (70°F). When potting on, use a loam-based mixture and pot firmly. Peaty mixtures are of little value to large plants.

Take care
Avoid saturated root conditions.

Dracaena marginata tricolor
(Variegated silhouette plant)
- **Good light**
- **Temp: 16-21°C (60-70°F)**
- **Avoid wet conditions**

This plant has a natural tendency to shed lower leaves as it increases in height. Nevertheless, it can be an elegant plant if carefully grown, having attractive light and darker colouring running along the entire length of the slender, pointed leaves.

The main stem of the plant will need a supporting cane to remain upright. Plants sometimes produce young shoots naturally along the main stem so that multiheaded plants result. Alternatively, one can remove the growing tip of the main stem when the plant is about 60cm (2ft) tall, so that branching is encouraged. If plants are grown in soil that is constantly saturated, the incidence of leaf damage will be much increased. The soil for these plants should always be on the dry side, especially so during winter.

Feeding is not desperately important, but weak liquid fertilizer during the spring and summer months will do no harm; winter feeding is not advised.

Take care
Keep warm, light and dry. 234♦

Dracaena terminalis 'Firebrand'
(Flaming dragon tree)
- **Good light**
- **Temp: 18-24°C (65-75°F)**
- **Keep moist and fed**

Few foliage plants can match the rich red colouring of this dracaena though it is not the easiest of potted plants to care for. The colourful leaves are erect and spear-shaped.

Plants are grown by the nurseryman in a very open mixture composed mainly of pine leaf mould; this ensures that when water is poured onto the soil it drains freely through. It is preferable to use rain water, and to ensure that the soil is saturated each time. Avoid bone-dry conditions, but endeavour to allow some drying out of the soil between each soaking.

Good light is needed for *D. terminalis* to retain its bright colouring, but full sun through glass window-panes may cause scorching of foliage, so plants should be protected from such exposure. While new leaves are growing it will be important to feed plants at regular intervals, but it is not normally necessary to feed during the winter months.

Take care
Avoid excessive watering. 233♦

Eucalyptus gunnii
(Blue gum)
- **Good light**
- **Temp: 7-16°C (45-60°F)**
- **Keep moist and fed**

In the tropics the blue gums are invasive major trees, but for our purpose the smaller-leaved variety, *E. gunnii*, makes a very acceptable indoor plant, and is hardy outside in many areas. Rounded leaves have a grey-blue colouring that can be very pleasing in plant groupings.

For cooler areas that offer adequate light these are excellent plants that will overwinter without trouble if roots are not excessively wet while temperatures are at lower levels. During their more active summer months they will need regular watering and feeding. These are quite vigorous plants and should be regularly potted on during their early stages of growth. Peat-based potting mixes will be fine for plants in their early development, but as they advance beyond the 13cm (5in) pot it will be essential to use a loam-based potting mixture. Also, as plants tend to become tall and thin it is advisable to use clay pots, which will provide a more stable base than plastic ones.

Take care
Avoid wet winter conditions. 235♦

231

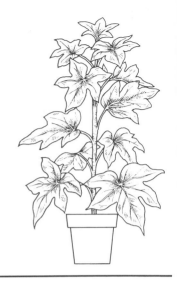

Euonymus japonicus medio-pictus
(Spindle tree)
- **Good light**
- **Temp: 7-18°C (45-65°F)**
- **Keep moist and fed**

This is another of the hardy outdoor plants that can be put to good use as subjects for indoor decoration. The leaves of this one are bright yellow in the centre with a green margin. With proper care it will grow to a height of 120cm (4ft). The woody stems can, however, be trimmed to a more manageable size at any time. There are other members of the euonymus family, such as the silver-foliaged *E. radicans*, which are more prostrate, and these will be the better for an annual clip into shape.

   Good light is essential so plants need a fairly bright windowsill, but full sun will be harmful. Excessive watering will be damaging, particularly during the winter months when growth is less active. Feeding can be undertaken while plants are growing but should be discontinued in winter. When potting on a loam-based mixture is ideal.

   Some branches will have a tendency to revert to green colouring, and it is best to cut these out.

Take care
Avoid hot, dry conditions. 237♦

Fatshedera lizei
(Ivy tree)
- **Light shade**
- **Temp: 4-16°C (40-60°F)**
- **Keep moist and fed**

This plant does not have the flexibility of the stems of *Hedera* (ivy), which is one of its parents, but is more in keeping with the stems of *Fatsia*, which is the other parent. Leaves have the shape of the ivy leaf and are glossy green in colour. For cooler locations the ivy tree is ideal, as it prefers low rather than high temperatures and is hardy in sheltered areas. Plants have a tendency to lose lower leaves, especially in hot, dry conditions.

   New plants may be propagated either from the topmost section of the plant with three firm leaves attached or from sections of stem with a single leaf attached. In both cases they will do well in a temperature of around 18°C (65°F) if inserted in peat and sand mixture. In order to provide plants of full appearance, it is best to put three or four rooted cuttings in the growing pot rather than a single piece. The soil for potting up cuttings should be on the peaty side.

Take care
Avoid hot conditions. 236♦

Above: **Dracaena 'Firebrand'**
*This brilliantly coloured plant grows
to a height of 60-90cm (2-3ft) and*
*needs light and warm conditions.
Leaf discolouration may result from
wet soil through bad drainage.* 231 ♦

Above:
Dracaena marginata tricolor
The striking colours of the narrow *leaves will develop well in good light. Soil should be kept on the dry side to prevent leaf drop.* 230♦

Above: **Dracaena fragrans
'Massangeana'**
*Strong, upright stems carry broad,
gracefully curved leaves.* 229♦

Below: **Eucalyptus gunnii**
*An attractive blue gum with small
leaves closely grouped on slender
stems. Hardy in sheltered areas.* 231♦

Above: **Euonymus japonicus**
Hardy out of doors, but also a fine bushy plant for cooler areas in the home. Good light will keep foliage colours really bright. 232♦

Left: **Fatshedera lizei**
The naturally glossy green leaves are attached to strong stems that should be supported so that the foliage can be seen to best advantage. 232♦

Below: **Fatshedera lizei variegata**
Yellow and white variegated forms are available, both of which need cool conditions to do well. 249♦

Left: **Ficus benjamina**
The elegant weeping fig has glossy green foliage and naturally cascading branches – a combination that produces one of the finest foliage plants. 249▸

Right: **Ficus benjamina 'Hawaii'**
Similar in appearance to the weeping fig, but of more erect habit and with brightly variegated leaves that are seen at their best in good light. 250▸

Below right: **Ficus lyrata**
Leaf shape gives the common name of fiddle leaf fig to one of the boldest and most vigorous indoor plants. Veined leaves are naturally glossy green. 251▸

Below: **Ficus europa**
Easily the best variegated form of broad-leaved rubber plants, with remarkably fine colouring and relatively easy to care for. 250▸

Left: **Ficus pumila**
Commonly named the creeping fig, it will also climb a damp wall or can be trained to a moss-covered support. The small, oval leaves are pale green and attached to wiry stems that have a natural twisting habit. 251♦

Right: **Fittonia argyroneura nana**
The silvery-grey colouring is heavily veined with a tracery of darker green that gives the oval leaves an attractive appearance. Plants have a creeping habit and need warmth and moisture. 252♦

Below: **Ficus robusta**
One of the symbols of the houseplant business, the rubber plant has broad glossy green leaves that are attached to stout upright stems. The leaves should be cleaned with a moist sponge. 252♦

Above: **Fittonia verschaffeltii**
Paper-thin leaves are of dull red colouring and are heavily veined, providing a plant of exotic appearance. Difficult to care for, the plant needs warm, moist, shady conditions. 253♦

Right: **Grevillea robusta**
When well grown the leaves of the silk oak have a silvery sheen that is most attractive. These vigorous plants need frequent feeding and cool, light conditions. 254♦

Below: **Gynura sarmentosa**
A member of the nettle family. The leaves are a vivid purple with a generous covering of tiny hairs that give the plant a rich glow of colour when seen in sunlight. 254♦

Above: **Hedera (small-leaved)**
There are many shapes and colours of these, all needing good light and cool conditions. Plants will climb or trail and all are hardy out of doors.

Top left:
Hedera maculata
With mottled greenish-gold foliage this is one of the larger-leaved ivies. It must have a supporting stake. 256♦

Left:
Hedera canariensis
In poor light the colourfully variegated foliage will revert to green. Offer good light. 255♦

Right: **Hedera helix 'Goldchild'**
Warm golden-yellow colouring places this ivy ahead of most foliage plants – it was once described as 'a bowl of sunshine'. 256♦

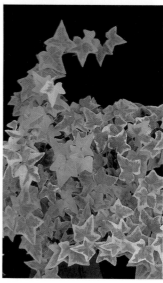

Above: **Helxine soleirolii**
*Minute bright green leaves are tightly
clustered and provide plants that are
neat hummocks of growth.* 257♦

Below: **Heptapleurum arboricola**
*Elegant, upright, green-foliaged
plants with palmate leaves that offer
a canopy of umbrella-like growth.* 257♦

Above: **Heptapleurum arboricola variegata**
Having the same habit as the green form but somewhat slower growing. The colouring is green and yellow with the latter predominating. 258♦

Above: **Hosta**
There are many attractive forms of these hardy plants, all developing into attractive clumps that need airy, light and moist conditions. 259♦

Below: **Hypoestes sanguinolenta**
The original spotted variety of this plant has been overtaken by a new one with much more pink. Needs light, moist conditions. 259♦

Fatshedera lizei variegata
(Variegated ivy tree)
- **Light shade**
- **Temp: 4-16°C (40-60°F)**
- **Keep moist and fed**

Most variegated plants are that little bit more difficult to care for than their green counterparts, and the variegated fatshedera is no exception. But provided it is not subjected to very high temperatures for long periods it will not prove too much of a problem.

Plants should be kept moist and well fed during the growing season and on the dry side with little or no feeding in winter. In agreeable conditions they will grow quite quickly on long single stems. However, the tip of the plant can be removed to encourage side shoots to grow and give the plant a more attractive appearance.

Besides the white variegated form there is now a cultivar with more golden foliage often labelled as *F. lizei aurea.* In my experience of growing the latter it would seem to be a marginally more difficult plant to care for, but none of the fatshederas can be classed as difficult.

Take care
Avoid hot and dry conditions. 237♦

Ficus benjamina
(Weeping fig)
- **Good light, no direct sun**
- **Temp: 16-21°C (60-70°F)**
- **Keep moist and fed**

Of very graceful weeping habit, *F. benjamina* will develop into tree size if provided with the right conditions. However, excess growth can be trimmed out at any time. To maintain plants in good condition with their glossy leaves gleaming it is important to feed them well while in active growth, and to pot them on into loam-based mixture as required. Little feeding and no potting should be done in winter, and it is also wise during this period to water more sparingly unless the plants are drying out in hot rooms. The weeping fig has a tendency to shed leaves in poorly lit situations.

Not many pests affect ficus plants, but scale insects seem to favour *F. benjamina.* These are either dark or light brown in colour and cling to stems and the undersides of leaves. Another sign of their presence will be dark sooty deposits on leaves below where the pests are clinging. It is best to wash them off with malathion.

Take care
Avoid placing in dark areas. 238♦

Ficus benjamina 'Hawaii'
(Variegated weeping fig)
- **Light shade**
- **Temp: 16-21°C (60-70°F)**
- **Keep moist and fed**

A recent introduction with white-and-green variegated leaves that seems likely to become a very successful indoor subject.

To get the best from these plants they need good light without bright sun, and the temperature should not fall below 16°C (60°F). Watering should follow the standard procedure for larger indoor plants, ie well watered from the top with surplus water clearly seen to drain out of the bottom of the container. The plant should then be left until the soil has dried out to a reasonable degree before watering again.

Younger plants should be provided with a supporting stake and the plant tied to the stake as new growth develops. However, a few strands should be allowed to hang over so that a plant with weeping growth all the way up results.

Like the green *F. benjamina*, this will tend to shed leaves at a rather alarming rate if it is placed in too dark a location.

Take care
Avoid placing in dark areas. 239♦

Ficus europa
(Variegated rubber plant)
- **Good light**
- **Temp: 16-21°C (60-70°F)**
- **Keep moist and fed**

Far and away the best variegated broad-leaved rubber plant ever to be produced. Leaf colouring is a bright cream and green and the stems are bold and upright. Unlike previous variegated rubber plants this one does not have the usual tendency to develop brown discolouration along its leaf margins, and it is altogether more vigorous.

Taller plants will require supporting stakes, and ample watering and feeding while new leaves are being produced. This should be all year except during the winter months. However, some plants are slow to get on the move and such plants should be watered with care until it is seen that new leaves are on the way at the top of the stem.

All the broad-leaved rubber plants will be the better for cleaning with a damp cloth or sponge periodically, but one should not be too enthusiastic when it comes to use of chemical cleaners.

Take care
Avoid wet winter conditions. 238♦

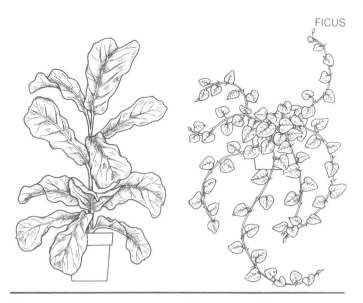

Ficus lyrata
(Fiddle leaf fig)
- **Light shade**
- **Temp: 16-21°C (60-70°F)**
- **Keep moist and fed**

One of the more majestic members of the fig family, *F. lyrata* develops into a small branching tree. Leaves are glossy green with prominent veins and, as the common name suggests, are shaped like the body of a violin. The original single stem of the plant will naturally shed lower leaves and the plant will produce leaf buds in the axils of the topmost four to six leaves, and in time these will become the branches of the tree.

It is important to seek out plants that have fresh, dark green leaves rather than those that may be marked or discoloured. Indoors they should be offered reasonable light and warmth, and in their early stages of development they will need careful watering; the plants are best kept on the dry side rather than too wet. More mature plants in larger pots will require more watering and more frequent feeding, with less of both being given in winter. The plant can be pruned at any time to improve its shape.

Take care
Avoid cold draughts. 239♦

Ficus pumila
(Creeping fig)
- **Light shade**
- **Temp: 16-21°C (60-70°F)**
- **Keep moist**

A simple plant, yet one of my personal favourites. Leaves are quite small as ficus plants go and are oval in shape. The plant may climb if provided with a support, or be allowed to trail in a natural manner. A good plant for mixed displays.

These plants must have reasonable temperature, and it is imperative that they be kept moist at all times; drying out of the soil will almost inevitably result in the loss of the plant. However, plants should not become sodden through standing permanently in water. They will tolerate drying out a little between waterings, but it must not be excessive. Feed them while they are growing, giving little or none in winter, and when potting on use a peaty mixture.

Cleaning individual leaves can be tedious, and I would suggest that a quick and adequate job can be done by inverting the plant in a bucket filled with soapy water and giving it a good swish around.

Take care
Avoid very dry conditions. 240♦

Ficus robusta
(Rubber plant)
- **Light shade**
- **Temp: 10-18°C (50-65°F)**
- **Avoid very wet conditions**

Almost the symbol of the modern-day houseplant business, the rubber plant is still grown and sold in large quantities. *Ficus robusta* now seems firmly established as the favourite rubber plant, and we seldom see its predecessors these days. The original variety was *F. elastica*, which in time was replaced by *F. decora*. The new plant is superior in almost every way, particularly in its ability to stand up to indoor conditions.

    Failure with these plants usually arises from overwatering. Permanently wet soil results in roots rotting away, which will mean loss of leaves. It is especially important to prevent plants becoming too wet during the winter months. During the winter it is also wise to discontinue feeding. Potting should be undertaken during late spring or early summer, using loam-based mixture. Leaves will be brighter if occasionally cleaned with a damp sponge.

Take care
Protect from sun through glass. 240♦

Fittonia argyroneura nana
(Little snakeskin plant)
- **Shade**
- **Temp: 18-24°C (65-75°F)**
- **Keep moist and humid**

The smaller-leaved version of the silver snakeskin plant is much less demanding than its big brother. The leaves are oval in shape and produced in great quantity by healthy plants. Neat growth and prostrate habit makes them ideal for growing in bottle gardens or disused fish tanks.

    Cuttings roots with little difficulty in warm, moist and shaded conditions. Several cuttings should go into small pots filled with peaty mixture, and it is often better to overwinter these small plants rather than try to persevere with larger plants. At all stages of potting on a peaty mixture will be essential, and it is better to use shallow containers that will suit the plant's prostrate growth.

    Not much troubled by pests; the worst enemy by far is low temperature allied to wet root conditions. Recommended temperature levels must be maintained, and this is especially important during cold weather.

Take care
Avoid wet and cold combination. 241♦

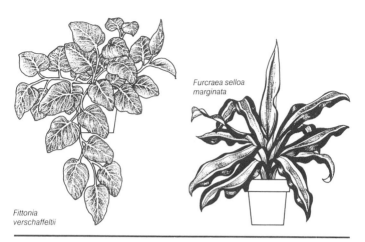

Fittonia
verschaffeltii

Furcraea selloa
marginata

Fittonia
(large-leaved)
(Snakeskin plant)
- Shade
- Temp: 18-24°C (65-75°F)
- Keep moist and humid

There are two of these that one will
be likely to come across, neither of
them very easy to care for. With large
reddish-green leaves there is *F.
verschaffeltii*, and with attractively
veined silver leaves there is *F.
argyroneura*. Both are of prostrate
habit, with leaves tending to curl
downwards over their containers. In
my experience these plants rarely do
well on the windowsill. They fare
much better in miniature
greenhouses, disused fish tanks or
bottle gardens. In such situations the
plants are free of draughts.

Bright sunlight will play havoc with
the tender foliage so these plants
must be in the shade, but not
necessarily in very dark locations.
When applying water it is best to
warm it slightly and to dampen the
area surrounding the pot as well as
the soil in which the plants are
growing. Frequent but small feeds
will be better than occasional heavy
doses – a little with each watering.

Take care
Avoid low temperatures. 242

Furcraea
- Good light
- Temp: 13-21°C (55-70°F)
- Keep moist and fed

There are several of these that one
may come across, and where
reasonable space can be offered
they can develop into spectacular
plants. The thick, fleshy leaves
radiate from the centre of the plant in
the form of a rosette and in some
varieties they may grow to a length of
120-150cm (4-5ft). For such
specimens adequate space is
essential, particularly as the larger
sorts have vicious-looking spines.

Growing these plants should not
be too much of a problem provided
they have a reasonable temperature
and are not allowed to become
excessively dry at their roots.
Feeding the more massive
specimens will have to be done with
some thoroughness and will mean
each time the plant is watered.

Besides the very large kinds there
is *F. foetida*, which produces leaves
45cm (18in) in length. But this one
will also present a few problems as
the spiny leaves are very stiff.

Take care
Be wary of the spined leaves.

Grevillea robusta
(Silk oak)
- **Light shade**
- **Temp: 4-21°C (40-70°F)**
- **Feed and water well**

An Australian plant, the silk oak makes a splendid tree in its native land, and is a fairly fast-growing pot plant in many other parts of the world. It is tough, has attractive, green silky foliage and is one of the easiest plants to care for. It can be readily raised from seed.

The grevillea will quickly grow into a large plant if it is kept moist and well fed, and if it is potted into a larger container when the existing one is well filled with roots. A loam-based soil is best. If plants become too tall for their allotted space it is no trouble to remove the more invasive branches with a pair of secateurs – almost any time of the year will do for this exercise.

During the summer months when the plant is in full vigour it will be important to ensure that it is obtaining sufficient water, and this will mean filling the top of the pot and ensuring that the surplus runs right through and out at the bottom drainage holes.

Take care
Water well in summer. 243♦

Gynura sarmentosa
(Velvet plant)
- **Good light**
- **Temp: 13-18°C (55-65°F)**
- **Keep moist and fed**

Scented flowers are a bonus with almost all plants, but the gynuras have been blessed with a scent that is obnoxious enough to be almost damaging to the senses. Weedy flowers appear in summer and should be removed before they have a chance to open. However, there are almost always compensations in nature and the gynuras are favoured with violet-tinged foliage that is hairy and very striking when seen in sunlight. They will grow at a rampant pace in light conditions if they are being watered carefully and fed regularly. Given a supporting cane plants can be encouraged to climb, but they are seen at their best when trailing from a pot or basket.

Untidy growth can be trimmed back at almost any time, and firm pieces may be used for propagating new plants. This should be done regularly as older plants tend to become untidy and lose their bright colouring. It is best to put several cuttings in each pot and to pinch out tips for bushy plants.

Take care
Replace older plants every year. 242♦

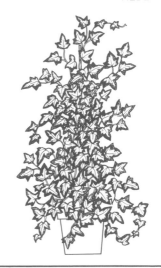

Hedera canariensis
(Canary Island ivy)
- **Good light**
- **Temp: 4-16°C (40-60°F)**
- **Keep moist and fed in summer**

This is one of the most rewarding indoor plants of them all, having bright green-and-white variegation and being reasonably undemanding to grow. The principal need is for light, cool conditions and a watering programme that allows for some drying out of the soil between each good soaking.

Plants can be encouraged to climb or trail, and they are excellent for those difficult cooler places such as hallways. In hot, dry conditions the plants are likely to become infested with red spider mite. These are minute insects that increase at an alarming rate if left to their own devices. In time the mites will make tiny webs from one part of the plant to another, but initially they are difficult to detect and are almost invariably found on the undersides of leaves. When infested with mite the leaves tend to curl inwards and appear hard and dry. Thorough and frequent drenching with insecticide is the best cure and should be done carefully out of doors on a still day.

Take care
Avoid hot, dry conditions. 244♦

Hedera Golden Heart
(Jubilee ivy)
- **Good light**
- **Temp: 4-16°C (40-60°F)**
- **Keep moist and fed in summer**

When well-grown there are few plants that can match the gold-and-green colouring of this small-leaved ivy. Large plants trained to a framework or growing against a wall can be especially pleasing. But the qualifying word here is 'well-grown', as these plants can often be thin single strands that do little for their surroundings. It is important to ensure that six, eight, or even 10 cuttings go into the propagating pot, so that the end result is a full and attractive plant. Pinching out the tips to induce a more bushy habit does not work with *H.* Golden Heart, which simply produces a single new shoot.

In good light the variegation will be improved, but bright sun should be avoided. In summer plants will have to be kept moist all the time and fed regularly, but in winter feeding should stop and much less water be given. During the summer months a sheltered spot out of doors will be much better than keeping plants inside, where the temperature may be too high.

Take care
Avoid wet winter conditions.

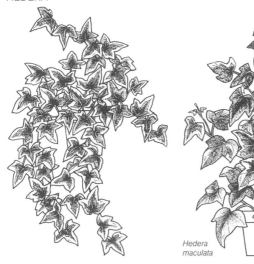

*Hedera
maculata*

Hedera helix 'Goldchild'

(Golden English ivy)
- **Good light**
- **Temp: 7-16°C (45-60°F)**
- **Keep moist and fed**

One of the loveliest ivies of them all, having green-and-gold foliage with the latter being much the more predominant. Shallow plastic saucers for larger flower pots are excellent for displaying them in. Saucers should have holes made in their base, and several young plants are then planted in the containers. The result will be a flat mass of golden greenery that I once heard described as 'a bowl of sunshine'. When incorporating ivies in indoor displays, however, it is important to ensure that the position is not too hot and dry.

Cool, light conditions are best, and will help considerably in reducing the incidence of red spider mite. Smaller-leaved ivies develop a black rot among their stems and foliage if they are allowed to become too wet and the conditions are dank and airless. When watering, give a thorough application and then allow to dry reasonably before repeating. Feed in spring and summer.

Take care
Avoid hot and dry conditions. 245♦

Hedera (large-leaved)
- **Light shade**
- **Temp: 4-16°C (40-60°F)**
- **Keep moist and fed**

There are several larger-leaved ivies, other than *H. canariensis*, that are good for use as backing plants in arrangements either indoors or out.

Possibly the best-known of these is *H. maculata*, with dull gold and green mottled foliage, which makes a fine plant when trained to a support. With larger, very dark green leaves, each with a dull yellow splash in the centre, there is *H.* 'Goldleaf', one of the quickest growing of all the ivies. Also with very dark leaves, but unrelieved by other colouring, there is *H.* 'Ravenholst'. Perhaps the best of the larger-leaved forms, albeit seldom available, is *H. marmorata*, which has stiff, twisting stems and firm, well-variegated leaves.

As with almost all the other hederas, these plants will do better in cooler conditions, and should be well fed and watered during the more active summer months of the year. They will also attract red spider mites, which can be very harmful to the plant if allowed to go unchecked.

Take care
Avoid high temperatures. 244♦

Helxine soleirolii
(Mind your own business)
- **Light shade**
- **Temp: 4-18°C (40-65°F)**
- **Keep moist**

There are green- and golden-foliaged kinds, with the latter being the better choice. Although they will become straggly and untidy in time, the helxines are generally seen as neat mounds of minute leaves that make a pleasant change from the usual run of houseplants. Almost any pieces that may be snipped off when tidying up will make new plants if placed in peaty compost.

Shallow pans suit their low growth best and they will do well on almost any light windowsill. Plants should be watered carefully by pouring water into the pot under the leaves; water poured over the leaves will disarrange the neat mounds of growth and mar the plants' appearance. Less water is needed in winter, and no feeding, although a weak feed regularly given in summer will be appreciated.

A loam-based compost will be best when it comes to potting on, and regular trimming around with scissors will maintain a neat shape.

Take care
Periodically renew older plants. 246♦

Heptapleurum arboricola
(Parasol plant)
- **Good light, no strong sun**
- **Temp: 16-21°C (60-70°F)**
- **Keep moist and fed**

In some parts of the world this plant may be seen labelled as *Schefflera*, which it strongly resembles. However, the difference lies in the size of the leaves. Both are green and palmate, but the schefflera leaf is very much larger.

Marginally more difficult to care for than *Schefflera* the parasol plant has an alarming habit of shedding leaves for no apparent reason. My view is that they often get much colder than the temperature recommended here. If plants are very wet at their roots and are subjected to low temperatures as well they will almost certainly lose leaves. There is some compensation, however, in that plants produce fresh growth later if the conditions improve.

Individual stems will grow to a height of 3m (10ft) in a comparatively short time. However, one can cut the stem back to more manageable size at any time of the year. As a result of this pruning treatment the plant will produce many more side growths.

Take care
Avoid winter wetness and cold. 246♦

257

Heptapleurum
'Geisha Girl'

Heptapleurum arboricola variegata
(Variegated parasol plant)
- **Good light, no strong sun**
- **Temp: 16-21°C (60-70°F)**
- **Keep moist and fed**

The fingered leaves and habit of growth are exactly the same as the green form, but the leaves are liberally splashed with vivid yellow colouring to give the plant a glowing brightness when it is placed among others in a large display. Elegance lies in the graceful and light distribution of leaves and stems, which enables one to see through and beyond to other plants in the display. And indoors it is equally important to have graceful plants rather than a solid wall of foliage.

In common with almost all the variegated plants this one should have a light location, but exposure to bright sun close to window-panes should be avoided if the leaves are not to be scorched. This is especially important if the leaves have been treated with chemicals. Most of the leaf-cleaning chemicals are perfectly suitable for the majority of plants, but one should never expose treated plants to direct sunlight.

Take care
Avoid winter wetness and cold. 247♦

Heptapleurum varieties
(Parasol plant)
- **Good light, no strong sun**
- **Temp: 16-21°C (60-70°F)**
- **Keep moist and fed**

One of the new green varieties is *Heptapleurum* 'Geisha Girl', which has more rounded leaves than the original and, when grown as a bushy plant with several pieces in the same pot, is in many ways superior.

Of dwarfer habit and with much smaller leaves there is *H. arboricola* 'Hong Kong', which has the added advantage of being easy to raise from seed. This one and all the others can be propagated from cuttings. These should consist of a piece of stem with a leaf attached and should be placed in small pots of moist peat in a temperature of not less than 21°C (70°F). Once rooted, all of the parasol plants will benefit from being potted on into slightly larger containers using loam-based potting mixture.

Active plants will require frequent watering and feeding during the summer months, but less water is required in winter and no feed should be given.

Take care
Avoid winter wetness and cold.

Hosta
(Plantain lily)
- **Light shade**
- **Temp: 4-21°C (40-70°F)**
- **Keep dry in winter, wet summer**

These are marginal houseplants, and have the added disadvantage that because they are deciduous they are often lost or forgotten during the winter months.

Despite these drawbacks I find them very useful as clumps in large tubs in cooler locations around the house, and we seem to be seeing new varieties all the time. All of them are superb when used as foliage accompaniment to flowers in mixed arrangements.

During the summer plants should be kept very moist and regularly fed. As they die down naturally in late summer only the minimum amount of moisture should be maintained in the soil until new growth is seen.

New plants are very easily made by dividing larger clumps in the autumn and planting them individually in pots. A peaty mixture with some loam added will suit them fine. Older plants can be planted successfully in the garden.

Take care
Avoid bright sun through glass. 248♦

Hypoestes sanguinolenta
(Freckle face; Polka dot plant)
- **Good light**
- **Temp: 10-16°C (50-60°F)**
- **Keep moist and fed**

In the last few years the hypoestes has enjoyed a new lease of life through the introduction of a much more colourful cultivar with a greater proportion of pink in its leaves.

Plants are easy to manage, although they frequently suffer through being confined to pots too small for the amount of growth that these quick growers will normally produce. Any purchased plant that appears to be in too small a pot should be potted into a larger one without delay. Use loam-based potting soil, as peat mixtures can be fatal for this plant if they dry out excessively. Also, it is wise to remove the growing tips so that plants branch and become more attractive. Untidy or overgrown stems can be removed at any time, and firm pieces about 10cm (4in) long can be used for propagation.

Extremely dry soil will cause loss of lower leaves, so check daily to ensure that the soil is moist.

Take care
Avoid drying out of soil. 248♦

Iresine herbstii
(Blood leaf)
● **Good light**
● **Temp: 13-18°C (55-65°F)**
● **Keep fed and watered**

These fall among the cheap and cheerful range of plants, and have foliage of a very deep, almost unnatural red. Cuttings root very easily and plants are quick to grow; they can be propagated successfully on the windowsill if shaded from direct sun.

Mature plants, however, must have a very light place if they are to retain their colouring, and will only need protection from strong midday sun. During the spring and summer plants must be kept active by regular feeding and ensuring that the soil does not dry out excessively. When potting on becomes necessary a loam-based mixture should be used; plants will soon use the nourishment in peat mixes even if fed regularly. At all stages of growth the appearance of the plant will be improved if the tips are periodically removed.

Besides the red-coloured variety there is *I. herbstii aureoreticulata*, which has yellow colouring and needs the same attention.

Take care
Feed well in summer.

Iris pallida
● **Good light**
● **Temp: 10-16°C (50-60°F)**
● **Keep on the dry side**

There are many hardy outdoor plants that are perfectly suitable as houseplants, and this is most assuredly one of them. In a pot it seldom grows more than 30cm (1ft) high, with overlapping fans of boldly striped green-and-white leaves.

Plants do best in shallow pans of loam-based potting mixture with plenty of drainage material in the bottom of the pan. If the soil is sluggish and slow to dry out the leaves will have a droopy, tired appearance; in a well-drained, dryish mixture the leaves will remain more attractively erect. Feeding is not desperately important, but very weak fertilizer given during the summer months will aid plants that have been in the same pots for a long time.

Propagation is simply a matter of removing plants from their pots, pulling the clumps of leaves apart and potting the divided pieces into small, shallow pots of their own.

Take care
Avoid excessive watering and feeding. 265♦

Kentia belmoreana
(Sentry palm)
- **Light shade**
- **Temp: 16-21°C (60-70°F)**
- **Water and feed well in summer**

This is also seen under its other name of *Howea belmoreana*. As a young plant it will be fine for indoor decoration, but as time goes on it will outgrow all but the largest of rooms. Growth can be contained to some degree in much the same way as trees are grown by the Bonzai method in Japan and elsewhere. The roots are hard pruned every second or third year causing the plant to become shorter and more stunted, with a bulbous base to its trunk. In one of my greenhouses I have two such plants that are almost 50 years old, yet they are only just over 3m (10ft) high.

Once these plants become old and well established they seem much easier to care for than in their early years. Mine are lightly shaded from the sun and are well watered during the summer months while they are producing their usual one or two leaves. They are kept on the dry side in winter.

Take care
Avoid wet winter conditions. 265♦

Kentia forsteriana
(Paradise palm)
- **Light shade**
- **Temp: 16-21°C (60-70°F)**
- **Water and feed well in summer**

Kentia forsteriana is one of the most elegant and interesting of all the plants grown in pots for indoor decoration, but it is tending to become increasingly expensive. Also known as *Howea forsteriana* – most of the seed for growing these plants commercially still comes from their natural home of Lord Howe Island in the South Pacific.

To grow well all palms need an open, fibrous potting mixture, and it is wise to put a layer of clay pot shards in the bottom of the container.

The long upright leaves of these plants are sensitive to many of the chemicals used for controlling pests and for cleaning foliage, so it is wise to test any products on a small section of the plant before going in at the deep end and treating it all over. When testing such chemicals one should wait for at least a week to see what the reaction may be. It is also very unwise to expose plants to full sun or to cold conditions following any application of chemicals.

Take care
Avoid wet winter conditions.

Leea coccinea rubra
- Light shade
- Temp: 16-21°C (60-70°F)
- Keep moist and fed

This is a relative newcomer that may well become a very popular and trouble-free houseplant. It belongs to the Araceae family and is compact and neat, with numerous leaves closely set together on short stout stems. Leaves are open and finely cut, and are of rich russet colouring. The habit is not unlike that of its relative, *Aralia sieboldii*. Although the colouring of the foliage is a little better in good light the plant does not seem to object unduly to growing in more shaded locations.

As small plants they do well enough in peaty mixtures, but clearly approve of being potted into loam-based soils when going into 13cm (5in) pot sizes and larger. The pot should have plenty of drainage material placed in the bottom and the potting soil must be reasonably firm. Water well after potting and then keep the soil on the dry side until the plant has established in the new mixture. Once settled, plants should be fed each week when active.

Take care
Keep out of cold draughts. 266♦

Maranta erythrophylla
(Herringbone plant)
- Light shade
- Temp: 18-24°C (65-75°F)
- Moist soil and atmosphere

With reddish-brown colouring and intricately patterned, rounded leaves, this is one of our more attractive smaller plants. Exotic colouring immediately suggests that it is difficult, but the reverse is true if sufficient warmth is maintained and reasonable care given.

These plants are best grown naturally with foliage trailing where it will. Unless the leaves are misted twice daily, hanging containers will usually prove to be too dry a location for them; it will be better to grow plants at a lower level. To improve humidity around the plant place the pot in a larger container with moist peat packed between the two pots.

Peaty mixture is essential when potting on, but one should not be too hasty in transferring plants to very large pots. Fertilizer should be very weak and given with each watering rather than in a few heavy doses.

In time the plants will become ragged and it may then be wise to start again with new cuttings.

Take care
Avoid bright sunlight. 267♦

Maranta kerchoeviana
(Rabbit's tracks)
- **Shade**
- **Temp: 16-21°C (60-70°F)**
- **Moist soil and atmosphere**

Dark spots on grey-green leaves give this plant its unusual common name; the dark spots are said to resemble the tracks left by a rabbit. One of the older established houseplants, it is one of the easiest of this family to care for. It needs protection from direct sunlight and must be reasonably warm. Frequent feeding with weak liquid fertilizer is best, and one should use a peaty potting mixture.

When watering the soil should be moist but not totally saturated for very long periods, especially in winter. The danger with peat mixtures is that they will soak up very much more water than the plant is ever likely to need and will become totally waterlogged – a dangerous condition for most plants. For this reason plants should not be watered from the bottom and allowed to absorb water from the pot saucer. It is very much better to water into the top of the pot, giving sufficient to ensure that surplus drains away.

Take care
Avoid bright sunlight. 266♦

Monstera deliciosa
(Swiss cheese plant; Mexican breadfruit)
- **Light shade**
- **Temp: 16-21°C (60-70°F)**
- **Moist roots, regular feeding**

The naturally glossy green leaves with attractive deep serrations make the monsteras among the most popular of all indoor foliage plants. The aerial roots produced from the stems of more mature plants are an interesting and often perplexing feature. Removing some excess roots will not be harmful, but in most instances it is better to tie the roots neatly to the stem of the plant and to guide them into the pot soil.

As plants mature they will naturally produce serrated leaves, but darker growing conditions can result in leaves that are smaller and complete, rather than cut out. Bright sunlight magnified by window glass can cause scorching of foliage and should be avoided, particularly while soft new leaves are maturing.

Monsteras belong to the Araceae family and in their natural jungle environment will tend to scramble along the floor before finding a tree trunk to climb.

Take care
Avoid exposure to direct sunlight. 268♦

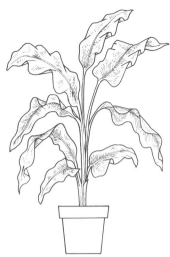

Mimosa pudica
(Sensitive plant)
- **Light shade**
- **Temp: 16-21°C (60-70°F)**
- **Keep moist and fed**

These are attractive little plants with fern-like foliage, which are grown as annuals, fresh seed being sown each spring and old plants discarded at the end of the summer. The main attraction of this particular plant lies in its habit of collapsing completely during the day when the foliage is touched. In time the plant becomes erect again, but it is an eerie sight.

These plants are frequently offered for sale in very small pots that have little nutrient left in the soil. These should be potted into standard houseplant mixture as soon as possible. The result will be a much greener, more vigorous plant.

Actively growing plants should be kept moist and fed regularly. Freshly potted plants should be allowed to establish in new soil before being fed. A position in light shade is suggested, but plants will tolerate some sunlight if not too bright.

New plants may be raised from spring-sown seed, or from cuttings of older plants taken in the autumn.

Take care
Pot on to avoid starvation.

Musa
(Banana plant)
- **Light shade**
- **Temp: 18-24°C (65-75°F)**
- **Keep moist and fed**

Any exotic fruit that can be grown as a potted plant indoors will give the owner a great deal of pleasure and excite the interest of almost every visitor. The banana plant is no exception. There are many different cultivars and some are much too large for indoor decorating. *M. cavendishii*, with its narrower and shorter leaves, is one of the best where space is limited.

All of these plants will require ample watering and feeding. Newly purchased plants should be promptly transferred to slightly larger containers using loam-based potting soil. In time plants may produce banana fruits, but this is unusual indoors. What is more likely is that the main stem, on attaining about 2m (6ft) in height, will begin to deteriorate as new shoots appear at the base. When no longer attractive the main stem should be cut out and the smaller plants given a chance to develop, as they most certainly will.

Take care
Check for red spider under leaves.

Above: **Iris pallida**
An attractive miniature iris with pale green-and-white coloured foliage. The neat clumps of growth can be divided at any time to make additional plants. Cool conditions and dryish soil at the roots. 260♦

Right: **Kentia belmoreana**
Majestic palms that will attain a height of 3m (10ft) with roots confined to pots. Green, fingered leaves radiate from a stout central trunk that will in time develop a bulbous base and add much to the appearance of the plant. 261♦

Above: **Leea coccinea rubra**
A fine, relatively new plant to the houseplant range with reddish foliage that is dense and compact. Does well in light or shade. 262♦

Right: **Maranta erythrophylla**
With reddish-brown and green-coloured leaves that are most intricately marked, these are very colourful foliage plants. 262♦

Below: **Maranta kerchoeviana**
With pale green, darkly spotted leaves, this is among the easiest of the marantas to care for. For best results offer moist, shaded and warm conditions. 263♦

Above: **Monstera deliciosa**
Interesting leaves are perforated in older plants and are deeply cut along their margins. Strong aerial roots are produced from the main stem and are a natural part of its attraction. 263♦

Left: **Neanthe bella**
The compact parlour palm is ideal for limited space, and does well in most locations other than cold and wet. Chemicals may damage foliage, more so if exposed to strong sun. 281♦

Right:
Neoregelia carolinae tricolor
Spectacular plants of the bromeliad family with flat rosettes of leaves overlapping at their base to make a watertight urn for water. 281♦

Left: **Nephrolepis exaltata**
Bold ferns of which there are numerous versions, all with strong green fronds spraying out from the centre of the plant pot. Shade and warmth are needed. 282♦

Below left:
Nephthytis 'White Butterfly'
Free-growing plants of the Araceae family needing moisture and shade to do well. Will climb or trail. 283♦

Right: **Palisota elizabetha**
Forms bold clumps of pale green leaves with white midribs. The plants can be propagated by dividing clumps into smaller sections. 283♦

Below: **Pandanus baptiste**
Magnificent plants needing ample space. Leaves are bright yellow in colour with spined margins and a spined keel on their undersides. 284♦

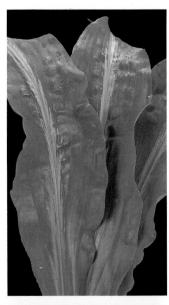

Above: **Pandanus veitchii**
*This resembles a pineapple plant
when young but becomes bolder
with age. Leaves radiate from a short
central trunk and are white and green
variegated with spined margins and
undersides.* 284♦

Right: **Pellionia daveauana**
*Naturally hanging or creeping plants
that are easy to care for. Leaves are
about 5cm (2in) in length and
multicoloured. New plants can be
propagated easily from cuttings.* 285♦

Below: **Pellaea rotundifolia**
*The button fern has very dark green,
rounded leaves that form into
densely foliaged plants in a
comparatively short time. Shaded,
moist and warm conditions.* 285♦

Above: **Peperomia argyreia**
With dark green markings on a silvery-grey background this is one of the most attractive of peperomias. Leaves have a natural shine. 286♦

Left: **Peperomia caperata**
The small leaves of this neat plant are produced in abundance and are a rich dark green in colour. A further attraction is their rough surface. 286♦

Right: **Peperomia hederaefolia**
Glossy, grey-coloured leaves are produced in quantity but remain small in size to form neat and compact plants that are in the easy-care category. 287♦

Above: **Peperomia magnoliaefolia**
*Most popular of the peperomias, with
glossy leaves that are brightly cream*
*and green variegated. Leaves are
fleshy and retain a lot of moisture, so
reducing the need for watering.* 287♦

Above:
Philodendron bipinnatifidum
Weedy plants when young but becoming most majestic with age. Keep moist. 288♦

Below: **Philodendron hastatum**
Glossy green leaves are broadly arrow-shaped. Plants attain stately proportions in time, but need supporting. 289♦

Above: **Philodendron scandens**
*The well-known sweetheart plant
has heart-shaped leaves that are
deep green in colour. Plants will
climb or trail.* 289♦

Right: **Phoenix roebelenii**
*When mature these palms are
among the most impressive of all
foliage plants, with fine leaves
radiating from a central stem.* 290♦

Below: **Phoenix canariensis**
*A tough tropical palm with coarse
foliage and a solid, gnarled trunk that
becomes a principal feature of the
plant as it ages.* 290♦

Above: **Pilea cadierei nana**
Foliage of the aluminium plant is
generously speckled with silver.

Regular pinching out of the growing
tips will produce plants of neat
appearance. Easy to care for. 291♦

Neanthe bella

(Parlour palm)
● **Light shade**
● **Temp: 16-21°C (60-70°F)**
● **Keep moist but well drained**

For people with limited space who wish to acquire a palm this is the answer, as the parlour palm presents a neat and compact plant throughout its life.

This plant is often used in bottle gardens, where it takes place of honour as the taller plant to give the miniature garden some height. One might add a word here to say that when planting bottle gardens it is most essential to ensure that small, non-invasive plants are selected.

The parlour palm should not be allowed to dry out excessively, although it should be a little on the dry side during the winter months, when growth is less active. It is important to ensure that the pot is well drained, and this will mean putting a layer of broken pieces of clay pot in the bottom of the new container before adding soil. Water poured onto the surface of the soil should be seen to flow fairly rapidly down through the mixture.

Take care
Avoid using chemicals on leaves. 268♦

Neoregelia carolinae tricolor

(Blushing bromeliad; Cartwheel plant)
● **Good light**
● **Temp: 13-18°C (55-65°F)**
● **Dry at roots, urn filled**

Although it does produce small and inconspicuous flowers in the centre of the rosette of leaves (the 'urn' or 'vase') this is very much a foliage plant. Overlapping leaves radiate from a short central trunk and are spectacularly striped in cream and green with the added attraction, as flowers appear, of the shorter central leaves and the base of larger leaves turning a brilliant shade of red.

Following this colourful display the main rosette will naturally deteriorate and in time will have to be cut away from the small trunk to which it is attached. Take care that the small plant or plants forming around the base of the trunk are not damaged during this operation, as these will be the plants of the future. Leave the young plantlets attached to the stump to grow on or, in preference, remove them when they have developed several leaves of their own and pot them into peaty mixture.

Take care
Periodically change the water in the central urn of leaves. 269♦

Nephrolepis exaltata
(Ladder fern; Sword fern)
- **Shade**
- **Temp: 16-21°C (60-70°F)**
- **Keep moist always**

There are now many fine cultivars of this excellent plant. Any purchased plants that appear too large for their pots should be potted on without delay into a slightly larger container. A peaty mixture containing some loam will give better results than a soil that is thin and lifeless. As an alternative to putting the new plant into a conventional pot, transfer it to a decorative hanging basket.

Bright sunlight for any length of time will be fatal, as will excessive drying out of the soil. It will also be harmful should temperatures drop too low, if the soil in the pot is excessively wet. Plants will respond to feeding, but they often do better if fed with a foliar feed rather than a more conventional fertilizer taken up through the root system. New plants are normally raised from spores taken from the undersides of leaves when ripe, but may also be grown from the plantlets that develop on the runners of older plants.

Take care
Protect from direct sunlight. 270♦

Nephthytis 'Emerald Gem'
(Goose foot plant)
- **Light shade**
- **Temp: 16-21°C (60-70°F)**
- **Keep moist**

Also offered as *Syngonium podophyllum* 'Emerald Gem', this is one of the easiest of the aroid plants to care for indoors. In bright sunlight the plant will quickly deteriorate, but given moist, warm and shaded conditions it should be trouble-free.

It is an adaptable plant that may be grown as a trailing subject or encouraged to climb by offering some form of support. Being an aroid it will develop natural aerial roots along the main stem. It will assist the plant if the supporting stake can be covered with a layer of moss; the moss should be bound tightly to the support with non-corrosive plastic-covered wire, and kept moist. These plants also do well when grown by water culture. Although moisture at their roots and in the surrounding atmosphere is important, exercise care when watering, and ensure that the soil dries out a little between waterings, particularly during the winter. Feed regularly except in winter.

Take care
Keep moist, warm and shaded.

Nephthytis 'White Butterfly'
(Goose foot plant)
- Light shade
- Temp: 16-21°C (60-70°F)
- Keep moist and fed

Also known as *Syngonium podophyllum* 'White Butterfly'; the common name of goose foot relates to the shape of the adult leaf. Pale green leaves are suffused with white, and the plant will trail or climb as required.

It will have to be kept moist at all times, with occasional misting of the foliage with tepid water. The goose foot has adapted amazingly well to hydroculture, the technique of growing plants in water with nutrient solution added. In this instance the plant has all the soil washed away from its roots before it is converted to water culture. The roots are then suspended in clay granules (a sort of artificial pebble), and a special nutrient is added to the water for the plant to feed on. If the simple directions concerning watering and feeding are followed, the goose foot will grow at three times the rate of the same plant in soil, and frequent pruning is needed.

Take care
Avoid dry conditions. 270♦

Palisota elizabetha
- Light shade
- Temp: 16-21°C (60-70°F)
- Keep moist and fed

Years ago at the Chelsea Flower Show I noted large clumps of this in the exhibit of one of our botanical gardens. A chat with the man in charge made it possible for me to exchange with one of my plants. The lance-shaped dense leaves are produced from soil level and have a pale yellow central colouring with darker green outside. For show purposes it is an ideal plant that can be placed almost anywhere to good effect, and is especially useful for concealing the cumbersome pots of taller specimen plants. But it does not seem to appeal much to Mr. Average when he selects plants for the home; perhaps one day there will be a change of heart.

The plant is very easy to care for, but must be kept moist and fed. To make new plants the older clumps can be divided into smaller sections and potted into loam-based mixture at almost any time. Regular feeding of established plants will be important.

Take care
Never allow to dry out. Keep warm. 271♦

283

Pandanus baptiste

(Screw pine)
- **Good light**
- **Temp: 16-21°C (60-70°F)**
- **Avoid too wet conditions**

This is probably the best-protected plant of them all. Vicious barbs are along the margins of the leaves, and a barbed keel runs the length of the underside of each leaf; all are capable of drawing blood if carelessly handled. However, it has the most incredible bright yellow colouring, which sets it apart from almost every other plant. The large recurving leaves are produced from a very stout trunk and will attain a length of 1.8m (6ft) and a width of 15cm (6in) or more when roots are confined to a pot. Should you be considering one of these for your home, be sure that you have a place large enough to accommodate it.

Older plants take on a further interesting dimension when they produce stout anchor roots from the main trunk; these extend in the manner of tent guy ropes around the plant to anchor it when hurricane winds hit its natural tropical island home. Maintain reasonable temperatures but treat them harshly to succeed.

Take care
Approach with caution! 271♦

Pandanus veitchii

(Screw pine)
- **Good light**
- **Temp: 16-21°C (60-70°F)**
- **Avoid too wet conditions**

Of the screw pines this is the most suitable for the average room, as it is reasonably compact and easier to accommodate. Leaves are green and white variegated and are produced in the shape of a large rosette, with leaves sprouting from a stout central stem. The screw pines all have vicious spines along the margins of their leaves, and a set of barbs running from the base to the tip of the leaf on the underside. Locate plants where they will be out of harm's way, perhaps by placing on a pedestal; this is also the best method of setting off these fine plants to advantage.

Being tough tropical plants that grow in exposed coastal areas, they are well adapted to harsh conditions. They will tolerate quite sunny locations and not be harmed provided they are not too close to the window-panes. Drought conditions seem to be taken in their stride, and they certainly prefer to be dry rather than too wet. Sharply draining, gritty soil is essential.

Take care
Handle plants with care. 272♦

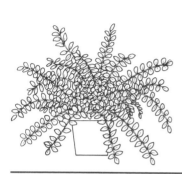

Pellaea rotundifolia
(Button fern)
- **Shade**
- **Temp: 16-21°C (60-70°F)**
- **Keep moist**

The button fern has dark green rounded leaves attached to firm, wiry stems, and forms a dense, attractive plant.

When potting use a peaty mixture and shallow pans. Almost all ferns in small pots will quickly become root bound and will lose their vigour if not potted on. However, inspection of roots can be misleading as these are very dark brown and the colour of the peaty soil in which they are growing, so careful inspection is needed before potting on.

Potting is best done in spring or summer and the new container should be only a little larger than the last. Roots ought to be moistened before it is removed from the pot, and after potting the soil should be well enough watered for surplus to be seen draining through the holes in the base of the pot. Then keep the newly potted plant on the dry side for several weeks — careful judgement is needed, as excessive drying out of the peaty mixture can be fatal as far as ferns are concerned.

Take care
Avoid direct sunlight. 272♦

Pellionia daveauana
- **Light shade**
- **Temp: 13-21°C (55-70°F)**
- **Keep moist and fed**

Very easy plants to care for, and easy to propagate, yet they never seem to make the grade as indoor plants. This is rather odd, as they adapt very well as hanging plants, or do well as a creeper, in the bottle garden, or simply as an addition to the windowsill collection. Leaves are oval-shaped and produced in quantity, and they have an interesting colouring of brown and dull yellow.

To propagate new plants, remove pieces of stem, any section, about 7.5cm (3in) long, and put four or five of these in small pots of peaty houseplant soil. Cuttings can go direct into hanging pots or small baskets if desired. When they get under way, remove the tips to encourage the plant to branch out. It is essential that plants be kept moist and warm, and out of direct sunlight. When potting on becomes necessary any of the many peaty houseplant potting mixtures will suit them fine, but avoid using very large pots.

Take care
Renew older plants periodically. 273♦

Peperomia argyreia
(Rugby football plant)
- **Light shade**
- **Temp: 13-18°C (55-65°F)**
- **Keep moist and fed**

Sadly, this is one of the older houseplants that is not seen so frequently these days. The leaves are an interesting grey-green colour with darker stripes that radiate from the centre of the leaf. The darker stripes give the plant its name of Rugby football plant.

These compact plants should be grown in shallow pans of soilless potting mixture. The location must be light, with protection from direct sunlight. Watering should be done with care; err on the side of dry rather than wet conditions. Established plants can be given weak liquid fertilizer with every watering from early spring to late summer, but none in winter. Sound leaves can be removed and cut into quarters that are placed in upright position in pure peat in warm conditions. The quartered leaf will produce roots and eventually leaves along the length of the cut edge below soil level. During propagation, ensure that the cuttings do not become too wet.

Take care
Avoid winter wetness and cold. 274♦

Peperomia caperata
(Little fantasy)
- **Light shade**
- **Temp: 16-21°C (60-70°F)**
- **Never overwater**

This plant is neat and compact and ideally suited to growing on the windowsill, where it will not become entangled with curtains. Leaves are a blackish green in colour, and have an undulating surface. The rounded leaves are attached to long stalks that sprout directly from soil level.

Cuttings made by inserting individual leaves in peaty mixture will root with little trouble if a temperature in excess of 18°C (65°F) can be maintained. Rooted leaves produce clusters of small plants that should be potted into peaty houseplant soil when large enough to handle. Small pots should be used initially and plants ought to be gradually potted on from one size container to the next. Also, when potting low-growing plants of this kind, it is important not to select pots of full depth; shallower pans (or half pots) are now freely available. After potting, the soil should be kept on the dry side and plants should not be fed for at least three months.

Take care
Avoid placing in dark corners. 274♦

Peperomia hederaefolia
(Silver ripple)
- **Light shade**
- **Temp: 16-21°C (60-70°F)**
- **Keep moist and fed**

Unusual glossy grey colouring sets *P. hederaefolia* apart from most other indoor plants. Stalked leaves are rounded in shape and emerge from soil level, there being no stem to speak of. At one time a great favourite in the houseplant league it now seems to have waned a little, probably resulting from other more interesting plants coming along to take its place. One of its main benefits lies in the fact that it occupies little space and is ideal for including in small planted arrangements of plants. Carboys are the typical example of close grouping that requires small plants that are not too invasive. Vigorous plants will quickly invade the growing space of every plant in the container.

This peperomia will enjoy a watering routine that allows the soil to dry out, but not bone dry, between each watering. It will also respond well to frequent weak feeds, but needs no feeding and less water in winter.

Take care
Avoid wet and cold combination. 275♦

Peperomia magnoliaefolia
(Desert privet)
- **Good light**
- **Temp: 16-21°C (60-70°F)**
- **Keep on dry side**

The common name and the thick fleshy leaves give some clues regarding the care of this neat and colourful little plant. The succulent fleshy leaves indicate that they are capable of holding a considerable amount of water, to withstand arid conditions.

The quickest way of killing desert privet is to keep it in poor light and on the cold side, and to have the soil very wet. One of the most important requirements will be to ensure that the soil dries out between each watering. Stem rot followed in all probability by the fungus disease botrytis will be the inevitable result of keeping plants too wet for too long.

Feeding is not important, but will have to be done occasionally – preferably not in winter and never in heavy doses. But in respect of nutrition there is one very important need, and that is, when potting plants on into larger containers, to use soilless potting mixture; anything else would be fatal.

Take care
Keep warm, light and dry. 276♦

Persea gratissima
(Avocado pear)
● **Good light**
● **Temp: 16-21°C (60-70°F)**
● **Keep moist and fed**

The foliage is green, coarse, and not particularly attractive, but there is the fascination of growing plants from the central stone of the fruit and no doubt a sense of achievement exists that encourages one to hang on to the plant. Very often they are left to become tall and ungainly when it would be better to pinch out the early growing tips of the plant to encourage it to branch out and adopt a better shape. Plants will also be thin and poor in appearance if they are allowed to languish in dark corners: good light is needed, but offer some protection from direct sunlight.

Raising plants from stones is relatively easy. Four cocktail sticks are pushed into the stone evenly spaced, and the stone is then suspended in a tumbler with the base submerged in about 5cm (2in) of water; in time the base of the stone will soften and roots will form in the water. When lots of roots are present the stone is potted in peaty soil.

Take care
Feed while actively growing.

Philodendron bipinnatifidum
(Tree philodendron)
● **Shade**
● **Temp: 16-21°C (60-70°F)**
● **Keep wet and fed**

There are numerous philodendrons of similar type to this one, all requiring ample space for their radiating leaves once they reach maturity. Because of their habit of growth these are essentially individual plants to be placed on their own rather than as part of a collection. Leaves are glossy green in colour and deeply cut along their margins, and held on stout petioles attached to very solid short trunks. In time aerial roots will be produced from the trunk; direct these into the pot soil when they are long enough. With older plants it may be necessary to remove some of these aerial roots, or they can be allowed to trail into a dish of water placed alongside.

Ample watering is a must, with marginally less being given in winter; and feeding should not be neglected. When potting on use a mixture containing some loam, as these are quite greedy plants. Most of them are raised from seed and young plants are usually available.

Take care
These plants need space. 277♦

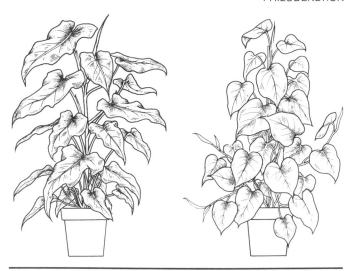

Philodendron hastatum
(Elephant's ear)
- **Shade**
- **Temp: 16-21°C (60-70°F)**
- **Keep moist and fed**

Again we have a touch of majesty from the splendid Araceae family of plants, and the common name immediately gives the game away that this is a rather large plant. The leaves are broadly arrow-shaped, glossy green and attached to very bold, tall-growing stems; in a greenhouse it may reach a height of 6m (20ft). Normally indoor growth is thinner and less robust, but the fact that the plant has a tough constitution makes it a reasonably trouble-free plant in agreeable conditions.

As a young plant it will trail, but it is much too important for this style of growing and when purchasing one you should also acquire a moss-covered support (preferably one that can be extended) to which the plant can be tied. If the moss is kept moist by regular spraying with water from a mister it will be found that in time the natural aerial roots of the plant will grow around and into the moss. Leaves can be occasionally wiped with a damp cloth to clean them.

Take care
Avoid dry and sunny positions. 277♦

Philodendron scandens
(Sweetheart plant)
- **Shade**
- **Temp: 16-21°C (60-70°F)**
- **Keep moist and fed**

One of the smallest-leaved of all the philodendrons and possibly the best suited to the relatively smaller rooms of today. The leaves are heart-shaped and glossy green, and it may be encouraged to either climb or trail.

Keeping the soil moist, not saturated, is important, and occasional weak feeding will suit it well. Young plants should be potted into soilless potting mixture, but older plants will respond better if potted into a mix that contains a small proportion of loam. In ideal conditions plants may be potted at almost any time, but in the average home they will do much better if the potting can be done at the start of the summer. I am often asked for plant suggestions for dark corners and the questioner invariably wants something colourful. But such plants are few and far between; it is better to select green foliage for difficult spots, and the sweetheart plant is ideal in most cases.

Take care
Avoid dry and sunny places. 278♦

Phoenix canariensis
(Feather palm)
- **Good light**
- **Temp: 16-21°C (60-70°F)**
- **Keep moist**

In their tropical habitat these stately palms will grow to 9-12m (30-40ft) in height, but they are less vigorous when their roots are confined to pots. Leaves are coarse and open, and attached to short, stout trunks. Leaves have short petioles armed with vicious short spines, which make it necessary to handle the plant with care. Older plants are normally beyond the purse of the average person, so seek out plants of more modest size when shopping.

Smaller plants can be potted on into loam-based potting soil. Good drainage is essential, so broken flower pots or some other form of drainage material ought to be placed in the bottom of the pot before any soil is introduced. Well-drained soil is needed, but regular and thorough watering will be of the utmost importance while plants are actively growing. During growth, feed plants at regular intervals using a proprietary fertilizer and following the maker's directions.

Take care
Check occasionally for red spider. 278♦

Phoenix roebelinii
(Feather palm)
- **Good light**
- **Temp: 16-21°C (60-70°F)**
- **Keep moist**

Not unlike *P. canariensis* as a young plant, but later more feathery and delicate and less coarse in appearance. It is also less robust, retains its shape better, and will attain a height of around 1.5m (5ft) when grown.

Select loam-based potting mixture with some body to it. Good drainage will ensure that the soil in the pot will remain fresh and well aerated, which is essential if palm roots are not to rot and die. During the summer, plants can go out of doors in a sheltered, sunny location.

Not many pests bother this plant, but the ubiquitous red spider will usually be lurking around if the growing conditions tend to be very hot and dry. One should suspect their presence if plants become harder in appearance and develop paler colouring than usual. Some insecticides are harmful to palm plants, therefore it is wise to check suitability with your supplier before purchasing.

Take care
Ensure soil is well drained. 279♦

Pilea cadierei nana
(Aluminium plant)
● **Light shade**
● **Temp: 16-21°C (60-70°F)**
● **Keep moist and fed**

With silvered foliage, this is by far the most popular of the pileas, but there are numerous others, all needing similar treatment.

Plants are started from cuttings taken at any time of the year if temperatures of around 18°C (65°F) and moist, close conditions can be provided. A simple propagating case on the windowsill can offer just these conditions. Top cuttings with four to six leaves are taken, the bottom pair is removed and the end of the stem is treated with rooting powder before up to seven cuttings are inserted in each small pot filled with a peaty mixture. Once cuttings have got under way the growing tips are removed and the plants are potted on into slightly larger containers in loam-based mixture.

Plants should have ample light, but not be exposed to bright sunlight. Although small, pileas need ample feeding during the growing months, if they are to retain their bright colouring.

Take care
Pinch out tips to retain shape. 280♦

Pilea involucrata (P. spruceana)
(Friendship plant)
● **Light shade**
● **Temp: 16-21°C (60-70°F)**
● **Keep moist and fed**

The friendship plant has reddish-brown colouring, and is easy to propagate; it may have acquired its common name as a result of surplus plants being distributed around the neighbourhood.

Several other pileas may be propagated with equal ease, and one or two of them will further oblige by producing an abundance of seed that will pop about in all directions when ripe, with the result that all the other pots surrounding the seeding pilea will provide a welcome bed of moist soil for the seed to germinate in. It will be wise to treat these as weeds and remove them before they take over the living room.

The friendship plant provides a neatly rounded, low-growing plant with an unusual colouring. It keeps its neat appearance for perhaps two years indoors and then begins to develop longer and more straggly stems, which spoil the plants' appearance; it could then be wise to start again with fresh cuttings.

Take care
Keep it out of bright sunlight. 297♦

Piper ornatum
(Ornamental pepper)
- **Good light**
- **Temp: 18-24°C (65-75°F)**
- **Keep moist**

The waxy leaves are 7.5-10cm (3-4in) long, deep green in colour and beautifully marked in silvery pink. Provide plants with a light framework onto which they can be trained so that they are seen to full effect.

Warmth is essential, and the air around the plant must not become too dry; spray leaves with tepid water from a hand mister. When potting on, avoid large pots; these plants prefer pots in proportion to the top growth. Soilless potting mixture suits them best, but it will be important to ensure that the plant is fed regularly (not in winter) and that soil never becomes too dry. Very wet conditions will be equally harmful, so allow some drying out between waterings. Plants lose much of their colouring if grown in dark corners. Provide good light but avoid direct sunlight.

Firm leaves with a piece of stem attached can be rooted in peat in warm conditions during spring in a propagating case.

Take care
Avoid winter cold and wetness.

Pisonia brunoniana variegata
- **Light shade**
- **Temp: 16-21°C (60-70°F)**
- **Keep moist and fed**

These small tropical trees are useful plants with leaves about 30cm (12in) long, closely grouped on firm, upright stems. They have a neat habit of growth and attractively variegated leaves.

Good light with some protection from direct sunlight is necessary if plants are to retain their colourful variegation. To keep them in good fettle a reasonable, stable temperature is also needed. During the growing months plants require much more water than in winter, when care will be needed to ensure that the soil is never excessively wet; wet conditions at this time will cause roots to rot, with consequent loss of the lower leaves. Feeding is not necessary in winter, but should not be neglected for active plants.

New plants can be made from stem sections with one or two leaves attached, taken in spring; put them into small pots of peat, and place in a heated propagator. Use loam-based soil for growing on.

Take care
Avoid wetness and cold in winter.

Pittosporum eugenioides
(Parchment bark)
- **Good light**
- **Temp: 13-21°C (55-70°F)**
- **Keep moist and fed**

In the course of my duties it is almost inevitable that I should have favourite plants. For at least 20 years I have supervised the care of a pair of *P. eugenioides* plants that are now in the region of 3m (10ft) high and of full and attractive appearance. The pots in which they are growing are little more than 38cm (15in) in diameter – much too small, in the opinion of most plant growers, but my plants are superb and are sustained solely on regular feeding throughout the year, with the exception of the winter months. These plants seem to prove conclusively that plant pots of enormous size are not really necessary if the culture is correct.

The colouring of the leaves, which have attractively waved margins, is predominantly grey with a little white relief, and leaves are attached to firm, wiry stems. Good light is necessary and one must avoid excessive watering in winter to prevent browning of leaf margins.

Take care
Avoid dark locations. 298♦

Pittosporum garnettii
(Parchment bark)
- **Good light**
- **Temp: 7-16°C (45-60°F)**
- **Keep moist and fed**

A little-known plant, but very hardy both indoors and in the garden. The leaves are oval in shape, slightly wavy at their margins, and with a speckled grey-white silvery sheen to them. Against the light-coloured foliage the black stems provide a splendid contrast. In the garden over a period of about six years, young plants grow to a height of around 120cm (4ft), with a diameter of about 75cm (2ft 6in). Plants growing in pots and about the same age are roughly half the size.

Good light is essential if plants are to retain their colouring – and their leaves. Cool conditions will be more acceptable than high temperatures. Plants are better standing in large saucers than in decorative outer pots, which tend to accumulate unnoticed surplus, causing the soil to become waterlogged. With saucers one can see surplus water accumulate and tip it away.

Take care
Avoid dark areas and wet conditions.

293

Pittosporum tenuifolium
(Parchment bark)
- **Good light**
- **Temp: 7-18°C (45-65°F)**
- **Keep moist and fed**

This is much used for flower arrangements by florists. Bright green leaves have wavy margins, and the black stems provide an interesting contrast. They are quite colourful, develop a neat, bushy shape, and will tolerate cooler conditions and enjoy them rather than object by shedding leaves.

Start off small plants in peaty mixture, but from the 13cm (5in) size pot and upwards a loam-based mixture will be better. As these plants like fresh air and sunshine, pot them into decorative patio planters rather than the more conventional flower pot, and put them out of doors in summer.

On taking them in again it is fatal to place them immediately in darker areas; have them as near to a natural light source as possible where the conditions will be cool and airy.

Trimming off pieces of the plant for flower arrangments will be beneficial provided one is not too severe. Trimmed plants become bushier.

Take care
Keep in good light. 297♦

Platycerium alcicorne
(Stag's horn fern)
- **Shade**
- **Temp: 16-21°C (60-70°F)**
- **Keep moist**

Essential requirements of all platyceriums are moist, warm and shaded conditions, and if one cannot offer all three of those then it will be difficult to grow these plants.

Plants are normally grown in pots filled with peat mixture and will seldom do well in anything that is too heavy and root-restricting. But besides the conventional pot they may be grown as mobiles, or for hanging on a wall. The plant is removed from its pot and the roots are wrapped in fresh sphagnum moss before the complete bundle is firmly secured to its support: plastic-covered wire is useful for this purpose. The plant can then be soaked thoroughly in a bucket of water and allowed to drain before it is put in position. Subsequent watering should follow the same lines.

Scale insects attaching themselves to all parts of the plant are by far the worst pest, and should be wiped off with a firm sponge that has been soaked in insecticide.

Take care
Avoid excessive drying out. 298♦

Pleomele reflexa variegata
(Song of India)
- **Good light**
- **Temp: 16-21°C (60-70°F)**
- **Keep on dry side**

These painfully slow-growing plants are not often available: anyone seeing a priced plant should stake a claim immediately! When mature and well grown, this is a fine plant. Stems are very woody, and leaves are miniature but bright yellow. Plants may be no more than 1.5-1.8m (5-6ft) tall, though at least 20 years old. Slow growth is one reason for their scarcity, and for the high price should any be on offer.

Plants enjoy good light, with shade from strong sunlight, and temperatures that fluctuate from 16 to 21°C (60 to 70°F). Water well when necessary, and allow to dry appreciably before watering again, but the surrounding area should be kept moist at all times. Feeding should be done on average once a week in summer, with none at all from the onset of winter to the early spring when new growth appears.

Few pests bother these fine plants, whose worst enemy is a combination of wetness and cold.

Take care
Ensure soil drains freely. 299♦

Podocarpus macrophyllus
(Buddhist pine)
- **Light shade**
- **Temp: 10-16°C (50-60°F)**
- **Keep moist, less in winter**

The open foliage of this small tropical tree provides a pleasing potful of greenery for cooler locations indoors. If grown on a single stem it may attain a height of about 1.5m (5ft); but remove the growing tip when the plant is young, and it will become more bushy.

It abhors overwatering, which can be particularly damaging during winter. Avoid the practice of placing plants in a saucer and filling it with water. With modern peaty potting mixtures there will be much more water taken into the peat by capillary action than the plant is ever likely to need, so leading to root rot. Instead, fill the space between the rim of the pot and the soil each time the plant is watered. When watering from the top, one should see the surplus draining through the holes in the bottom of the container. Before watering again, allow the soil to dry.

When growing podocarpus plants indoors they do much better in cool, light conditions, and abhor heat.

Take care
No winter feeding required. 300♦

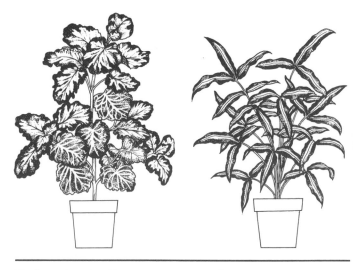

Polyscias balfouriana
(Dinner plate aralia)
- **Light shade**
- **Temp: 16-21°C (60-70°F)**
- **Keep moist and fed**

This is another painfully slow grower that will take at least 10 years to reach 3m (10ft) in height, but in limited space this could be an advantage. Stems are woody and the leaf colouring is variegated white and green. Growth is very erect and plants seldom need to be staked. As the plant ages and increases in height, the lower stem will have a natural tendency to shed leaves.

Red spider mites seem to find this plant particularly appetizing. Although minute in size, these pests can increase at an alarming rate and completely blanket the plant to such an extent that it may well not recover. The layman often finds it difficult to believe that such minute pests can be so destructive. When they are detected, take action right away, by preparing a recommended insecticide solution and thoroughly saturating the undersides of all foliage. This task ought to be done out of doors on a warm day, and rubber gloves and a mask worn.

Take care
Check for pests under leaves. 301♦

Pteris cretica albo-lineata
(Variegated table fern)
- **Shade**
- **Temp: 16-21°C (60-70°F)**
- **Keep moist**

The variegated form of *P. cretica* has a pale green outer margin to its leaves and a cream-coloured central area. There are several other variegated forms available, and all will respond well to shaded and warm conditions where a reasonable degree of humidity can be maintained. They will also benefit from regular feeding once they have become established in their pots. Many of these smaller ferns do very well if fed with a foliar feed, which is sprayed onto the leaves.

Fern plants do very much better if they can be grouped together. Large plastic trays are easily obtainable, and these are ideal for placing groups of ferns and other types of indoor plants. The tray is filled with gravel and well watered before the plants are placed on the surface; it is important that the plant pot base should not stand in water, as this would make the soil much too wet. The wet tray will provide a continual source of essential humidity.

Take care
Never subject ferns to direct sun. 300♦

Above: **Pilea involucrata**
Sometimes known as the friendship plant because its ease of propagation makes its distribution among friends a simple matter. Neat hummocks of growth result if the leading growing tips are removed when they appear to be overgrowing. Frequent feeding is an essential need, and warm, light conditions will be a benefit. 291♦

Right: **Pittosporum tenuifolium 'Irene Patterson'**
One of the many improved forms of the New Zealand pittosporums. Glossy, evergreen foliage springs from woody stems and provides attractive plants in pots where the temperature is on the cool side and good light is available. Can be planted out of doors but is not altogether hardy, so needs protection from severe weather. 294♦

297

Above: **Pittosporum eugenioides**
*With grey-and-white variegated
foliage, these are essentially pot
plants for the cooler location indoors.
Good light is a further important
need. Stems are woody and leaves
have wavy margins.* 293♦

Right: **Pleomele reflexa variegata**
*Commonly named song of India, this
is an aristocrat among potted plants.
Foliage is almost entirely bright
yellow, with narrow leaves about
15cm (6in) long.* 295♦

Below: **Platycerium alcicorne**
*The foliage has a bluish-coloured
bloom that adds much to the
appearance of this fern. Anchor
fronds are intended to hold the plant
in position, while main fronds
resemble stags' antlers.* 294♦

Left: **Podocarpus macrophylla**
Mature trees in their native habitat, these plants have numerous, narrow, evergreen leaves and make fine bushy plants for cool places. 295♦

Right:
Polyscias balfouriana 'Pinnochio'
Leaves are rounded with pale cream and green variegation. Stems are woody and the plant is generally slow growing. It needs careful culture if the leaves are not to be shed prematurely. Red spider mites are troublesome. 296♦

Below: **Pteris cretica albo-lineata**
An attractive fern with pale green and off-white variegation, and one of the easiest ferns to care for. Needs moist and warm shaded conditions to thrive. Bright sun and dry air conditions cause leaf scorch. 296♦

Left:
Sansevieria trifasciata Laurentii
*The true type has bright yellow
margins to the leaves with mottled
variegation in the central areas.
These plants tolerate direct sunlight
and can be very durable if not
overwatered.* 315♦

Right: **Saxifraga sarmentosa**
*Aptly named the mother of
thousands because of the many
perfectly developed plantlets that
hang naturally from the parent plant,
this is essentially a trailing subject.
Propagation is a simple matter of
rooting plantlets.* 316♦

Below: **Schefflera digitata**
*With large-fingered leaves that are
attached to stout petioles, this is one
of the finest indoor green plants. The
leaves are naturally glossy green and
are attached to a strong central stem
that needs no form of support.* 317♦

303

Above:
Scindapsus 'Marble Queen'
One of the more difficult indoor plants. White dominates. 318♦

Top left: **Schefflera venusta**
A comparative newcomer, with narrow, palmate, undulating leaves. Colouring is a rich glistening green and the plant is of upright habit. 317♦

Left: **Scindapsus aureus**
Perhaps the best of all the foliage plants, with yellow and green variegation that is retained even in poor light. Will climb or trail. 317♦

Right: **Sedum morganianum**
A naturally trailing succulent plant with bluish-grey leaves that hang perpendicularly from the growing pot, which must be suspended. 318♦

Above: **Setcreasea purpurea**
*A member of the tradescantia tribe.
The leaves of this plant are purple all
over and attached to firm succulent
stems. The colour develops most
effectively when the plants are in
good light.* 320♦

Left: **Sparmannia africana**
*Large, pale green leaves of coarse
texture branch freely from stout
stems with many branches. It will in
time attain a height of about 2.4m
(8ft). An easy-care plant.* 321♦

Right: **Stenotaphrum secundatum**
*Amazingly vigorous plants that will
quickly fill their allotted space. They
can be used effectively in hanging
baskets. Leaves are narrow with
cream and green variegation.* 321♦

Above: **Tetrastigma voinierianum**
*A rampant member of the vine family
and perfect for covering an interior
wall with its invasive, pale green
growth and leaves. Natural tendrils
will cling to any support.* 322♦

Left: **Stromanthe amabilis**
*Similar in appearance to some of the
marantas, these plants form neat low
mounds of growth but need careful
culture to succeed. Warm conditions
suit them best.* 322♦

Below: **Tolmiea menziesii**
*The most endearing feature of this
plant is the way in which perfectly
shaped young plants form on the
stalks of parent leaves. Needs cool
conditions.* 323♦

Above: **Tradescantia 'Quicksilver'**
*Fine, easy-care plants with bright
silver variegation. Best in hanging
baskets.* 325♦

Below: **Vriesea mosaica**
*A rare member of the bromeliad
family with mainly reddish-brown
colouring.* 325♦

Above: **Yucca aloefolia**
Stately plants for difficult locations, as they are very durable if not overwatered. These plants are normally seen as stout stems with tufts of growth at the top. 326♦

Above: **Zebrina pendula**
*From the lowly tradescantia tribe, but
a surprisingly colourful plant when*
*seen as a well-grown specimen in a
hanging basket. The foliage of better
plants has a silvery sheen.* 326♦

Rhoeo discolor
(Moses in the cradle)
- Shade
- Temp: 16-21°C (60-70°F)
- Keep fed and watered

Related to the tradescantias, *R. discolor* is not a particularly attractive or exciting plant to have around, but it is interesting. Besides the common name above, there are several others, such as three men in a boat or Moses on a raft, all of them relating to the white flowers that nestle in a boat-like bract which develops at the base of the leaves. The leaves are green on their upper surface, striped with cream in the variegated form, and deep purple on the reverse of the leaf.

It will produce flowering bracts in time and these scatter seed in and around the pot, making propagation simple. This is a good thing, as plants tend to lose their attraction with age, and are better replaced periodically. A reasonable temperature is essential, and plants will do best in a lightly shaded location; they should be kept fairly moist at all times. Feeding need be undertaken only when growth is active. Potting soil should contain some loam.

Take care
Replace plants every second year.

Rhoicissus rhomboidea
(Grape ivy)
- Light shade
- Temp: 13-18°C (55-65°F)
- Keep moist and fed

Grape ivy is a tough old plant that seems to outlast all others. The three-lobed leaves are a bright glossy green. The plant should be offered some form of support through which it can entwine itself; but although generally considered to be a climber it will also do very well in a hanging container.

Plants are started from cuttings taken at any time if moist and warm conditions can be provided. When cuttings are potted put five or six into a small pot of peaty mixture.

Although tough enough to withstand harsh treatment they will fare better if kept moist and fed regularly in a location that offers reasonable light but not full sun. In bright sunlight, or if plants are starved, they become pale brown, and leaves will be generally smaller. Plants that have taken on a harder appearance may be in need of potting on, so root condition should be checked and plants potted if need be in loam-based mixture.

Take care
Avoid strong sunlight.

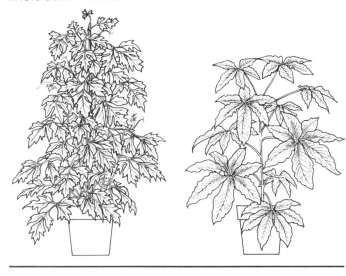

Rhoicissus rhomboidea 'Ellendanica'
(Grape ivy)
- **Light shade**
- **Temp: 13-21°C (55-70°F)**
- **Keep moist and fed**

The tri-lobed glossy foliage of *R. rhomboidea* should be familiar to everyone associated with indoor plants, but we now have from Denmark a plant with lightly waved leaf margins that add much to its attraction. The glossy foliage in well-grown plants has a burnished tinge.

It can withstand harsh conditions and survive happily. Of natural climbing habit, it will not take too unkindly to darkish locations indoors, but will obviously fare better in reasonable light, not direct sun. Keep plants moist and fed in spring and summer.

Pests are not a great problem, but mealy bug can sometimes cause difficulties. These bugs are easily seen, as small groups that resemble cotton wool, inside which the young bugs are protected. Mature bugs, with a white mealy appearance, will be in the vicinity. Apply insecticide or methylated spirit direct.

Take care
Avoid strong sun.

Ricinus communis coccineus
(Castor bean)
- **Good light**
- **Temp: 13-18°C (55-65°F)**
- **Keep moist and fed**

Oil extracted from this tropical African tree is used in medicine, and the leaves have an oily sheen. The coccineus form is superior, with a reddish hue to its leaves; it should be the one selected if there is a choice. In nature a height of 12m (40ft) is not out of the ordinary, but when roots are confined to pots it will be nearer 1.2-1.5m (4-5ft). Growth is fairly rapid, and plants may be stood outside during the summer.

A light position indoors will suit them best, and the room temperature should be cool rather than too hot. When potting on use a loam-based mixture and ensure that established plants are fed regularly: this will usually mean at every watering as new leaves develop.

In hot, dry conditions red spider mites will become a problem. Mites are generally on the undersides of the upper leaves and cause light brown discolouration.

Take care
Avoid hot, dry conditions.

Sansevieria 'Golden Hahnii'

(Golden bird's nest)
- **Good light**
- **Temp: 16-21°C (60-70°F)**
- **Avoid overwatering**

This one is rarely offered for sale today, because the plant is incredibly slow growing. There is also a plain green *S*. 'Hahnii', but it is not in the least attractive compared to the golden-coloured variety. Both make neat rosettes of overlapping leaves 10cm (4in) in length.

One of the best homes for them is a dry bottle garden; or they can be used in a dish garden. Like the more conventional sansevierias, both 'Hahnii' varieties abhor wet conditions, and will quickly succumb should the prevailing conditions offer a combination of wet and cold. Warm and dry will suit them very much better; in winter they will go for weeks on end without any water, and in some situations they could well go through the winter completely dry, as do most of the cacti and succulents. Feeding is not important, but a loam-based potting mix will be much better than one that is entirely peat.

Take care
Avoid cold and wetness.

Sansevieria trifasciata Laurentii

(Mother-in-law's tongue)
- **Good light**
- **Temp: 16-21°C (60-70°F)**
- **Keep dry**

This plant is almost indestructible. The leaves are about 60cm (2ft) long, thick and fleshy, holding a lot of moisture which the plant can draw on as needed; in view of this, it is important not to overwater, nor to give any more than the plant requires.

A good watering once each month in summer should suffice, with none at all during the winter months. This may seem harsh, but if plants are to be exposed to colder winter temperatures they will get through much better if the soil in the pot is dry rather than wet. Potting ought not to be done too frequently, and one can leave the plant until it actually breaks the pot in which it is growing – the swelling bases of leaves within the pot are quite capable of breaking clay as well as plastic pots. Loam-based soil is essential when potting on, and clay pots will help to maintain the balance of these top-heavy plants.

Take care
Avoid cold and wetness together. 302♦

315

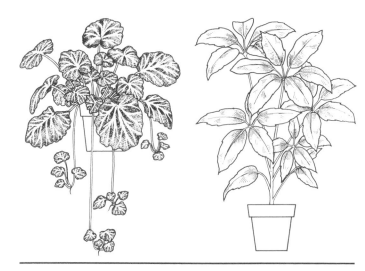

Saxifraga sarmentosa
(Mother of thousands)
- **Light shade**
- **Temp: 16-21°C (60-70°F)**
- **Keep moist and fed**

This is one of the simplest plants to propagate: you just detach the perfectly made plants when of reasonable size and press them into small pots filled with houseplant potting mixture. Grow the parent plant in a hanging basket with a curtain of tiny plants hanging from it and attached to threads of growth that may be 60cm (2ft) or more in length; the family of young plants will provide continual interest.

These plants are very easy to care for. Offer them reasonable light and warmth, with water and feed in moderation, bearing in mind that plants suspended from the ceiling will tend to dry out more rapidly than similar plants growing at a lower level in the same conditions. The amount of feed given will very often depend on the vigour of the plant, and during the winter months little or no feed is required.

Inspect these saxifrages regularly for pests: mealy bug, red spider or aphids might be present.

Take care
Suspend plants for best effect. 303♦

Schefflera digitata
(Umbrella plant)
- **Light shade**
- **Temp: 16-21°C (60-70°F)**
- **Keep moist and fed**

Even with roots confined to a pot, this majestic indoor tree may attain a height of 3m (10ft) or more. The glossy green palmate leaves radiate from the leaf petiole like the fingers of a hand. Unlike some houseplants, the schefflera does not produce more than one new shoot when the top is removed, so overgrown plants lose much of their charm when the growing top is severed. Also, as plants increase in height they tend to shed lower leaves.

New plants are raised from seed, normally sown in high temperatures in spring. When large enough, seedlings are put into small pots containing peaty mixture, later into larger pots of loam-based soil.

Indoors they respond to light, airy conditions, and the ideal temperature should be in the region of 18°C (65°F). They grow more vigorously in the warmer months, and need more water and regular feeding; in winter less water is needed and no feeding.

Take care
Avoid extremes of temperature. 303♦

Schefflera venusta 'Starshine'
(Umbrella plant)
- **Light shade**
- **Temp: 18-24°C (65-75°F)**
- **Keep watered and fed**

This comparative newcomer has dark green glossy leaves, attached to the petiole like the fingers of a hand. Unlike the more common larger schefflera, it has narrow, undulating leaves, with the result that the plant has a deal more elegance. It is also a much more compact plant, and will be better suited to the average home than the bolder schefflera types such as *S. digitata*. Avoid excessive watering and feed when active.

One problem is that the plant seems to attract mealy bugs, which will quickly spoil the appearance with their sticky, black honeydew if not dealt with. Honeydew is in fact a nice term for the excreta of the mealy bug, which drop onto the leaves below where the bugs are present, with the result that black fungus mould will form on the excreta. The latter can be wiped off with a sponge, and the mealy bugs can be removed with a swab of cotton wool soaked in methylated spirit.

Take care
Keep warm and draught-free. 304♦

Scindapsus aureus
(Devil's ivy)
- **Light shade**
- **Temp: 16-21°C (60-70°F)**
- **Keep moist**

S. aureus used to be one of those varieties that were difficult to propagate and to care for indoors. Yet we now have a plant with the same name that is one of the most reliable and one of the most colourful foliage plants available. It can only be that by constant re-selection a much tougher strain of the same plant has been evolved; there is now little difficulty in propagating it, and it seems to have an almost charmed life indoors.

Belonging to the Araceae family it needs a reasonable amount of moisture in the pot and, if possible, also in the surrounding atmosphere. The variegated leaves are green and gold, and for a variegated plant it has the truly amazing capacity of being able to retain its colouring in less well lit places. Most other variegated plants deteriorate or turn completely green if placed in locations offering insufficient light. The devil's ivy will also climb or trail as desired, and does well in hydroculture.

Take care
Avoid hot, dry conditions. 304♦

Scindapsus 'Marble Queen'
(Variegated devil's ivy)
- **Light shade**
- **Temp: 18-24°C (65-75°F)**
- **Keep moist and fed**

The white variegated devil's ivy will test the skill of the most accomplished grower. Most plants with a large area of white are a problem, and this is no exception.

A temperature over 18°C (65°F) is needed, particularly in winter. Also, it will be necessary to create a humid atmosphere around the plant. (This should not be confused with watering the plant to excess.) The simplest way is to provide a large saucer or tray filled with pebbles on which the plant can stand; the saucer can be partly filled with water, but the level should never be above the surface of the pebbles, as it is important that the plant pot should not stand in water. In a warm room such a saucer will continually give off moisture around the plant. Moist peat surrounding the pot in which the plant is growing is another way of providing moisture; and there are numerous types of troughs with capillary matting for placing plants on; these are useful at holiday time.

Take care
Keep moist and warm. 305♦

Sedum morganianum
(Burro's tail)
- **Light shade**
- **Temp: 13-18°C (55-65°F)**
- **Keep on dry side**

The burro's tail is a rather fascinating plant in that the fleshy grey leaves are closely grouped on slender hanging stems that give the strands of plants the appearance of a very meticulously plaited length of rope. One problem is that the small pads of growth are easily dislodged with handling. It should be grown in a hanging pot or basket.

However, suspending small pots overhead is fraught with danger as far as the plants are concerned, as it is extremely difficult to water them satisfactorily, and one also tends to forget them. When utilizing burro's tail as a hanging plant it is suggested that several small plants be put into the same container to give a bolder display and make their care easier. Mention is made above of hanging plants *above* one's head, but it is better to hang them at about head level so that they can be easily checked and tended. Use porous potting mixture, and keep plants on the dry side and in good light.

Take care
Handle carefully in transit. 305♦

Selaginella
(Creeping moss)
- Shade
- Temp: 18-24°C (65-75°F)
- Keep moist

These challenging plants, which will test the skills of the most accomplished grower of indoor plants, resemble miniature moss-like ferns, and are available in a number of varieties.

They require warm, moist conditions, and any drying out of the roots or the atmosphere results in shrivelling of foliage. When potting plants, use a mixture that will retain the maximum amount of moisture – a peat and fresh sphagnum moss composition is best. Foliage should be frequently misted over with tepid rain water, and the pot placed on wet gravel or plunged in damp peat. However, given all these requirements it will still be hard to keep these plants in an ordinary room. The moist, humid conditions they need are best created by using a sealed glass container, which will be free of draughts and has its own damp environment. Also ensure that plants are not exposed to direct sunlight, or close to radiators.

Take care
Ensure moist and warm conditions.

Senecio macro-glossus variegata
(Cape ivy)
- Good light
- Temp: 13-21°C (55-70°F)
- Keep moist and fed

In appearance these vigorous climbing plants strongly resemble the small-leaved ivies, and they must have some form of support for their rapid growth. During their growing season, provide moist conditions and regular feeding; less water is required in winter, and no feeding.

However well the plants may be cared for, in time the top growth extends and lower branches begin to shed their leaves. Replace older and less attractive specimens by starting afresh with a new batch of cuttings. Senecio will root like a weed during the summer if given warm and shaded conditions. Stem cuttings with two leaves attached should be prepared, and up to seven of these put into each small pot filled with peaty potting mixture.

This plant is prone to attack by aphids, which seem to find the tender succulent new growth particularly appetizing; inspect the tips for aphids, and treat with insecticide as soon as possible.

Take care
Inspect frequently for aphids.

Setcreasea purpurea
(Purple heart)
- **Good shade**
- **Temp: 10-16°C (50-60°F)**
- **Avoid wet conditions**

The humble tradescantia has many interesting relatives, including *S. purpurea*. Brilliant purple leaves are seen at their best when the plant is growing in good light with some direct sun, but very strong sun should be guarded against. They are impressive when grown in hanging pots or baskets: with all hanging plants one should endeavour to achieve a full effect, so lots of cuttings should go into each pot.

Cuttings of pieces of stem some 10cm (4in) long will not be hard to root in conventional houseplant potting mixture. Enclosing the cuttings in a small propagator, or even a sealed polythene bag, will reduce transpiration and speed up the rooting process. Several cuttings, up to five in each 7.5cm (3in) pot, will provide better plants than single pieces in the pot.

Like most of the tradescantia tribe, this one should be well watered and allowed to dry appreciably before watering again. Feed occasionally.

Take care
Replace old plants by cuttings. 306♦

Sonerila margaritacea
(Frosted sonerila)
- **Light shade**
- **Temp: 18-24°C (65-75°F)**
- **Keep moist**

A neat and colourful plant, with prominent silver markings on the upper surface of leaves, and purple underneath. They are extremely difficult to manage if treated simply as a potted plant for the windowsill.

Low temperatures, draughts, full sun and overwatering all make life difficult for the tender sonerila. Sonerila demands even temperature and even amount of moisture above all. A glass case or bottle garden offers draught-free conditions that can also be maintained at an evenly moist level much more easily than can be done if plants are simply placed on a windowsill among cold draughts and fluctuating temperatures.

Use tepid rain water, not water drawn direct from the tap. Feed regularly with weak liquid fertilizer while plants are producing new leaves; when potting, they will do best in soilless mixture. Ensure that soilless mixtures do not become excessively wet or dry.

Take care
Avoid cold and wetness in winter.

Sparmannia africana
(Indoor lime)
- **Light shade**
- **Temp: 16-21°C (60-70°F)**
- **Keep moist and fed**

The sparmannia may produce a few flowers but is principally a foliage plant. The leaves are very large and fresh green in colour and are produced in quantity from woody stems. Small plants have straight stems, but they will begin to branch while reasonably young, and develop into attractive small trees.

The number of leaves and vigour of growth immediately suggest that this is a hungry plant that will require adequate and frequent feeding to retain its pleasing colour and maintain its vigor without loss of leaves. Older plants can be quite severely pruned at any time of year. Firm pieces of stem with a few leaves attached can be very easily rooted in peaty mixture in a temperature around 18°C (65°F). Use peat to start them off, but pot on into loam-based potting soil as soon as they have a reasonable amount of roots.

Mealy bug can be a problem, but is easily detected and can be wiped off with methylated spirit.

Take care
Remember to feed and pot on. 306♦

Stenotaphrum secundatum
(St Augustine's grass)
- **Light shade**
- **Temp: 10-16°C (50-60°F)**
- **Keep very moist and fed**

This amazingly invasive grass bounds away in all directions once it has established a foothold. It is not unattractive, with cream and green variegation, the cream being predominant. Its major drawback is that as the plant produces fresh growth, so the older growth shrivels and dies, leaving dry brown leaves hanging from the lower parts of the plant. However, if one has time to remove these as they appear, the plant can be kept looking attractive.

Tufts of grassy leaves with a thicker base are produced in profusion; any removed and pushed into pots of peaty soil root almost at once. When plants appear to be past their best, root fresh cuttings and dispose of the aged parent. This is best done in the autumn, so that one will have more manageable plants to care for over the winter.

These plants will grow anywhere if there is moisture and warmth, and are very welcome as something different in the way of hanging plants.

Take care
Renew older plants regularly. 307♦

Stromanthe amabilis
- **Shade**
- **Temp: 18-24°C (65-75°F)**
- **Keep moist**

This plant belongs to the same family
as the calatheas and marantas. The
oval-shaped leaves come to a point
and are a bluish green in colour with
bands of stronger colour running the
length of the leaf. They overlap one
another and are produced at soil
level from a creeping rhizome. They
reach a length of about 15-23cm (6-
9in) and a width of 5cm (2in).

New plants are easily raised by
dividing existing clumps into smaller
sections and potting them up as
individuals. The soil for this ought to
be a good houseplant mixture
containing a reasonable quantity of
peat. Being squat plants they will
also be better suited to shallow pans
rather than full-depth pots. Shade is
essential, as plants simply shrivel up
when subjected to strong sunlight for
any length of time. Soil should be
kept moist, but it is absolutely
necessary to ensure that it is
moistness that is the aim and not
total saturation.

Take care
Maintain warmth and humidity. 308♦

Tetrastigma voinierianum
(Chestnut vine)
- **Light shade**
- **Temp: 16-21°C (60-70°F)**
- **Keep moist and well fed**

Given moist conditions in a warm
greenhouse and reasonable cultural
care you can almost stand and watch
this plant putting on new growth! The
lobed leaves are a soft green in
colour and are seen at their best
when the plant has freedom to climb
a supporting stake or framework. As
new small leaves appear, so do the
fascinating hair-covered tendrils
which reach out in search of an
object to cling to. This is probably the
quickest growing of all indoor plants,
and is ideal if one needs a climber to
cover a wall trellis in the minimum
time.

Being vigorous plants, they have
to be kept on the move with frequent
feeding, doubling the fertilizer dose
that the manufacturer recommends.
It also means that potting on cannot
be neglected: large plants of
chestnut vine in small pots will never
do well. The potting mixture must be
a loam-based one and the potting
should be done with a degree of
firmness.

Take care
Provide generous feeding. 309♦

Tillandsia usneoides
(Spanish moss)
- **Light shade**
- **Temp: 16-21°C (60-70°F)**
- **Spray foliage frequently**

One of the most fascinating plants of them all, in that it does not require any soil in which to grow. The plant has very slender stem-like leaves that form a tangled mass resembling a bundle of silvery-grey tangled wire. In their native Everglades of America these plants hang in dense masses from the branches of every tree.

A decorative few pieces on something like a small decorated bromeliad tree that is kept moist by frequent spraying can be a fascinating feature in the conservatory, where excess moisture will be easier to tolerate. Plants need only be hung over a branch. The clump will increase in size, and the strands in length. Ensure that the foliage is moistened regularly during the course of the day. Propagation means little more than teasing pieces away from the parent plant and hanging them up individually. Feeding is not necessary: other than water, the main need is for adequate warmth.

Take care
Keep foliage moist.

Tolmiea menziesii
(Pick-a-back plant)
- **Light shade**
- **Temp: 7-18°C (45-65°F)**
- **Keep moist and fed**

Interesting plants that develop into soft mounds of pale green foliage that are attractive at low level or suspended from the ceiling. Mature leaves develop perfect young plants that are carried on their backs. These can be detached when of reasonable size and potted up individually in peaty houseplant mixture. To succeed, plants should be kept in a light and airy place and be watered and fed with moderation. For mature plants use loam-based potting soil. Although they will tolerate very low temperatures and survive, they are better kept at around 16°C (60°F).

Hot and dry conditions increase the possibility of red spider mite infestation, which will in time considerably weaken plants. A sign of red spider presence will be a general hardening of the topmost leaves of the plant, which also become much paler. Check the undersides of leaves periodically with a magnifying glass; mites are very difficult to see otherwise.

Take care
Avoid hot and dry conditions. 309♦

Tradescantia blossfeldiana

- **Good light**
- **Temp: 10-16°C (50-60°F)**
- **Keep on the dry side**

This interesting and robust plant has pale green hairy foliage and stout stems, and is capable of withstanding rough treatment. There is also a variegated form, with pale cream to yellow colouring suffused through the paler background green, and a purplish underside to the leaves. Both produce the typical three-petaled tradescantia flowers, which are purple with white tips.

One frequently sees very weedy examples of these plants about, and the trouble seems to be that the initial plants had only a single, straggly cutting put in the pot. With plants that produce lots of growth, as tradescantias do, always put several cuttings in the pot when propagating; you will then have a full and handsome final plant.

With hanging baskets of plants that become ragged in appearance, remove the tops of half a dozen shoots and insert them where there are gaps. Tradescantia cuttings root almost anywhere.

Take care
Never overwater or overfeed.

Tradescantia purpurea

(Wandering Jew)
- **Light shade**
- **Temp: 13-18°C (55-65°F)**
- **Keep moist and fed**

This tradescantia has a brownish-red upper surface to its leaves and a purple underside, with fleshy, paler stems. Not so trailing as many of the tradescantias, it looks better growing in a shallow pan on the windowsill rather than in a hanging basket.

Cuttings with about three leaves can be taken during spring or summer and rooted in a houseplant potting mixture. Peat will not encourage them to root any better, and frequently results in the small plants being starved once they get under way. As with all the freer-growing tradescantias it will be best to put five to seven cuttings in the pot to ensure a fuller final plant. Excessive watering should be guarded against, but plants must remain moist during summer, and should also be regularly fed over this period. Towards the end of the summer more vigorous plants will have taken on a straggly, tired appearance, and it is then advisable to trim back any untidy growth.

Take care
Renew with cuttings periodically.

Tradescantia 'Quicksilver'
(Wandering Jew)
- **Good light**
- **Temp: 10-16°C (50-60°F)**
- **Keep on the dry side**

There are numerous varieties of *T. fluminensis,* but this one is bolder and much brighter than any of the others; all, however, require very similar treatment.

Good light is important if plants are to retain their silvered variegation, but protection from bright sun will be necessary. The soil should be free to drain and at no time become waterlogged. These plants respond well to regular applications of liquid fertilizer while they are in active growth. The view that when plants are fed they tend to lose their variegation is nonsense, as variegation depends on available light and whether or not the plants are allowed to become green. In poor light leaves tend to become green; and green shoots will in time take over, if not removed.

For baskets there are no better foliage plants, and small baskets or pots can be started by placing cuttings directly into the basket potting soil.

Take care
Remove green growth. 310♦

Vriesea mosaica
- **Light shade**
- **Temp: 16-21°C (60-70°F)**
- **Water into urn of leaves**

Some of the vrieseas are quite small and produce their flowering bracts at an early age, whereas others, such as *V. mosaica,* are grown principally for their decorative foliage. The colouring of *V. mosaica* is a dull reddish-brown, and there are interesting variations of colour through and across the leaf, as the name suggests.

This plant is quite rare and seldom offered for sale, but others of similar type are seen occasionally. Most have intricate patterns and colours in their recurving leaves, and grow to considerable size. They also have the typical bromeliad rosette of recurving leaves that makes a watertight urn into which water can be poured for the plant to live on. The urn should be kept topped up and the water replenished occasionally, but there is seldom need to water the soil in the pot – spillage from the urn is usually enough to keep the soil moist enough. All bromeliads do better in a mix of peat and coarse leaf mould.

Take care
Give very little water to the soil. 310♦

Yucca aloefolia
(Boundary plant)
- **Good light**
- **Temp: 10-21°C (50-70°F)**
- **Keep on the dry side**

The woody lengths of stem are imported from the tropics in very large quantities; they come in an assortment of sizes and are rooted at their destination, then potted and sold with their attractive aloe-like tufts of growth at the top of the stem.

Further benefits of this plant are that they are pleasing to the eye when grouped together, and little trouble to grow.

They do best in well-lit, coolish rooms if given the minimum of attention. The soil should be allowed to dry out quite appreciably between waterings and feed should be given once every 10 days during the summer months.

Purchased plants are normally in pots relevant to their height, so the pot is often quite large; as a result of this, the plant is growing in a container in which it can remain for two years or more. Plants should be potted on only when they have well filled their existing pots with roots. Use loam-based soil for this job when it is done.

Take care
Never overpot or overwater. 311♦

Zebrina pendula
(Silver inch plant)
- **Good light**
- **Temp: 13-18°C (55-65°F)**
- **Keep moist and fed**

This very common member of the tradescantia family has extraordinary colouring in its leaves, all of which have a plain purple reverse. It is one of the easiest plants to care for indoors, but the ease of care sometimes results in the plant being neglected.

Plants are very easily started from cuttings taken at any time other than winter. These should go into small pots filled with peaty soil, six or seven cuttings in each pot. Once established, put three or four pots of cuttings into a small hanging basket filled with a good houseplant potting soil, and keep the basket at a low level until the plants have obviously got under way; then the basket can be suspended at about head level. (If baskets are suspended immediately after planting, their care is often neglected.) Put plants in a light position out of direct sunlight, and water and feed them well while they are active; keep them dryish in winter, with no feeding.

Take care
Renew old plants every second year for an attractive display. 312♦

Part Three

CACTI AND SUCCULENTS

Gymnocalycium mihanovichii 'Hibotan'

Authors

Peter Chapman and Margaret
Martin are enthusiastic growers
and collectors who have
collaborated for over 20 years to
photograph and write about cacti
and other succulent plants. They
have co-authored two books and
contributed articles to countless
other books and magazines. The
advice they give in this section
comes from first-hand
experience.

Opuntia microdasys var. albispina

Index of Scientific Names

The plants are arranged in alphabetical order of Latin name.
Page numbers in **bold** refer to text entries; those in *italics* refer to photographs.

Index of Common Names

Introduction to Cacti and Succulents

Although it is common practice to refer to 'Cacti and Succulent Plants', with one exception (the pereskias) all cacti are succulent to varying degrees and belong to one family, the Cactaceae, whereas succulents can belong to many different plant families. They all have in common the ability to store water in their tissues in order to survive periods of drought, and this makes them ideal plants for the busy or forgetful person; many can survive days or even weeks of dryness. Cacti in particular can be divided into desert and jungle types; the latter live on trees as epiphytes, often in association with orchids, in tropical rain forests. Epiphytes use trees for support only; they are not parasites. Such cacti are represented by the epiphyllums, rhipsalis species, the Christmas cactus, and similar plants.

Often any thick-leaved or spiny plant is called a cactus, sometimes incorrectly. A unique feature of cacti is the 'areole', a small, pin-cushion-like structure arranged in numbers over the stems, from which any spines or hairs grow. All cacti have areoles but they are not always easy to see. The cactus flower is also characteristic and is often large and beautiful. Many cacti bloom annually; but a few can never become large enough in an average amateur collection to do so. Cacti are 'stem succulents', that is, water is stored in greatly thickened stems and, apart from the exception mentioned earlier (the pereskias) and a few other rarities, they have no real leaves. Other succulents, coming as they do from many different families, have flowers as diverse as the families themselves. They have no areoles; any spines resemble rose thorns. Some African euphorbias are virtually leafless, and with their ribbed, thorny, succulent stems they closely resemble cacti.

Cacti come from the American continent and those found elsewhere in the world have been introduced at some time in the past. Many other succulents are native to Africa.

Naming
Few of these plants have generally accepted common names, and their botanical names are prone to occasional change due to the latest fashionable scientific opinion. In this section we have used the most familiar names and given the recent alternative where applicable.

Situation and temperature
Almost all cacti and most other succulents can be overwintered at a temperature of 5°C (41°F) if kept dry, and cacti grown for flowers usually need this cold winter rest; indoors the window of an unheated room is the best place. Individual entries mention when a plant needs a rather higher winter temperature; greenhouse specimens can be brought indoors to save extra heating. Good light is essential for most succulents, and indoors the sunniest window should normally be used, remembering that the light is one-sided and the plants should be turned occasionally. In sunnier climes full sun in a greenhouse can cause scorching. The risk is reduced by good ventilation and few plants will scorch anywhere in the open air.

Potting mixtures and potting

Cacti and other succulent plants do not require an elaborate potting mixture; the mixture really only needs to be well-drained. Either peat- or loam-based mixtures will do, but it is usually an advantage to mix in about one third of extra drainage material such as sharp sand or perlite, as the one thing all these plants dislike is any degree of waterlogging of the soil. Potting on – that is, transferring to a larger pot – is necessary when the plant has formed a mass of roots; it may or may not be necessary every year, depending on the rate of growth of the particular plant. Repotting can be carried out by shaking off as much of the old potting mixture as possible from the roots and replacing the plant in the same pot (thoroughly cleaned first) in fresh mixture. Spiny plants can be held in a fold of newspaper. The best time for this is early spring, at the beginning of the growing season; withhold watering for a few days afterwards to enable the roots to recover.

Watering and feeding

Most succulents grow in spring and summer when water can be freely given each time the potting mixture appears almost dry. In winter, any surplus water can easily cause rotting and complete dryness is normally necessary with greenhouse plants, but indoors an occasional watering may be needed to prevent undue shrivelling. (Any exceptions are mentioned in the text.) Many succulents, notably the freely flowering ones, benefit from a dose of fertilizer every two weeks during the spring and summer. A high-potassium type, such as is designed for tomatoes, should be used. But plants in soilless, peat-based potting mixtures, which contain no natural food, will need this throughout the growing season.

Propagation

Succulent plants can be raised from seed, which unless bought from a specialist nursery will probably be 'mixed'. Sow as for any greenhouse perennial at a temperature of 18-24°C (65-75°F). Be in no hurry to prick out; most seedlings can remain in the same pan for a year, unless very crowded. Keep them slightly moist and not too cold for their first winter. Plants that form offsets can be propagated by removing one or more, allowing them to dry for a few days to reduce the risk of rot before potting them.

Pests

The main pest of these plants is the mealy bug, often seen as white cotton-wool patches and sometimes mistaken for a fungus. The pest itself hides within this, but sometimes appears, looking like a minute white woodlouse. Treatment with a proprietary spray will usually control these bugs. But watch out for a more insidious relative, the root mealy bug, when you are repotting; minute white patches on the roots indicate this. Dip the infected roots in an insecticide before repotting and water occasionally with a similar substance.

Right:
Acanthocalycium violaceum
A most attractive globular cactus beautifully spined and producing splendid colourful blooms. It does not become too large. 345♦

Far right: **Agave filifera**
Although a potential giant, this succulent is slow-growing, and it makes a very distinctive specimen when small. The narrow leaves have sharp spines at the tips. 346♦

Below right: **Agave parviflora**
This is one of the smaller agaves and makes an attractive addition to any collection. Offsets are usually formed around the base. It is an easy plant to raise from seed. 346♦

Below:
Aeonium arboreum var. **nigrum**
The almost black leaves of this succulent make it a most unusual plant. Good light is needed to keep the leaves from becoming green. 345♦

Above: **Agave victoria-reginae**
Probably the most beautiful of all the agaves, this slow-growing succulent does not usually form offsets, but is readily raised from seed. The attractive leaves are each tipped with a sharp spine. 347♦

Left: **Aloe jacunda**
This very attractive dwarf succulent soon produces offsets from the base to form a group, and is free-flowering. Its need for partial shade makes it ideal as a room plant, for a not too sunny window. 348♦

Above right: **Aloe variegata**
The very well-known Partridge Breast Aloe is ideally suited to the living-room as it thrives in shade. Pink flowers are sometimes produced at the end of a long stem. Very little water is needed. 349♦

Right: **Ancistrocactus scheeri**
A slow-growing cactus with very beautiful spines and flowers. As it has a thick, fleshy root, it is prone to rotting and needs very careful watering. Offsets are not usually produced. 350♦

Left: **Aporocactus flagelliformis**
The popular Rat's Tail Cactus, with its long hanging stems and colourful flowers, is a 'must' for a basket _ really the only way to grow it. 351♦

Right: **Ariocarpus fissuratus**
Looking more like a chunk of stone than a cactus, this plant can in fact produce a most beautiful flower. It is very slow-growing. 352♦

Below right: **Astrophytum asterias**
Another unusual cactus, entirely without spines, but producing most attractive yellow flowers. Well worth the extra care it needs. 353♦

Below: **Aporocactus mallisonii**
Another ideal subject for a hanging basket, this cactus – which is actually a hybrid – has masses of trailing stems and large flowers. 351♦

Left: Astrophytum myriostigma
A simple astrophytum to cultivate and also easy to handle, being quite spineless. The silvery hairy scales give it a rock-like appearance. 354♦

Below: Astrophytum ornatum
A spiny astrophytum, which needs to be fairly large before flowering but is nevertheless an interesting addition to any collection. 354♦

Bottom: Borzicactus aureispinus
This somewhat unusual cactus needs careful positioning to allow for the beautiful long stems with their golden spines. 355♦

Left: **Carpobrotus edulis**
This succulent can be grown out of doors in mild regions of temperate countries, ideally in a sunny rock garden, where its sprawling stems and colourful flowers are a delight. Edible fruits are produced. 357♦

Below: **Cephalocereus senilis**
'Old Man Cactus' aptly describes this plant, with its mass of twisted white hairs and almost no spines. Although large in nature, it makes an ideal pot specimen. 357♦

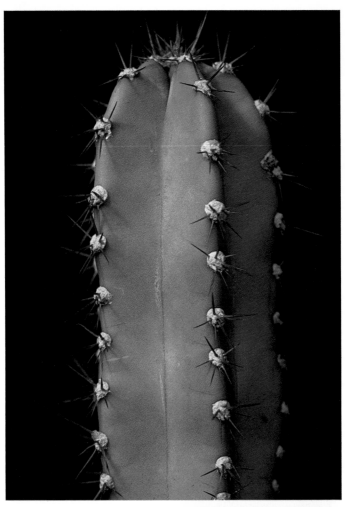

Above: **Cereus peruvianus**
Although it can be a giant in the wild, the attractively spined, slender stems of this cactus make an ideal contrast with the more globular plants in the collection. It is grown for its shape and form rather than its flowers, which are not produced by small specimens. 358♦

Right: **Ceropegia woodii**
This succulent, with its long trailing stems, needs to be grown on a plastic trellis or similar support, where it can show off its curious but most attractive flowers and small fleshy leaves to the best advantage. Otherwise, let the stems trail over the edge of the pot. 358♦

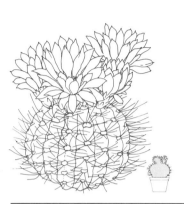

Acanthocalycium violaceum

- **Full sun**
- **Temp: 5-30°C (41-86°F)**
- **Water with care**

Acanthocalycium violaceum is a cylindrical plant about 12cm (4.7in) in diameter. During summer, it produces large numbers of beautiful violet flowers, about 5cm (2in) across. Even during winter the plant is attractive, and the stout yellow spines show up well against the dark green of the stem. This cactus does not offset easily, certainly not as a young plant; many apparently solitary plants do occasionally form offsets with age.

A good potting mixture is two parts of loam- or peat-based material to one part of sharp sand or perlite. *A. violaceum* should be watered with caution even during the summer growing period. Always allow it to dry out between waterings and if possible water on a sunny day. Feed every two weeks with a high-potassium (tomato) fertilizer when the buds form. If it should lose its roots, allow the plant to dry for two or three days and repot in fresh, well-drained mixture. Keep in a well-lit position.

Take care
Water sparingly. 336♦

Aeonium arboreum 'Nigrum' ('Zwartkop')

- **Full sun**
- **Temp: 5-30°C (41-86°F)**
- **Water occasionally in winter**

An attractive, robust succulent with almost black glossy leaves arranged in a rosette that can be as much as 20cm (8in) across. The stem carrying it is about 1.5cm (0.6in) thick and as it gradually elongates one is left with a rosette of leaves on about 30cm (12in) of bare stem, any lower leaves having fallen off. Cut off the leafy top with a short piece of the stem, let it dry for a couple of days and then just push it into the surface of fresh potting mixture. It will soon rot to form a flat, compact plant once more. Keep the old stem; it will send out many small rosettes, which in their turn can be removed and rooted.

This aeonium makes a good houseplant but needs plenty of light or the leaves will tend to lose their beautiful dark colour and turn greenish. Although it will withstand a lower temperature, it does not need it and will thrive in a normal living-room. Use any good standard potting mixture.

Take care
Mealy bugs like to live between the leaves. 336♦

Agave filifera
- Full sun
- Temp: 5-30°C (41-86°F)
- Water with care

Agave filifera forms a rosette 65cm (26in) across; each leathery leaf is 3cm (1.2in) wide and ends in a stout spine. The leaves are dark green in colour with white threads along the edge. This agave will eventually throw up a flower stem 2.5m (8ft) high, on the end of which are purple and green bell-like flowers. The main rosette dies after flowering, but new rosettes will form at the base of the old plant. The lifespan of the main rosette is 8-25 years.

Because of its tough leaves, *A. filifera* is very resistant to a dry atmosphere. If it is kept indoors during the winter months, place it outdoors during the summer. It needs sun during the growing period to keep it a good colour and shape. It is ideal for a patio or veranda.

This agave will grow in any loam- or peat-based medium. Water generously during very hot weather but keep only slightly moist during winter or periods of cloudy, damp weather.

Agave parviflora
- Full sun
- Temp: 5-30°C (41-86°F)
- Do not overwater

One of the smallest of the agaves, *Agave parviflora* is ideal for a small greenhouse. The adult rosette is 18cm (7in) across, and the slender dark green leaves have white edges and white marginal threads. Eventually the plant will flower and die. The flower stem is about 1m (39in) high and carries pale yellow flowers. The agave will probably be over five years old when it flowers, and young plantlets will form around the dying rosette. These should be removed and potted up. Because of its attractive form, *A. parviflora* makes a good houseplant. When warm weather comes, put the plant outdoors in full sun; this will keep it in good health.

A good loam- or peat-based medium will suit this plant. It should be repotted annually. During hot weather, water freely: but keep it just moist during the winter and wet, cloudy weather. Agaves, with their tough leaves, present a problem to any insect pests.

Take care
Beware of the stout spines. 337♦

Take care
Repot each year. 337♦

Agave victoria-reginae
- **Full sun**
- **Temp: 5-30°C (41-86°F)**
- **Water with care**

Agave victoria-reginae is the most
beautiful of the small agaves. It is a
densely leaved rosette: the leaves
are 15cm (6in) long, dark green in
colour with beautiful white markings.
Each leaf ends in a terminal spine,
which should be treated with
respect. *A. victoria-reginae* can
withstand a very dry atmosphere and
may be used as a houseplant during
the winter months, but in the
summer growing period it needs full
sun to bring out its beautiful
colouring.

Like all agaves, this species has a
long flower stem, 3-4m (10-13ft) in
height. The flowers are cream. After
flowering the rosette dies, and
unfortunately there are unlikely to be
any offsets. But you may well have
had the plant for 10 years before it
flowers.

Any good loam- or peat-based
potting mixture is suitable for this
plant. It should be repotted annually.
The plant may be watered freely
during hot sunny weather but should
be kept fairly dry at other times.

Take care
Avoid the sharp spines. 338♦

Aloe aristata
- **Partial shade**
- **Temp: 5-30°C (41-86°F)**
- **Water occasionally in winter**

Although some aloes are impossible
giants, this one is ideal for a
greenhouse or windowsill collection.
It forms tough green rosettes about
10-15cm (4-6in) across; clumps of
up to 12 rosettes may eventually be
produced. But this is no problem,
because individual rosettes can
easily be detached and grown as
new plants. Narrow leaves within the
rosette are 8-10cm (3.2-4in) long
with slightly raised white spots.
Small greenish flowers are produced
in a cluster on the end of thin stems
up to 50cm (20in) high.

Preference for partial shade
makes this and other aloes ideal
houseplants, but do not put them in
any dark corner; merely avoid full
summer sunlight. If kept in a living-
room give some water in winter, but
in a colder greenhouse this
succulent is best allowed to be
almost dry; only water if it shrivels. *A.
aristata* is easy to grow in any good
potting mixture, and extra drainage
material is not necessary.

Take care
Divide the plant before it becomes
too large.

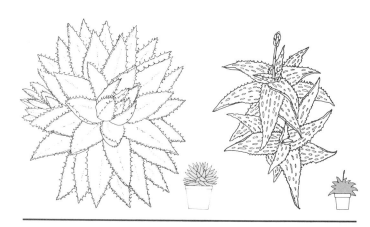

Aloe brevifolia

- ● **Partial shade**
- ● **Temp: 5-30°C (41-86°F)**
- ● **Keep slightly moist in winter**

Although this succulent can make a large clump of 12 or more heads, the individual plants are only up to 8cm (3.2in) across, and these can easily be separated before the plant becomes unmanageable. So it is one of the easiest plants to propagate. Each head consists of about 30 fleshy leaves, up to 6cm (2.4in) long and 2cm (0.8in) broad at the base. Upper surfaces are smooth and the few soft spines are confined to the undersides; the edges are furnished with blunt white teeth. A flower stem of about 30cm (12in), with small scarlet tubular flowers at the end, enhances the beauty of this plant, which is very easy to grow. Its need for some shade from summer sun and its wide temperature tolerance make it an ideal houseplant. It is also tolerant with regard to its soil requirements; any good standard potting mixture, either loam- or peat-based, will be quite satisfactory. Water this aloe quite freely in spring and summer, and give enough in winter to prevent shrivelling.

Take care
Avoid dark corners indoors.

Aloe jacunda

- ● **Partial shade**
- ● **Temp: 5-30°C (41-86°F)**
- ● **Keep slightly moist in winter**

A true dwarf succulent plant, this is one of the most attractive of the aloes. It consists of prettily mottled fleshy leaves, forming a compact rosette 8-9cm (3.2-3.5in) across. Individual leaves are up to 4cm (1.6in) long and 2cm (0.8in) broad at the base. This delightful little aloe branches freely from the base and soon forms an attractive clump. Excess heads can easily be removed, complete with roots, for propagation. Typical small, tubular aloe flowers, rose-pink in colour, are produced on stems up to 30cm (12in) long.

Any good potting mixture normally drains well enough for this aloe. Grow it indoors by all means, keeping it in a light window, but avoid full sun. It can even be planted out in the garden during spring and summer. It should be watered freely in spring and summer. Indoors in winter it will need more water than in a greenhouse.

Take care
Watch out for slugs on plants in the garden. 338♦

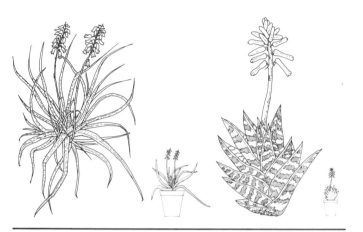

Aloe x 'Sabra'
- **Partial shade**
- **Temp: 5-28°C (41-83°F)**
- **Water occasionally during winter flowering**

This hybrid aloe was produced by an English nurseryman and named in honour of his daughter. It is a very pretty, relatively small-growing succulent with long, narrow, finely toothed, purplish-green leaves dappled with white. Individual leaves grow up to 20cm (8in) long, but are only about 12mm (0.5in) wide at the base. The plant forms offsets freely, eventually producing a clump of heads, each of which can give rise to a flower stem up to 20cm (8in) long, tipped with about 30 pinkish-white blooms, opening in succession from the top. A clump about 13cm (5in) across would probably consist of five to eight heads.

This aloe flowers in the winter and it is essential to give the plant some water at this time, with a short, almost dry, resting period after flowering, until early spring. During the rest of the year it may be watered freely. A good, well-drained potting mixture is needed; add about one third of sharp sand or perlite to a standard mix.

Take care
Full summer sun can cause the leaf tips to dry out.

Aloe variegata
(Partridge breast aloe)
- **Partial shade**
- **Temp: 10-30°C (50-86°F)**
- **Keep dry in winter**

This is certainly one of the best-known succulent plants. It thrives on many windowsills in homes and offices, and its success indicates the chief cultivation tip – it is better as a houseplant than in a greenhouse environment. The surprising thing is how little water the plant seems to need, even indoors. The leaves have a thickened 'V' section and are up to 15cm (6in) long in mature plants, though most specimens are much smaller. They are bright green, marbled with whitish bands. Although so common, this is a delightful plant, enhanced occasionally by the appearance of bright pink, tubular flowers on a stem up to 30cm (12in) long.

Although this aloe seems to thrive on neglect, it is possible to go too far in this respect, witness the miserable, dried-up specimens sometimes seen! Add about one third extra sharp sand or perlite to any good potting mixture, either loam- or peat-based.

Take care
Water only in spring and summer when almost dried out. 339♦

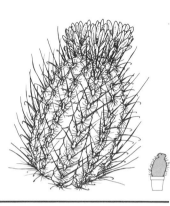

Aloinopsis schooneesii

- **Full sun**
- **Temp: 5-30°C (41-86°F)**
- **Keep dry in winter**

Aloinopsis schooneesii is often listed in catalogues under its older name of *Nananthus schooneesii.* This little South African plant is a leafy succulent; each head has about 10 fleshy blue-green leaves. The plant clusters, but may be kept for several years in a 7.5cm (3in) pot. It must be placed in a sunny position if it is to flower well.

The golden-yellow flowers are produced continuously through the summer months. Each flower lasts for several days. The flowers are about 1.5cm (0.6in) across.

This succulent needs a very open soil; half loam-based mixture and half sharp sand or perlite is suitable. It is not necessary to repot annually; it is better to break the cluster up every three or four years in the spring. Pull the heads off, dry for two days and then pot up.

Water the plant freely during summer, allowing to dry between waterings.

Take care
Do not water during winter.

Ancistrocactus scheeri

- **Full sun**
- **Temp: 5-30°C (41-86°F)**
- **Keep dry in winter**

A beautifully spined, very attractive cactus that is well worth the little extra attention needed to cultivate it. The roughly spherical stem, which does not normally form offsets, carries strong yellowish spines, sometimes as long as 4cm (1.6in). A good specimen is around 7cm (2.8in) across. The funnel-shaped flowers, yellowish-green in colour, are about 2.5cm (1in) wide.

Admittedly, this is not one of the easiest of cacti to grow, but it should thrive if its requirements are understood. The main difficulty is that it has large, fleshy roots that have a tendency to disappear at the slightest amount of excess water, and for this reason some specimens are grown grafted. But all should be well if you use a very open potting mixture, made by using equal parts of sharp sand or perlite and a standard loam- or peat-based mix; water only in spring and summer.

Take care
If roots are lost, cut to clean tissue, dry and repot. 339♦

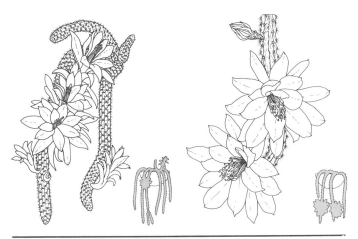

Aporocactus flagelliformis

(Rat's-tail cactus)
- **Diffuse sunlight**
- **Temp: 5-30°C (41-86°F)**
- **Keep moist all year**

A beautiful plant for a hanging basket, this cactus will grow happily in a window. The long slender stems may reach a length of 2m (6.5ft); they are closely ribbed and densely covered with small brown spines. In early spring, the stems are covered with vivid cerise flowers; these are tubular, 5cm (2in) long, and last for several days.

A loam- or peat-based mixture is suitable for this plant. Feed with a liquid tomato fertilizer once every two weeks during the growing period. Repot annually. Never allow the plant to become completely dry, even in winter. In summer, water generously.

When the plant becomes too large, one of the tails may be cut off, dried for two days and potted up. Early summer is the best time for rooting cuttings. Mealy bug can be a serious pest. It is easy to overlook them on a large plant. Treat the plant with a systemic insecticide.

Take care
Never let this plant dry out. 340♦

Aporocactus mallisonii

- **Diffuse sunlight**
- **Temp: 5-30°C (41-86°F)**
- **Keep damp all year**

An excellent plant for a hanging basket, this cactus will thrive in a warm living-room but does need plenty of light. The stout stems reach a length of about 1m (39in); they are deeply ribbed and covered in short spines. In early summer, large numbers of brilliant red flowers are carried along the stems.

A good loam- or peat-based mixture is needed. Repot annually. During the summer growing period, water generously and use a liquid tomato fertilizer every two weeks.

A. mallisonii (now known as x *Heliaporus smithii*) is a hybrid and can only be propagated vegetatively. When the plant has outgrown its accommodation, cut off one of the stems. Dry for two days and pot up. Propagation is most successful in early summer. Mealy bug is the chief pest that attacks this cactus. Inspect the stems regularly. Spray with a proprietary insecticide if an infestation is found.

Take care
Never let this plant dry out. 340♦

Argyroderma octophyllum

- **Full sun**
- **Temp: 5-30°C (41-86°F)**
- **Keep dry in winter**

This is a stemless plant with one pair of fat, egg-shaped leaves, which are blue-green in colour. This plant will never grow more than 3cm (1.2in) long, and is ideal for a small, sunny greenhouse. The yellow flowers appear from the cleft between the leaves in late summer. The flowers are about 2cm (0.8in) across and open on sunny afternoons, closing in the evening. The flowers last for several days.

During spring, the old pair of leaves will start to shrivel and a new plant will emerge from between them. No water should be given until the old leaves have completely dried up. Continue watering on sunny days until the autumn. Keep dry through the winter.

Grow in a mixture of half loam-based medium and half sharp sand or perlite. Repot every three or four years. Mealy bug and root mealy bug can be serious pests; water with a proprietary insecticide.

Take care
Never overwater, or the plant will become bloated.

Ariocarpus fissuratus var. lloydii

(Living rock)

- **Full sun**
- **Temp: 5-30°C (41-86°F)**
- **Always water carefully**

Ariocarpuses are among the rarest and most interesting of the cacti but are suitable only for greenhouse cultivation. These plants grow in desert conditions in the blazing sun. For successful cultivation they need the maximum sunlight, a very open mixture (half loam-based medium, half sharp sand or perlite) and careful watering. Water on sunny days in summer, and keep dry in winter.

A. fissuratus bears a close resemblance to a chunk of rock. It has a thickened taproot crowned by large flattened tubercles. The tubercles are greyish in colour with creamy wool among the new growth. The large satiny pink flowers appear from the centre of the plant. They open in late autumn or early winter. A mature specimen is 15cm (6in) across, and may have taken 20 years to reach that size. Mealy bug may attack the new, tender growth. Inspect the woolly centre of the plant for signs of these pests. If found, treat with a suitable insecticide.

Take care
Never overwater. 341

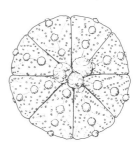

Ariocarpus trigonus
- Full sun
- Temp: 5-30°C (41-86°F)
- Water very carefully

Ariocarpus trigonus is a rare and unusual cactus. The plant has long upright tubercles arranged like a crown on the large taproot. Most specimens seen in cultivation are not more than 13cm (5in) across. The tubercles are brownish-grey in colour. The flowers are produced from the centre of the plant in late autumn or early winter. They are pale yellow with a satiny sheen.

Water with the greatest care, on sunny days only, so that any surplus moisture dries up quickly. Keep dry in the winter. The soil must be very well drained: a loam-based mixture to which an equal volume of sharp sand or perlite has been aded is suitable. Although slow-growing, ariocarpuses can swell at the neck of the plant just below soil level and jam themselves in their pots. Make sure there is a space of about 1cm (0.4in) between the plant and the rim of the pot. Because of its need for strong light, *A. trigonus* needs greenhouse cultivation.

Take care
Do not let soil get compacted.

Astrophytum asterias
- Full sun
- Temp: 5-30°C (41-86°F)
- Do not overwater

Astrophytum asterias looks like a grey-green sea urchin; it could never be confused with any other cactus. Eventually it forms a flattened hemisphere about 10cm (4in) across. The stem is made up of eight spineless ribs, and the skin is covered with white spots. These vary from plant to plant: some specimens are beautifully covered in white polka dots, whereas others may have very few markings. The flowers open continuously through the summer; they are pale shiny yellow with a red throat, and sweetly scented. Seedlings about 2.5cm (1in) across will flower.

Never overwater and keep the soil completely dry during winter. A very open soil, half loam- or peat-based mixture and half sharp sand or perlite, is suitable. To ensure continuous flowering, keep the plant in the sunniest part of the greenhouse and feed every two weeks with a tomato fertilizer when the buds form.

Take care
Avoid watering on dull days. 341▶

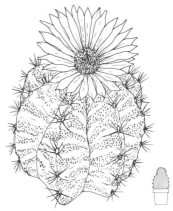

Astrophytum myriostigma
(Bishop's mitre)
- **Full sun**
- **Temp: 5-30°C (41-86°F)**
- **Dry winter rest**

Astrophytum myriostigma is a cylindrical plant eventually reaching a diameter of 20cm (8in). The dark green skin is completely covered with silvery scales. The number of ribs varies from four to eight. They are spineless, but the prominent areoles give the plant the appearance of having been buttoned into its skin. The flowers appear on the top of the plant continuously throughout the summer. They are yellow with a reddish throat and a sweet scent.

This is the easiest of the astrophytums to grow. A loam-based or peat-based mixture plus one third extra grit is suitable. Water freely throughout the summer, giving a liquid tomato fertilizer every two weeks, but keep dry in winter. This cactus is a native of the Mexican deserts and in cultivation needs the maximum light available. Mealy bug and root mealy bug can be a nuisance. Small white mealy bugs look very much like white scales.

Take care
Allow to dry between waterings. 342♦

Astrophytum ornatum
- **Full sun**
- **Temp: 5-30°C (41-86°F)**
- **Water with care**

Astrophytum ornatum does not bloom until it is about 15cm (6in) high, and it will probably take about 10 years to reach flowering size. But even without flowers, this is an attractive cactus. The stem is divided by eight ribs, which carry stout amber-coloured spines. The dark green skin has bands of silvery scales running across it. The pale yellow flowers are carried on top of the plant and are sweetly scented.

To keep the vivid colouring of this cactus, it needs sun. A useful mix is two parts loam- or peat-based medium plus one part sharp sand or perlite. Water generously throughout the summer, allowing to dry out before watering again. When the buds form give a dose of tomato fertilizer every two weeks. Keep the soil dry throughout the winter. Repot the plant annually, and inspect the roots for any grey ashy deposits, a sign that root mealy bug is present; if it is, water with an insecticide.

Take care
Make sure drips in the greenhouse do not spoil winter dryness. 342♦

Borzicactus (Matucana) aureiflora

- Full sun
- Temp: 5-30°C (41-86°F)
- Keep dry in winter

The two names given for this cactus indicate that it also has been subjected to re-classification and it is more likely that you will meet it under *Matucana*. Although in nature the globular stem can reach a diameter of 30cm (12in), specimens in cultivation are likely to be much smaller, with a flattened rather than a globular stem. A number of blunt ribs carry colourful, stout spreading spines. Bright yellow flowers, usually about 3cm (1.2in) across, are formed at the top of the stem in summer.

Use a porous potting mixture, which you can make by adding about one third of sharp sand or perlite to a standard loam- or peat-based material. Water this cactus quite freely in summer and feed once every two weeks or so with a high-potassium fertilizer, such as is given to tomatoes. Really good light will help to develop the fine spine coloration; give it full sunlight if at all possible.

Take care
If in a room, put it in the sunniest window.

Borzicactus aureispinus

- Full sun
- Temp: 5-30°C (41-86°F)
- Keep dry in winter

The long elegant stems of this unusual cactus make it a fascinating addition to any collection. *Borzicactus* was previously called *Hildewintera aureispina* and *Winterocereus aureispinus*, being a victim to the name changes that take place all too frequently among cacti (and other plants!). With stems up to 50cm (20in) long and 4-5cm (1.6-2.0in) wide, it is somewhat of a challenge to manage. Branches come freely from the base, so that a cluster of stems is eventually formed. Either tie them to a stout cane pushed into the pot or use a half-pot, letting the stems trail over the edge and along the greenhouse staging or a shelf. The stems glisten with bright golden spines, and beautiful salmon-pink flowers can be expected on older specimens.

Grow borzicactus in a good standard loam- or peat-based potting mixture, to which has been added a third sharp sand or perlite.

Take care
Mealy bugs can hide among the dense spines. 342♦

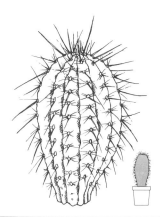

Caralluma europaea
- Full sun
- Temp: 10-30°C (50-86°F)
- Keep moderately dry in winter

A delightful little succulent plant which, although related to the 'carrion' flowers, has nothing unpleasant about it. The four-angled, slightly toothed stems (no spines) branch freely and reach a length of about 10cm (4in). The plant has a somewhat creeping habit. Star-shaped yellow flowers with deep purple markings, 2cm (0.8in) across, are produced in summer.

Caralluma europaea is an easy plant to cultivate, the only likely trouble being winter care. Although it will survive lower temperatures than the suggested 10°C (50°F), it may succumb to fungus attack (usually indicated by black marks on the stems) unless completely dry, when it is likely to shrivel badly. So keep it warmer, indoors if necessary, and give enough water in winter to prevent shrivelling. With a good, well-drained potting mixture (one part sharp sand or perlite to two parts of a standard mix) you can water it freely in summer.

Take care
Avoid cold and damp conditions.

Carnegia gigantea
(Saguaro)
- Full sun
- Temp: 5-30°C (41-86°F)
- Keep dry in winter

Symbolic of many Western films and also used as the state sign of Arizona, this is one of the largest cacti, but because it is very slow-growing it is quite suitable as a pot plant. Although in nature it can reach a height of 15m (50ft), it takes about 200 years to do so; hardly likely to embarrass the collector! An average domestic specimen would be about 15cm (6in) high in ten years. It forms a green, ribbed column with short spines, and will not produce the up-pointing arms characteristic of giant desert plants; it is unlikely to flower in the owner's lifetime. Although not particularly spectacular as a potted cactus, it is nevertheless of interest because of its association with the desert giants.

Grow *C. gigantea* in a particularly well-drained potting mixture; add one part of sharp sand or perlite to two parts of a good standard loam- or peat-based material. A top dressing of gravel 1cm (0.4in) thick will help to avoid rotting at the base.

Take care
Never overwater this cactus.

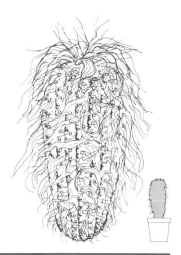

Carpobrotus edulis
(Hottentot fig)
- **Full sun**
- **Frost-free conditions**
- **Water generously in hot weather**

Like many shrubby succulents, *C. edulis* does better if planted outdoors during warm weather. It can either be lifted in the autumn, or cuttings can be taken in late summer and wintered indoors. In mild regions it can remain outside.

The plant is a strongly growing shrub with prostrate branches 1m (39in) long. It can be grown against a small wall and the branches allowed to trail over it. The large triangular leaves are grass-green in colour. Although this is not a prolific flowerer, the blooms are large, about 10cm (4in) across, and a vivid magenta, yellow or orange in colour.

If grown outdoors the plant will suffer from the same pests as other garden plants, and should be given similar treatment. It should be placed in a sunny position and given an occasional watering during prolonged dry weather. Cuttings should be wintered on a light windowsill or in a frost-free greenhouse. Keep slightly moist.

Take care
Restart when it becomes untidy. 343♦

Cephalocereus senilis
(Old man cactus)
- **Full sun**
- **Temp: 7-30°C (45-86°F)**
- **Water very carefully**

In its native Mexico, this cactus forms a column 12m (40ft) high and 45cm (18in) across. These plants are said to be 200 years old, so there is little fear of a seedling outgrowing its accommodation. The white flowers are not produced until the plant is 6m (20ft) high, so this cactus must be grown for the beauty of its form.

The pale green stem with its yellow spines is completely hidden by long, white hairs. These will pick up dust, so to keep the plant gleaming white, shampoo it with a dilute detergent solution and rinse thoroughly; choose a hot sunny day. With advancing age, the lower hairs will inevitably become permanently discoloured. The upper part of the stem may be cut, dried for three days, and potted up. Take cuttings in late spring.

A very open soil – half loam-based mixture and half grit – and a dry winter rest are essential. Keep this cactus in the warmest, sunniest position available.

Take care
Avoid cold, damp conditions. 343♦

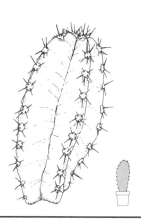

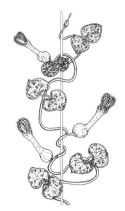

Cereus peruvianus
- **Full sun**
- **Temp: 5-30°C (41-86°F)**
- **Water generously in summer**

This columnar plant forms a handsome addition to any cactus collection. It is a vigorous plant and in a matter of a few years will form a blue-green column about 2m (6.5ft) high. The stem is ribbed, and the ribs carry stout spines. It is possible to flower this cereus in cultivation; the large white flowers open at night. In the wild, this plant will reach a height of 9m (30ft). When it reaches the roof of the greenhouse, cut the cereus about 1m (39in) from the top, dry for three days, and then pot up the top. The base will send out branches, which can be used for propagation.

Grow in a loam-based mixture and repot annually. Water generously during summer, and feed about once a month with a liquid fertilizer with a high potassium content (tomato fertilizer). Keep dry in winter. *C. peruvianus* is tough and vigorous, and unlikely to be bothered by pests.

Take care
Do not allow this plant to become potbound. 344♦

Ceropegia woodii
- **Full sun**
- **Temp: 7-30°C (45-86°F)**
- **Keep slightly moist in winter**

This plant has small heart-shaped leaves on long wiry stems. If the plant is kept moist, the leaves are thin and green; but if it is kept dry, the leaves thicken and attractive silvery markings develop. *C. woodii* makes a pretty plant for a hanging basket. But it looks even better if the stems are coiled around the top of a pan. Then the flowers stand up from the stems like tiny purple candles. The stems will root into the soil and form small tubers. After flowering, horn-shaped seed pods may develop. Inside the pod are flat seeds, each attached to its own tiny parachute.

A rich but porous soil and a sunny position are needed. Water fairly generously in summer, but keep just slightly moist in winter. *C. woodii* forms small tubers but the actual root system is shallow, so grow it in a pan or a half-pot. If seeds set on the plant, sow the seed as soon as released and small seedlings should come up quickly.

Take care
Avoid winter cold and dampness. 344♦

Chamaecereus silvestrii

(Peanut cactus)
- **Full sun**
- **Temp: 0-30°C (32-86°F)**
- **Keep dry in winter**

Sometimes recently listed as *Lobivia silvestrii* (another victim of botanical name changes), it seems more appropriate here to use the name of so many years standing. The spreading stems are somewhat finger-like in shape and size, bright green in colour and covered with short spines. Offsets, somewhat resembling green peanuts, appear along the length of the stems, hence the popular name. They detach themselves at the slightest touch, and can be potted up at once – surely the easiest cactus to propagate! But the great joy of this plant is the brilliant scarlet flowers, 4cm (1.6in) across; produced in profusion, they almost cover the stems during spring and summer.

This is not a fussy plant, so grow it in any good potting mixture. Water freely in spring and summer. One of the hardiest cacti, it will survive in a cold frame if quite dry.

Take care
Keep cold in winter to encourage good flowering. 361♦

Chamaecereus silvestrii, orange hybrid

- **Full sun**
- **Temp: 0-30°C (32-86°F)**
- **Keep dry in winter**

Taking advantage of the close relationship between *Chamaecereus* and *Lobivia*, plant breeders have produced hybrids between these two groups of cacti. The result is a compact plant with short, stubby, upright, branching stems. Offsets are still formed and do not fall off so readily as with *C. silvestrii* itself, but propagation by means of these is still very easy. Flowers, in this case bright orange and about 4cm (1.6in) in diameter, are freely produced in spring and summer. Other similar hybrids exist with red and also yellow blooms.

Water this cactus freely in spring and summer and feed every two weeks with a high-potassium fertilizer, from when the buds form. This will encourage flowering, as will a cold winter rest; use an unheated room in the house. Grow in a good standard loam- or peat-based potting mixture. Extra grit is needed only if there is doubt about drainage.

Take care
Watch for mealy bugs. 361♦

359

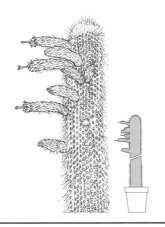

Cleistocactus straussii

(Silver torch)
- ● **Full sun**
- ● **Temp: 5-30°C (41-86°F)**
- ● **Water generously in summer**

Cleistocactus straussii is a slender column that will reach a height of 2m (6.5ft); the stem branches from the base. The plant is densely covered in short white spines, which give the plant a silvery gleam in the sunlight. Mature specimens flower freely in cultivation. The carmine flowers are carried on the sides of the columns and have a very characteristic shape: they consist of a long narrow tube with an opening only large enough for the stamens to protrude.

This is a vigorous cactus and to keep healthy it needs a good loam-based mixture and an annual repotting. Water generously during summer, give an occasional high-potassium liquid feed, and keep it dry in winter. To encourage flowering, put it in the sunniest position available. Some of the stems may be removed and used as cuttings if the plant is becoming too crowded.

Take care
Do not let this cactus become potbound. 362♦

Conophytum bilobum

- ● **Full sun**
- ● **Temp: 5-30°C (41-86°F)**
- ● **Give completely dry rest**

Conophytums are ideal plants for the small greenhouse but they need full sun. *C. bilobum* is one of the easiest species to grow. The two stemless leaves are fused to form a heart-shaped plant body, which is smooth and pale green in colour. The shining yellow flowers appear from the cleft between the leaves in late summer.

When to water can be a problem. Conophytums grow in late summer and autumn; but conditions in the greenhouse and the climatic conditions outside can influence growth, and watering is best based on observation. When watering stops, the plant body will slowly shrivel. Eventually two or three new heads emerge from the old plant. When the previous year's growth has shrivelled to a paper-thin skin, regular watering can start. It is advisable to give conophytums one good soaking in spring. Pot in very open mixture.

Take care
Make sure the winter dryness is not spoilt by drips in the greenhouse. 362♦

Top: Chamaecereus silvestrii
*The Peanut Cactus is very popular
and easy to grow. Finger-like stems
are covered with brilliant flowers in
spring and summer.* 359♦

Above:
Chamaecereus yellow hybrid
*One of the many attractive hybrids of
this cactus. A more compact plant
than the top one.* 359♦

Far left: Cleistocactus strausii
This beautiful silvery column can reach a height of over 100cm (39in) but is unlikely to out-grow its welcome in the average collection. Branches usually form at the base; small flowers are produced on older plants but do not open fully. 360◆

Left: Conophytum frutescens
Possibly the most attractive of a delightful group of miniature succulents. The plant consists of two very fleshy leaves to each head, from between which the flower grows. 377◆

Below left: Conophytum bilobum
This conophytum, one of the 'stemless mesembs', readily forms compact little clumps with masses of quite large yellow flowers. A most interesting collection can be made of conophytums alone, as they are all beautiful and take up very little space. 360◆

Below: Copiapoa cinerea
Flowers are not readily produced on these little cacti in temperate climates, but their compact growth and the attractive contrast between plant and spine colour make them nevertheless well worth growing. 377◆

Far left: Coryphantha vivipara
A free-flowering small cactus, which usually forms a clump of globular stems. With a good, well-drained soil it can survive low temperatures. 378♦

Top left: Crassula deceptrix
This miniature succulent has a mass of branched stems closely clad with unusually shaped leaves. Very pretty, but the flowers are tiny. 379♦

Centre left: Dolichothele (Mammillaria) longimamma
The extra-long tubercles make this cactus rather different from most mammillarias. Detached tubercles can be used for propagation. 380♦

Below left: Crassula arborescens
This can make a large shrub but it is also a good houseplant. It is best to take cuttings and restart when it becomes too large. 378♦

Below: Delosperma pruinosum (D. echinatum)
The tiny bristles of this delightful little succulent glisten like glass in the sunlight. Good light will keep it compact. 380♦

Above: **Echeveria derenbergii**
Being one of the most beautiful of the echeverias and also one of the easiest to grow makes this perhaps the ideal succulent. The brightly coloured flowers are carried on quite short stems. 381♦

Above right: **Echeveria gibbiflora** var. **carunculata**
A curious rather than beautiful plant grown mainly for the strange warty growths that appear on older leaves. When stems become 'leggy' restart by beheading. 382♦

Far right: **Echeveria harmsii**
The large flowers are really the showpieces of this echeveria and they are freely produced. The plant itself is straggly and is best kept under control by taking cuttings annually and restarting. 382♦

Right: **Echeveria 'Doris Taylor'**
A cultivated hybrid echeveria with beautiful velvety leaves and multicoloured flowers. Offsets often have roots while still on the parent plant, which makes propagation very easy. 381♦

Top: **Echeveria setosa**
The compact hairy rosette of this succulent is attractive in itself apart from the magnificent array of flowers shown here. 383♦

Above: **Echinocactus grusonii**
Only really large specimens of this cactus will flower. Winter cold can cause brown markings, so best moved to a living-room. 384♦

Above:
Echinocereus pentalophus
*The sprawling stems of this cactus
are more than compensated for by
the large reddish-purple flowers
abundant even on small plants.* 385♦

Left:
Echinocereus horizonthalonius
*This cactus is a challenge to cultivate
but worth the effort.* 384♦

Below:
Echinocereus knippelianus
*A clump-forming cactus, easy to
grow and flower.* 385♦

Above: **Echinopsis multiplex**
*The pink flowers of this easy cactus
are unusual in that they are sweetly
scented, but unfortunately they
usually fade away after one or two
days. The large flower and long tube
are typical of echinopsis.* 388♦

Above left:
Echinocereus perbellus
*This small, globular cactus has a
most distinctive spine formation and
is worth growing for that alone. The
large flowers are produced even on
quite young plants.* 386♦

Far left:
Echinocereus salm-dyckianus
*One of the softer-stemmed
echinocerei, this has more upright
stems than most. Flowers well.* 386♦

Centre left:
Epiphyllum 'Ackermannii'
*Probably the most common and best
epiphyllum hybrid in cultivation.* 390♦

Left: **Epiphyllum 'Cooperi'**
*Unusual among epiphyllum hybrids
in producing flowers from the base.
They are sweetly scented.* 390♦

Above: **Echinopsis Paramount hybrid 'Peach Monarch'**
A vigorously growing echinopsis hybrid. The flowers have a beautiful satiny texture. 389♦

Left: **Echinopsis Paramount hybrid 'Orange Glory'**
This is probably the most strongly spined of the hybrid echinopsis. Radiant, large orange flowers. 389♦

Below:
Epiphyllum 'Deutsche Kaiserin'
A particularly floriferous hybrid with masses of pink blooms along the straplike stems. 391♦

Right: Epiphyllum 'Gloria'
Epiphyllum hybrids are grown for their flowers rather than for the somewhat uninteresting stems. This one produces truly immense blooms in spring or summer, when it should be shaded from full sunlight and given an occasional feed. 391♦

Below: Euphorbia bupleurifolia
A particularly choice succulent euphorbia. The flowers are small but attractive, and the warty stems most unusual. The male and female flowers are on separate plants. Never overwater this plant and make sure drainage is good. 392♦

Above right: Euphorbia horrida
Euphorbia flowers are mostly small and somewhat insignificant, but if examined closely they are really beautiful. Well worth using a magnifier to study them. 409♦

Right: Euphorbia horrida
The resemblance to a cactus is only superficial; this plant is a non-cactus succulent. The sexes are on separate plants, the presence of pollen indicating a male. 409♦

Far right: Euphorbia mammillaris var. variegata
The daintily variegated stems and compact growth of this succulent make it a most attractive plant, though it has small flowers. 409♦

Above: Euphorbia milii
Although not strictly a succulent, this euphorbia is certainly an 'honorary' one, as it is commonly included in collections and is a popular houseplant. In parts of the world where it can be grown outside all the year it makes a dense hedge; else-where it needs winter warmth. 410♦

Right: Euphorbia resinifera
One of the rather cactus-like succulents, which eventually forms quite a large clump. It is an easy plant to cultivate, provided it has a well-drained potting mixture and is kept dry in winter. Like all euphorbias, it has a milky sap that is extremely irritant. 411♦

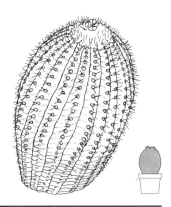

Conophytum frutescens
- Full sun
- Temp: 5-30°C (41-86°F)
- Give completely dry rest

Conophytum frutescens is sometimes listed under its old name of *C. salmonicolor*, which well describes the beautiful orange-pink flowers. The single pair of leaves is fused into a heart-shaped body about 3cm (1.2in) high. The leaves are green with light dots, and the flower emerges from the cleft in mid-summer. With age this plant develops stems, and ends up as a small shrub about 15cm (6in) high. If the plant seems to be deteriorating, remove the heads, leaving a short piece of stem attached to each head, and treat these as cuttings. Cuttings should be taken at the beginning of the growing period.

The soil should be very open: half loam-based mixture and half sharp sand or perlite. Repot every four or five years. During the resting period keep the plant completely dry; when the old plant body has completely shrivelled and the new heads have emerged (mid-summer), start watering, and continue until late autumn.

Take care
Keep the plant in full sun. 363♦

Copiapoa cinerea
- Full sun
- Temp: 5-30°C (41-86°F)
- Water cautiously

Copiapoa cinerea is one of the most beautiful cacti to come out of South America. It is grown for the beauty of its form; it rarely flowers in cultivation, probably because it is difficult to give it sufficient light to stimulate bud formation away from the burning sun of its native desert. Most plants seen in cultivation are the size of a grapefruit. It is chalky-white in colour, and the ribs carry glossy black spines that contrast beautifully with the white skin.

Copiapoas need very good drainage; use an open soil, of half loam-based mixture and half sharp sand or perlite. In the winter keep it dry, but during the summer water freely, allowing it to dry out between waterings. Keep this cactus in the sunniest part of the greenhouse; this will keep the plant brightly coloured.

With age, the plant will form offsets along the ribs. These may be used for propagation. *C. cinerea* looks more attractive when grown as a solitary plant.

Take care
Avoid damp winter conditions. 363♦

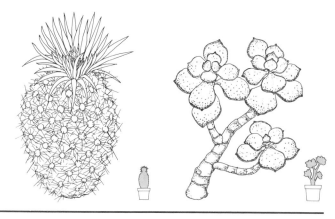

Coryphantha vivipara
- ● **Full sun**
- ● **Temp: 5-30°C (41-86°F)**
- ● **Water carefully**

Coryphanthas are small, globular cacti, very suitable for collectors with limited space. *C. vivipara* is a freely clustering plant; it is grey in colour and the stem is divided into tubercles. The tips of the tubercles carry white spines. The reddish flowers are borne on the top of the plant during the summer. The plant may be left as a cluster or some offsets used for propagation.

Any good potting mixture, either loam- or peat-based, may be used, with about one third of extra grit. During the late spring and summer, water freely, allowing the soil to dry out between waterings. Feed every two weeks with a high-potassium fertilizer when the buds form. Keep it dry in the winter. A sunny position is needed, because strong light stimulates bud formation and keeps the spines a good colour.

Mealy bug and root mealy bug are the pests most likely to be found; if so, water with a proprietary insecticide. If root mealy bugs are discovered, wash all the old soil off the roots and scrub the pot.

Take care
Do not let the soil get soggy. 364♦

Crassula arborescens
- ● **Full sun**
- ● **Temp: 5-30°C (41-86°F)**
- ● **Keep moist all the year**

Crassula arborescens is one of the largest of the crassulas, forming a shrub over 2m (6.5ft) high. It is an impressive background plant for a large greenhouse or may be used to decorate a paved area of the garden during the summer months. It has stout, woody stems, and the broad leaves are grey-green. The flowers are pink, but it is not an easy plant to flower; it is best regarded as a foliage plant.

A porous soil, consisting of two parts loam- or peat-based mixture and one part sharp sand or perlite, will ensure that the roots do not become waterlogged. This plant does not have a definite resting period and should be kept moist all the year. Crassulas require good light, but if the leaves start to look a little shrivelled, move the plant to a slightly shadier spot.

This plant is not greatly bothered by pests but scale insects can be a nuisance. They should be picked off by hand. If possible, avoid spraying, as this may mark the leaves.

Take care
Do not allow to dry out. 364♦

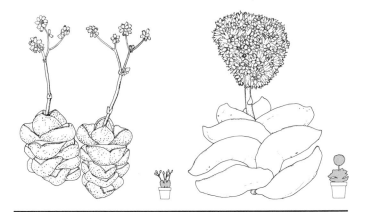

Crassula deceptrix
- **Full sun**
- **Temp: 7-30°C (45-86°F)**
- **Keep slightly moist all year**

This is a beautiful miniature plant, ideal for a small greenhouse or a sunny windowsill. The stems are 5cm (2in) high and are completely hidden by the closely packed leaves. The succulent leaves are covered with a white coating and the plant looks as if it were carved from white stone. The stems branch from the base. This is a slow-growing plant and may be kept in a 7.5cm (3in) pot for a number of years. The white bell-shaped flowers are carried on slender stems. It flowers freely in cultivation.

C. deceptrix is easily propagated. Cut one of the stems, dry it for two days, and pot up. Although this species does not have a dry resting period, it should never be overwatered. A very porous mixture – one part loam-based potting medium and one part grit – is suitable; always allow it to dry out before watering again.

White mealy bugs on a white plant can often remain unnoticed. Inspect regularly, and pick off any mealy bugs with forceps.

Take care
Water will mark the leaves. 365♦

Crassula falcata
- **Full sun**
- **Temp: 7-30°C (45-86°F)**
- **Keep moist all year**

Crassula falcata has such colourful flowers that it is a popular 'florist's plant' and is the parent of many beautiful hybrids. It is a small shrub, 30cm (12in) high. The large bluish-grey leaves are sickle-shaped. The stout flower stem carries a mass of tiny scarlet flowers; each individual flower is bell-shaped and they are arranged in a large, flat inflorescence. If the plant is grown in a greenhouse border, it will branch.

The crassulas may be propagated from leaf or stem cuttings. Shrubby crassulas tend to become untidy with age and should be restarted in the early summer. Grow in a well-drained soil, two parts loam-based mixture to one part sharp sand or perlite. Keep moist all the year but allow to dry out between waterings and keep a little drier immediately after flowering. When the buds begin to form, feed with a liquid tomato fertilizer once every two weeks.

This succulent makes quite a satisfactory houseplant if it can be given a window in full sun.

Take care
Restart leggy plants.

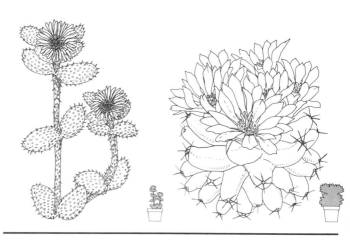

Delosperma pruinosum (D. echinatum)

● **Full sun**
● **Temp: 5-30°C (41-86°F)**
● **Keep moist all year**

Delosperma pruinosum is a small much-branched bush with plump, succulent leaves. These are covered with papillae, which have tiny bristles that give the leaves a glistening effect in the sun. The plant flowers continuously through the summer; the flowers, 1.5cm (0.6in) across, are whitish or yellow. The flowers open in the sunshine and close at night; they do not open on cloudy days or if the plant is in continuous shade.

   D. pruinosum is most successfully grown in a sunny border where it can have a free root run. In climates where there is no danger of frost, it can be left outdoors permanently. Otherwise, take small cuttings during the summer, which can be wintered in a light position indoors. When it is grown outdoors the usual garden pests will be attracted and *D. pruinosum* can receive the same garden insecticides.

Take care
If grown as a pot plant, do not allow it to dry out. 365♦

Dolichothele (Mammillaria) longimamma

● **Full sun**
● **Temp: 5-30°C (41-86°F)**
● **Keep dry in winter**

Dolichothele longimamma is a free-flowering small plant, ideal where space is limited. The bright, glossy yellow flowers are 6cm (2.4in) across and are produced on and off all summer. The cactus itself is bright green with very pronounced tubercles, which have weak spines on their tips. The plant grows from a pronounced thickened tap root. With age, a few offsets are formed: these may be removed and used for propagation. *D. longimamma* can also be propagated from tubercles: remove a tubercle, dry it for two days, and pot up separately.

   A good open mixture for this plant consists of two parts loam-based potting medium and one part sharp sand or perlite. During the spring and summer growing period water freely, but keep it dry during the winter. Sunlight is necessary to stimulate flower bud formation. Once the buds appear, water every two weeks with a high-potassium fertilizer.

Take care
Avoid cold, damp conditions. 365♦

Echeveria derenbergii

(Painted lady)
- **Full sun**
- **Temp: 5-30°C (41-86°F)**
- **Keep moist all year**

Echeveria derenbergii is a charming small plant that does equally well in the greenhouse or on a sunny windowsill. It is a small, tightly leaved rosette, which forms offsets to make a small cushion. The bluish-grey leaves end in a red tip. The plant flowers freely during summer; the petals of the small bell-shaped flowers are yellow inside and orange outside.

Echeverias are easy to cultivate, in a loam- or peat-based medium, with moderate watering in summer, plus a dose of high-potassium fertilizer every two weeks. In winter, keep slightly moist. In the wild, echeverias shed their lower leaves during the winter dry period, as a way of conserving moisture. In cultivation, even though the plant is not short of water, the lower leaves still shrivel, leaving a rather untidy plant in the spring. Remove the offsets and re-start the plants in early spring.

Take care
Do not let water collect in the centre of the rosette. 366♦

Echeveria 'Doris Taylor'

- **Full sun**
- **Temp: 5-30°C (41-86°F)**
- **Never allow to dry out**

Echeverias are such charming small pot plants that a number of hybrids have been developed. 'Doris Taylor' is a cross between *E. setosa* and *E. pulvinata*. It is a freely branching plant that looks its best in a half-pot. The pale green leaves are densely covered with white hairs and are carried on reddish-brown stems to form neat rosettes. The reddish-orange flowers are bell-shaped, and open in the spring.

'Doris Taylor' should be grown in loam-based potting mixture in a light position – either in a greenhouse or on a windowsill. Water generously during spring and summer, and feed every two weeks with a high-potassium fertilizer. Keep slightly moist in winter. During the winter, the lower leaves shrivel: they should be removed or fungus will grow on them, which can cause the death of the plant. In spring, the plant will be leggy. Behead the main rosette and remove the smaller ones for potting.

Take care
Avoid cold, wet winter conditions. 366♦

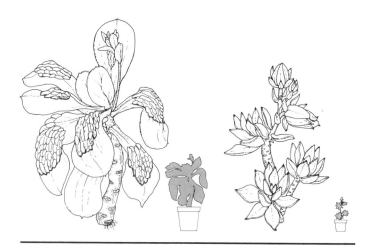

Echeveria gibbiflora
var. **carunculata**
- **Full sun**
- **Temp: 5-30°C (41-86°F)**
- **Keep slightly moist in winter**

Echeveria gibbiflora is one of the tall echeverias and seldom branches. The large leaves, 25cm (10in) long, are a lovely lavender-pink, and covered with large protuberances that are bluish to green. The protuberances are formed in autumn, so young plants may have completely plain leaves, but they will get their markings when autumn comes. The light red flowers open during the winter.

This plant tends to become leggy, and in the spring it should be beheaded. The base should be kept and with luck one or two offsets will form at the old leaf scars. These can be removed when about 2.5cm (1in) across and potted up. The top of the plant is, of course, also potted up. This is the only way to propagate this plant. Any good loam-based potting mixture may be used. Water generously during spring and summer. Keep just moist during the winter.

Take care
Do not splash the leaves with water, as it will mark the waxy coating. 367♦

Echeveria harmsii
- **Full sun**
- **Temp: 5-30°C (41-86°F)**
- **Keep moist all year**

Echeveria harmsii is the one echeveria that is grown for the beauty of its flowers rather than for its highly coloured leaves. The plant forms a small branching shrub with rosettes at the ends of the stems. These are made up of long, soft leaves covered in downy hair. The flowers are bell-shaped, 2.5cm (1in) long, and scarlet with a yellow tip.

Grow this plant in a loam- or peat-based potting mixture and keep it on a sunny windowsill. During summer, feed every two weeks with a high-potassium fertilizer and water generously, but give less water in the winter. If the plant looks untidy in spring, cut the rosettes off and treat as cuttings.

Echeverias are prone to harbour mealy bug. Pick the insects off, and if badly infested water the soil with a systemic insecticide. Since the plant is re-rooted every year, root mealy bug should not occur, provided the cuttings are planted in clean pots.

Take care
Do not let water collect in the centre of the rosettes. 367♦

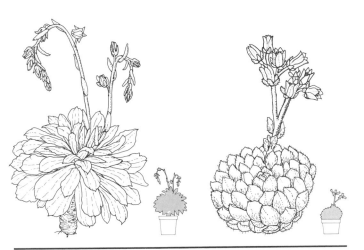

Echeveria hoveyii
- Full sun
- Temp: 5-30°C (41-86°F)
- Water with caution

Echeveria setosa
- Full sun
- Temp: 5-30°C (41-86°F)
- Water with caution

Echeveria hoveyii is a pretty plant for a sunny windowsill or greenhouse. It consists of a cluster of loose rosettes on short stems. The long, narrow leaves are greyish-green with cream and pink stripes. The colour is at its brightest in spring. For really intense colour, keep in full sun and do not overwater. Occasionally the plant may grow a rosette without any markings; these should be removed.

Like many clustering plants, *E. hoveyii* looks its best when grown in a pan or bowl. Make sure there is a drainage hole. A loam- or peat-based growing medium with about one third extra grit is suitable for this plant. Allow to dry out between waterings.

During winter go over the plant weekly and remove any shrivelled leaves; if left on the plant, these can rot and become infested with fungus. In spring, the plant may well be untidy. Cut off the rosettes and re-root them. If any mealy bugs are seen, pick them off.

Take care
Remove any plain rosettes.

Echeveria setosa is a flat, almost stemless rosette about 15cm (6in) across. The soft, dark green leaves are covered with dense white hairs, which gives the plant an attractive furry appearance. This plant needs a sunny position. In the spring, mature specimens flower; the blooms are red and yellow.

The leaves of this echeveria are pressed very closely to the ground. Even in summer, the plant should be carefully inspected, and any shrivelled or rotting lower leaves removed. If left on, a grey mould will attack the decaying leaves.

A loam-based potting mixture will suit this plant, which should be grown in a half-pot. Water all the year round but allow it to dry out between waterings. When the flower buds start to form, feed every two weeks with a high-potassium (tomato) fertilizer. Mature specimens produce an occasional offset, which may be removed for propagation.

Take care
Do not allow water to collect in the centre of the rosette. 368♦

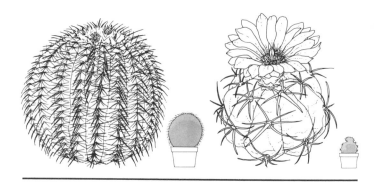

Echinocactus grusonii
(The golden barrel)
- ● **Full sun**
- ● **Temp: 7-30°C (45-86°F)**
- ● **Keep dry in winter**

Young specimens of *E. grusonii* have very pronounced tubercles and look like golden mammillaria. After a few years, the tubercles re-arrange themselves into ribs, usually about 28 per plant. *E. grusonii* is very long-lived and eventually reaches a diameter of 1m (39in). But in cultivation a plant of 15cm (6in) is a good-sized specimen and will be about 10 years old. The awl-shaped spines are pale golden-yellow and there is golden wool at the top of the plant. The small yellow flowers are produced on very large plants but only if exposed to very strong sunlight. In cooler climates, this plant is grown purely for the beauty of its colouring.

It needs an open soil, a loam- or peat-based mixture plus one third sharp sand or perlite. Water generously during summer, but allow it to dry out between waterings. Keep dry in winter. The chief pests are mealy bug and root mealy bug.

Take care
Avoid a cold, damp atmosphere. 368♦

Echinocactus horizonthalonius
- ● **Full sun**
- ● **Temp: 7-30°C (45-86°F)**
- ● **Water with care**

Echinocactus horizonthalonius is the baby of the genus, the only species that can be flowered in a pot. The flowers are pink and form a ring around the top of the plant. This cactus is a flattened plant, bluish-green in colour, with thick greyish spines. A flowering sized plant is 30cm (12in) across.

Although a very choice plant, *E. horizonthalonius* is not the easiest plant to cultivate. It is an extreme desert plant, and in its native state it bakes in the sun and has perfect drainage. The best treatment is to place the plant in the sunniest part of your greenhouse and grow it in a very open potting mixture. A loam-based mixture plus an equal quantity of sharp sand or perlite is suitable. Water on sunny days during spring and summer, but always allow the plant to dry out between waterings. Keep it dry during the winter.

Take care
Never allow to stand in water. 369♦

Echinocereus knippelianus
- **Full sun**
- **Temp: 5-30°C (41-86°F)**
- **Keep dry in winter**

Although this cactus may consist of a single oval or globular stem, about 5cm (2in) thick, for a few years, it will eventually form branches from the base, resulting in a compact clump. The stems have five ribs with a few short, bristly spines along them. Not being fiercely spined, it is quite an easy plant to handle. The deep pink flowers, 4cm (1.6in) or so across, appear from around the sides of the stems in spring and summer, and contrast delightfully with the dark green of the stems. Propagate this cactus by carefully cutting away a branch of at least 2.5cm (1in) across in spring or summer, letting it dry for a few days, and pushing it gently into fresh potting mixture.

Good drainage is essential, so grow this cactus in a mixture of two parts good standard potting material (peat- or loam-based) and one part sharp sand or perlite. When buds form, feed every two weeks with a high-potassium fertilizer.

Take care
Cut out any rotted branch. 369♦

Echinocereus pentalophus
- **Full sun**
- **Temp: 5-30°C (41-86°F)**
- **Keep dry in winter**

The small upright stem of this cactus soon branches and the ultimate result is a mass of sprawling shoots up to about 12cm (4.7in) long and 2cm (0.8in) thick. The spines are quite short and soft. On the whole perhaps it is not a particularly striking plant, but the magnificent blooms more than compensate for any lack of beauty in the cactus itself. Quite small specimens (one stem) will produce reddish-purple flowers up to 8cm (3.2in) across.

The stems, being rather soft and fleshy, are prone to rot with any excess water, so it is particularly important to use a well-drained potting mixture with no risk of waterlogging. Make this by adding one part of sharp sand or perlite to two parts of a standard potting mixture, which can be either peat- or loam-based. Propagate it by removing a suitable branch in summer, letting it dry for a few days, and potting up.

Take care
Water freely in summer. 369♦

Echinocereus perbellus
- Full sun
- Temp: 5-30°C (41-86°F)
- Keep dry in winter

One of the so-called 'pectinate' echinocerei, this shows a completely different type of stem from the more prostrate species. Here we have a predominantly solitary cactus, which may nevertheless form a low cluster with age. The stem is at first almost spherical and about 5cm (2in) across, but may eventually become more elongated. This stem is beautiful in itself; its many small ribs, closely decorated with short white spreading spines ('pectinate', or 'comb-like'), give a delightful, clean, neat appearance. The deep pink to purple flowers add to the attraction: about 5cm (2in) across, they open from hairy buds.

This cactus is almost completely hardy and can withstand dry freezing conditions in winter; but, to be on the safe side, keep to the recommended temperature, if possible. Grow it in a standard potting mixture to which has been added about one third of sharp sand or perlite.

Take care
Mealy bugs may hide among the spreading spines. 370♦

Echinocereus salm-dyckianus
- Full sun
- Temp: 5-30°C (41-86°F)
- Keep dry in winter

There are two types of echinocereus: those with fairly soft, mostly sprawling stems; and the pectinate (or comb-like) ones, with stiffer, elegantly spined, upright stems. This cactus belongs to the former group. Although small specimens consist of a single, upright stem, this soon branches at the base, eventually forming a clump of ribbed stems about 20cm (8in) long and 5cm (2in) thick, with short yellowish spines. It is probably the most attractive among the echinocerei, an attractiveness emphasized by the appearance of the funnel-shaped, pinkish flowers. These are about 7cm (2.8in) wide and can be up to 10cm (4in) long.

Grow in a mixture of one part sharp sand or perlite to two parts of any good standard material, to give the good drainage essential to this cactus. A gravel top dressing will protect the base. Feed every two weeks during the flowering season, to keep the flowers going.

Take care
Ensure a cold winter rest. 370♦

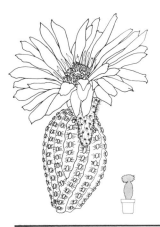

Echinocereus websterianus
- **Full sun**
- **Temp: 5-30°C (41-86°F)**
- **Keep dry in winter**

Another delightful echinocereus from the pectinate (comb-like) group. This cactus has a bright green stem divided into about 20 narrow ribs; along the length of each are groups of short, stiff, spreading white spines. In its native southern USA it can become quite large, but a good pot specimen would be about 15cm (6in) high and 5cm (2in) thick; branches are not usually formed. Blooms can be as wide as the plant itself, but usually on smaller specimens only one appears at a time, opening from a large bristly bud. The green and yellow centre of the flower contrasts splendidly with the lavender-pink petals.

Make up a well-drained potting mixture by adding one third of extra sharp sand or perlite to any good standard mix. With this you can water freely in spring and summer. Give this echinocereus a cold winter rest to ensure next year's flowers. If it is part of a living room collection, try to overwinter it in an unheated room.

Take care
Check for root loss in winter.

Echinofossulocactus lamellosus
- **Full sun**
- **Temp: 5-30°C (41-86°F)**
- **Keep dry in winter**

This group of cacti was formerly called *Stenocactus* and it is rather unfortunate that specialists have substituted the much longer name, if only because of the difficulty of writing it on a label! This is one of the prettiest, with a blue-green globular stem becoming rather cylindrical with age, and a diameter of up to 10cm (4in). The many thin ribs are wavy, which is characteristic of echinofossulocacti. White flattened spines are 1-3cm (0.4-1.2in) long, some curved upwards. This very attractive cactus will often produce its flowers when quite small; they are pink in colour, red inside, and tubular in shape, about 4cm (1.6in) long.

Coming as it does from sun-baked mountain regions, this plant can take all the sun you can give it in order to produce good spines and flowers. For this reason it is not so good as a houseplant. Water it freely in spring and summer, provided you grow it in a porous potting mixture of one part sharp sand or perlite to two parts soil.

Take care
Give this species a cold winter rest.

Echinopsis aurea
- **Full sun**
- **Temp: 5-30°C (41-86°F)**
- **Keep cool and dry in winter**

Echinopsis multiplex
- **Full sun**
- **Temp: 5-30°C (41-86°F)**
- **Keep cool and dry in winter**

Echinopsis aurea is still sometimes listed in catalogues under its old name of *Lobivia aurea*, which can be confusing. The plant has a cylindrical stem about 10cm (4in) high, which is ribbed, the ribs carrying short spines. A few offsets are formed on the main stem, and these may be removed and potted up.

The flowers are a beautiful lemon-yellow, which is an uncommon colour for an echinopsis. The main flush of flowers is in late spring, but odd flowers appear in summer.

Echinopsis plants need to be treated generously. Grow in loam-based mixture, which should be renewed annually. When buds appear, water once every two weeks with a liquid feed, the high-potassium type used for tomatoes. Like most desert cacti, *E. aurea* needs full sunlight to stimulate bud formation. Strong light also produces stout, well-coloured spines.

Take care
Feed generously when in bud, and during flowering.

The delicate pink flowers of this cactus open during the night and remain open during the following day. The flowers have a long tube about 20cm (8in) long and a sweet lily-like scent.

The genuine *E. multiplex* has long thick spines, but many pink-flowered echinopsis plants sold under this name are very short-spined hybrids, probably with *E. eyriesii*.

E. multiplex produces a profusion of offsets. To enable the main plant to reach flowering size quickly and to keep the plant within bounds, most of the offsets should be removed.

Large numbers of flowers are produced in early summer, and the plant should be fed during the flowering period with a tomato fertilizer. Any good potting mixture, either loam- or peat-based, is suitable for this species. Repot annually. Water freely during spring and summer, allowing the compost to dry out between waterings.

Take care
Watch for mealy bug. 371♦

Echinopsis Paramount hybrid 'Orange Glory'
- ● Full sun
- ● Temp: 5-30°C (41-86°F)
- ● Keep cool and dry in winter

'Orange Glory' is one of the beautiful *Echinopsis x Lobivia* hybrids that have been produced in the USA. The flowers are a deep glowing orange, a colour not found in pure echinopsis species. The cactus itself is cylindrical, with many ribs; the ribs carry short spines. A few offsets are produced on young plants; these may be left on the plant if a large specimen is desired, or removed for propagation.

This cactus may be grown in any loam- or peat-based mixture. Repot annually. Water freely during the spring and summer months, when the plant is in vigorous growth, but allow to dry out between waterings. When flower buds form feed every two weeks with a tomato fertilizer.

This is a desert plant and needs to be grown in full sunlight to stimulate bud formation and to encourage the growth of strong, well-coloured spines. This plant is tough and resistant to most pests.

Take care
Give plenty of sunshine. 372♦

Echinopsis Paramount hybrid 'Peach Monarch'
- ● Full sun
- ● Temp: 5-30°C (41-86°F)
- ● Feed while flowering

Echinopsis species have possibly the most beautiful flowers of any desert cacti, and among the most colourful are the hybrids developed in Paramount, California.

The peach-pink flowers of 'Peach Monarch' open during early summer, and there may be a dozen long-tubed flowers open at one time. Once the buds begin to form, the cactus should be kept moist and fed every two weeks. The best liquid feeds are those with a high potassium content.

'Peach Monarch' is 15cm (6in) high and 10cm (4in) across; short spines are carried on the numerous ribs. A few offsets are formed on young plants; use for propagation.

Echinopsis plants are easy to grow, in either a loam-based or a soilless compost. They are greedy plants, so repot annually. Give the plant a position where it will get maximum sunlight: strong light is necessary for bud formation.

Take care
Repot each year. 373♦

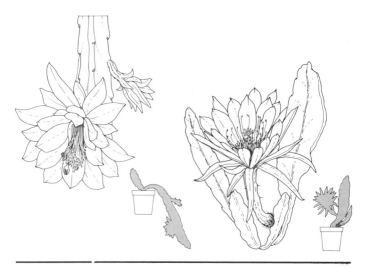

Epiphyllum 'Ackermannii'

(Orchid cactus)
- **Partial shade**
- **Temp: 5-27°C (41-81°F)**
- **Keep almost dry in winter**

Epiphyllums (also known as Epicacti) are among the most un-cactus-like cacti and are often grown by plant lovers who profess no interest in conventional cacti. Nevertheless, they are true cacti, but living naturally in tropical rain-forests rather than in the desert. Plants normally cultivated are hybrids between the various wild species and other cacti; such plants are hardier and have more colourful flowers. 'Ackermannii' is a typical example and is one of the oldest in cultivation, but its flowers have not been surpassed in beauty of colour. They are about 8cm (3.2in) across and brilliant red, but not perfumed. The blooms appear along the notched edges of the stems and may last for several days.

You can grow epiphyllums in a standard houseplant mixture, but if you add extra peat or leafmould to it, this is beneficial. Also, good drainage is important.

Take care
Feed with high-potassium fertilizer when in bud and flower. 371♦

Epiphyllum 'Cooperi'

(Orchid cactus)
- **Partial shade**
- **Temp: 5-27°C (41-81°F)**
- **Keep almost dry in winter**

The white flowers of this hybrid epiphyllum are perfumed; quite unusual for a cactus! Unlike those of other similar cacti, the flowers come from the base of the plant, not along the side of the stem. When the large buds are fully formed in spring or summer, they will open in the evening, and if they are in the living-room, a strong lily-like perfume will pervade the whole room at about 10pm. One can almost watch the buds unfold, to give brilliant white blooms maybe 10cm (4in) across.

This cactus will survive at the lower temperature in winter, but will do better if rather warmer. This is easy indoors, in a shady window. Water freely in spring and summer, and keep moister indoors in winter than in a greenhouse. But it appreciates a moist atmosphere; an occasional spray with water will help. Use a good standard potting mixture and feed occasionally.

Take care
Too much nitrogen in feed can cause brown spots. 371♦

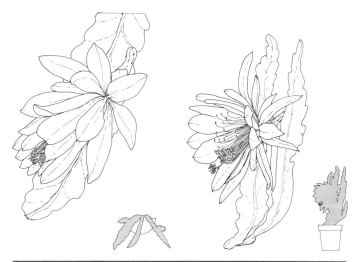

Epiphyllum 'Deutsche Kaiserin'

(Orchid cactus)
- **Partial shade**
- **Temp: 5-27°C (41-81°F)**
- **Keep slightly moist in winter**

The parentage of many of the epiphyllum hybrids is somewhat obscure, and this one probably has no true epiphyllum ancestry at all, being a hybrid between two jungle cacti. But it is so like an epiphyllum in appearance and cultivation requirements that it is normally included with these plants. Most epiphyllums need staking when the stems reach a length of about 30cm (12in), but this one is really pendent, making it ideal for a hanging basket. In spring and summer the trailing stems, which may be up to 60cm (24in) long, are covered with masses of deep pink flowers, about 5cm (2in) across – a truly magnificent sight.

Grow this beautiful jungle cactus in a good standard potting mixture; if you add extra leafmould or peat it will be appreciated, as well as a feed every two weeks in spring and summer with a high-potassium fertilizer. Spray it occasionally and avoid full sunshine.

Take care
Never let this cactus dry out. 373♦

Epiphyllum 'Gloria'

(Orchid cactus)
- **Partial shade**
- **Temp: 5-27°C (41-81°F)**
- **Keep almost dry in winter**

There are literally dozens (if not hundreds) of epiphyllum hybrids available, and space prevents the mention of more than a few. But they all require much the same treatment. A good, nourishing potting mixture is important; add extra sharp sand or perlite if it looks at all compacted. Leafmould is not too readily available, but if you have any mix some with the potting mixture. Never add limestone or chalk. Never let the plant dry out completely, and water it freely in spring and summer, feeding every two weeks or so.

'Gloria' is a particularly attractive hybrid with immense orange-pink flowers up to 20cm (8in) across. But like those of most of the day-flowering types, these blooms are without scent. This hybrid is reasonably hardy, and a cool greenhouse is perfectly adequate. In the drier conditions of a living-room, an occasional spray with clean lime-free water is beneficial.

Take care
Keep out of full sunshine. 374♦

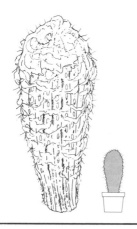

Espostoa lanata
- **Full sun**
- **Temp: 10-30°C (50-86°F)**
- **Keep dry in winter**

Although this cactus can reach tree-like proportions in its native state, 'seedling' plants are perfectly suitable for the collection, where they may reach a height of 30cm (12in) and a thickness of 5cm (2in) but will take many years to reach even this size. Specimens offered for sale are pretty little plants covered with a mass of white woolly hairs. It looks nice enough to stroke, but beware! Under the hair are needle-sharp spines; a trap for the unwary. As the cactus ages, these spines become larger and are visible outside the hair. Do not expect flowers; these are normally produced only on mature plants.

Grow in the usual well-drained potting mixture, made by adding about one third of sharp sand or perlite to a standard material. It is possible to overwinter this cactus in a cool greenhouse at a temperature of 5°C (41°F), but this is risky, and it is better to bring it indoors, unless it is already kept as a houseplant.

Take care
Plants in a window need to be turned.

Euphorbia bupleurifolia
- **Full sun**
- **Temp: 10-30°C (50-86°F)**
- **Keep dry in winter**

A choice, less common euphorbia, and although not one of the easiest to grow, it should not be too difficult for the careful collector. It is a small, spineless succulent, usually reaching a height of about 10cm (4in). The thick stem, which rarely branches, is covered with warty tubercles, and a tuft of leaves appears on the top during spring, and usually falls off at the approach of winter. The plant is grown more for its appearance than for the small flowers, which are produced in spring.

If greenhouse heating is kept low in winter, it is best to bring this plant indoors to an unheated room before any really cold weather, but put it in your lightest window.

Good drainage is essential for this plant, so add about one third of extra drainage material (sharp sand or perlite) to the potting mixture, which can be either loam- or peat-based. Water in spring and summer, but only when the soil is almost dry.

Take care
Avoid cold and wet conditions. 374♦

Top: **Euphorbia obesa**
An extreme succulent. This is a female plant with seed pods at the top of the single stem. 410♦

Above: **Faucaria tigrina**
An almost stemless succulent with pairs of leaves looking like tiny jaws. An easy plant to grow. 411♦

Top: **Ferocactus acanthodes**
*Normally only large specimens of
this cactus will flower, but the
colourful spines are beautiful.* 412♦

Above: **Ferocactus horridus**
*'Horridus' here means spiny, and
this cactus is very spiny indeed. Only
larger plants are likely to come into
flower. Never overwater.* 413♦

Above right: **Ferocactus latispinus**
*This ferocactus is quite likely to
flower, but usually only if the weather
is warm and sunny.* 413♦

Right: **Gasteria maculata**
*An ideal plant for the house or office
if given reasonable light, without full
sun, and not allowed to become
desiccated.* 415♦

Above: **Gymnocalycium bruchii**
*A small, compact cactus, soon
forming a freely flowering clump.
This plant is sometimes listed in
catalogues as G. lafaldense.* 418♦

Right: **Gymnocalycium andreae**
*The bright yellow flowers make this
an unusual gymnocalycium. Single
heads soon form offsets resulting in
a neat clump.* 417♦

Far left: **Glottiphyllum linguiforme**
Too much water will cause these succulents to become bloated rather than to rot, but they need enough to prevent shrivelling. Strike the happy medium and they are quite attractive plants with pairs of very fleshy leaves and magnificent flowers. They need plenty of light. 416♦

Left: **Gymnocalycium denudatum**
Sometimes known as the 'Spider Cactus' because of the short spreading spines clustered over its surface. The magnificent flowers are produced freely during spring and summer; they usually last for several days, and may be followed by seed pods. The seeds can be sown. 418♦

Below:
Gymnocalycium horridispinum
The unusually coloured flowers of this cactus make it outstanding even in this group of beautiful plants. Like most free-flowering desert cacti, this gymnocalycium needs a cool, dry winter rest in order to perform well the next year. Water in summer. 419♦

Above: **Gymnocalycium mihanovichii 'Hibotan'**
A novelty cactus that must always be grown on a graft, as it contains no food-making chlorophyll. Never let it become too cold. 419♦

Above right: **Haworthia maughanii**
One of the more unusual haworthias; it has flattened leaf tips, with transparent 'windows' to allow light to reach the inner tissues. In nature only the tips are exposed. 422♦

Far right: **Huernia zebrina**
The flowers are the chief attraction of this little succulent. They are large for such a small plant and most strange in appearance, with a slight, unpleasant smell. 423♦

Right: **Haworthia attenuata**
Haworthias make good houseplants as they enjoy reasonably shady conditions. Best grown under the staging in a greenhouse. 421♦

Above:
Kalanchoe daigremontiana
Tiny plantlets are freely produced along the edges of the leaves. The large mature leaves make this an impressive plant, but it is best to discard it and restart when it becomes straggly. 424♦

Right: **Kalanchoe blossfeldiana**
This is well-known as a houseplant. Its thickened leaves show that it is definitely a succulent. It produces masses of brilliant flowers in winter and spring. Restart it from cuttings if it becomes straggly. 423♦

Below: **Kalanchoe pumila**
A very free-flowering little succulent with pearly-grey leaves; the shade is due to their mealy coating. The thin stems eventually cause the plant to sprawl somewhat, making it very suitable for a hanging basket. 424♦

Left: **Lithops aucampiae**
Lithops or 'living stones' are extremely succulent plants, each head consisting of a pair of leaves without a stem. This is one of the larger species, with considerable variation in the leaf colour and pattern. Yellow flowers appear from between the leaves in autumn. A good, porous potting mixture is necessary and care in watering. 441▸

Below left: **Lithops bella**
The flower can be seen emerging from between the leaves in this photograph. Lithops do not have the range of flower colour found in the somewhat similar conophytums; they are either yellow or white. This one is slightly scented. The transparent 'windows' on top of the flattened leaves serve to admit light to the interior of the plant. In the wild these tops are level with the soil. 442▸

Below: **Lithops marmorata**
Surrounded by a mass of stones, this lithops would be difficult to find when not in flower; hence the term 'living stones' or 'stone mimicry plants' applied to this group in general. Lithops are easy plants to cultivate. Towards late autumn withhold all water and restart only in the spring when the old leaves have completely shrivelled away. New ones develop from the old. 443▸

Above: **Lobivia famatimensis**
Though it starts as a single stem, this attractive small cactus soon produces offsets from around the base to form a clump. Flower colour may vary from yellow to red. 444♦

Above left: **Lobivia backebergii**
The large, brilliant flowers of this lobivia make it a showpiece in any collection. The almost globular stem is usually solitary but sometimes offsets are formed at the base. It is a very easy cactus to grow. 443♦

Left: **Mammillaria bocasana**
The rounded, silky heads of this cactus and its ease of cultivation make it a popular mammillaria. But, beware! The silk conceals hooked spines, ready to catch on clothing. Easily raised from seed. 445♦

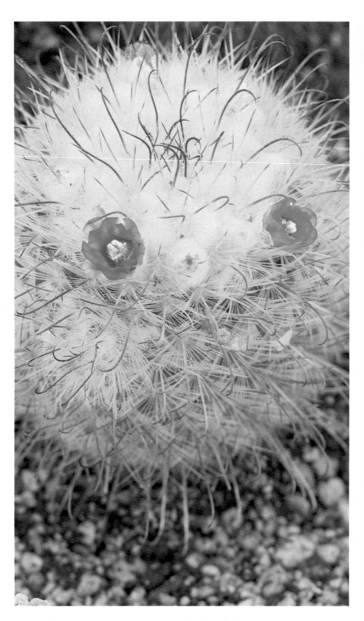

Above: **Mammillaria bombycina**
One of the attractions of mammillarias is the great variation of shape and spine formation, not to mention the usually freely produced flowers. This species is not one of the best for flowering, at least not in the case of young plants; but its delightful appearance more than compensates, and the flowers are small but beautiful. 445♦

Above right:
Mammillaria zeilmanniana
This is one of the most free-flowering of all mammillarias; a complete ring of blooms can be produced. 447♦

Right:
Mammillaria zeilmanniana alba
A white-flowered variety of the species above. A clump of rounded heads is eventually produced. 447♦

Above:
Neoporteria mammillarioides
Large flowers are freely produced at the top of this beautifully spined cactus and they may last for a week. *Needs a cold winter rest.* 449▸

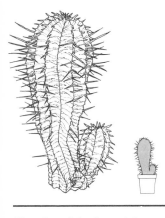

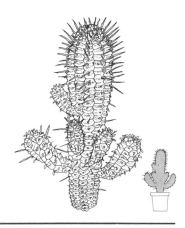

Euphorbia horrida
- Full sun
- Temp: 5-30°C (41-86°F)
- Keep dry in winter

Euphorbia mammillaris
var. **variegata**
(Corn cob)
- Full sun
- Temp: 5-30°C (41-86°F)
- Keep dry in winter

Although a very cactus-like plant, this is one of the 'other succulents'. The very small flowers and stout spines (not needle-like) give it away. It is not a 'horrid' plant; the name *horrida* means 'spiny'. In its native South Africa it can reach quite a large size, but a good cultivated specimen is not likely to be more than about 20cm (8in) high and 5cm (2in) thick. The attraction of this succulent is more in its shape than in its tiny flowers, although when clustered at the top these can be quite pretty. Plants are male or female.

E. horrida can be propagated from seed (but remember you need a pair) or from the branches that sometimes form at the base. If you remove the branches, wash off the oozing latex and let the cutting dry for a week before potting up. For this plant use a mixture of three parts standard soil and one part sharp sand or perlite.

Take care
Keep any white latex away from your eyes or mouth. 374/5♦

A beautifully variegated form of *E. mammillaris* (itself an attractive little succulent), this plant attains a height of around 20cm (8in) and a thickness of 5cm (2in). Grow it for its form and colour rather than its insignificant flowers. The freely produced branches soon give rise to a small bush of deeply ribbed stems, variegated with white, on which the blunt spines appear in bands.

If you want to propagate this euphorbia, remove a branch, wash off the sappy latex, and let it dry for a week before planting. A pity to spoil the look of the plant, but sometimes an ill-positioned branch can be found. To grow this euphorbia well, use any good standard potting mixture with about one third of sharp sand or perlite added. With the consequent good drainage, watering can be quite liberal during spring and summer.

Take care
Keep the latex away from your eyes or mouth. 375♦

409

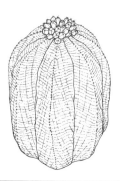

Euphorbia milii var. splendens

(Crown of thorns)
- Full sun
- Temp: 10-30°C (50-86°F)
- Keep slightly moist in winter

This delightful little shrub, only slightly succulent, is very popular as a houseplant, and deservedly so, as it is more suited to a well-lit living-room window in winter than to the average colder greenhouse, where it will certainly lose its long leaves, and probably its life also!

The plant's great attraction is its brilliant scarlet flower-like bracts, about 1.5cm (0.6in) across, produced freely in spring and summer. There is also a yellow version.

If the stems become too long, encourage more bushy growth by cutting them down to size; this also provides ample cuttings for spare plants. Keep any sap away from your eyes or mouth. Let the pieces dry for a few days and pot up; they should root fairly easily in spring and summer. Grow this euphorbia in any good loam- or peat-based potting mixture, and water freely in spring and summer.

Take care
Avoid cold draughts in winter. 376↓

Euphorbia obesa

- Full sun
- Temp: 5-30°C (41-86°F)
- Keep dry in winter

A true succulent in every sense of the word; there could hardly be a greater difference between this euphorbia and the preceding one. It has a most distinctive spineless, leafless greyish-green stem with a pale purple pattern. At first almost spherical and up to about 7cm (2.8in) across, it usually becomes taller with age. Having neither offsets nor branches, propagation is only from seed, which requires both male and female plants, as the sexes are separate. Tiny flowers with a delightful, delicate perfume are formed at the top of the plant, and followed by seed pods in the case of a female plant that has been pollinated.

Grow this attractive novelty in a well-drained medium consisting of two thirds of a standard potting mixture and one third sharp sand or perlite. This euphorbia tends to have a long tap root, so use a fairly deep pot for it.

Take care
Water in spring/summer only. 393↓

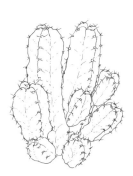

Euphorbia resinifera
- **Full sun**
- **Temp: 5-30°C (41-86°F)**
- **Keep dry in winter**

Faucaria tigrina
(Tiger's jaws)
- **Full sun**
- **Temp: 5-30°C (41-86°F)**
- **Keep almost dry in winter**

This is probably the oldest known succulent plant of all, having been discovered by an eastern king about 25BC! In cultivation it is a low, much-branched shrub, with four-angled bright green stems up to 30cm (12in) high. There are short spines in pairs along the edges of the branches. Flowers are seldom or never produced on cultivated plants, but if they were, they would be tiny and rather insignificant. Branches can be cut away and used for propagation, but the cut ends 'bleed' profusely with a white milky sap; this should be washed off with water and the branch allowed to dry for a week. Do this only during spring and summer.

Grow this euphorbia in a good, well-drained potting mixture of three parts standard peat- or loam-based material with one part of sharp sand or perlite. Water it quite freely in spring and summer but then gradually reduce for its winter rest.

Take care
Keep any trace of the white sap away from eyes or mouth. 376♦

Faucarias are not only pretty, but also easy to grow. These small succulents will grow on a sunny windowsill or in a sunny greenhouse. *F. tigrina* is a low-growing plant consisting of rather crowded succulent leaves, each of which has an edging of 'teeth'. The leaves are grey-green in colour, and covered with tiny white dots. The large golden-yellow flowers appear in autumn; they open in the afternoon if it is sunny, and close at night.

If overwatered, faucarias tend to become too large. Grow them in a soil consisting of half loam-based material and half sharp sand or perlite. Water freely in summer, but allow them to dry out in between. Give only an occasional watering in winter. With age, faucarias develop pronounced woody stems. In late spring, cut the heads off, with about 0.5cm (0.2in) of stem, and dry for a day before potting up.

Take care
It is not necessary to repot more than once every three years. 393♦

Fenestraria rhopalophylla

- **Full sun**
- **Temp: 5-30°C (41-86°F)**
- **Completely dry in winter**

Fenestraria rhopalophylla has grey-green cylindrical leaves that end in a transparent 'window'. In the desert regions of south-west Africa, the leaves are buried in the ground up to their tips and the light is filtered down to the chlorophyll through the 'window'. In cultivation the plant is grown completely above ground, partly because of the poorer light and also to prevent rotting.

The leaves, about 2.5cm (1in) long, grow in little clusters. The plant is vigorous and will soon fill a pan. The growing period starts early in spring and continues through the summer. White flowers appear in summer; they open in the sunshine and close again at night.

Grow in a sandy soil. It does not need repotting annually; when potting on, be careful not to disturb the roots. Water freely during spring and summer but keep completely dry during autumn and winter. Propagate by removing the heads during early summer.

Take care
Allow to dry out between waterings.

Ferocactus acanthodes

- **Full sun**
- **Temp: 5-30°C (41-86°F)**
- **Keep dry in winter**

'Ferocactus' means 'ferocious cactus' and this aptly describes these plants, with their array of sharp, tough spines. *F. acanthodes* is a particularly attractive member of the group. It is spherical, becoming more elongated with age, and the many ribs are furnished with reddish spines up to 4cm (1.6in) long, some of them curved. A giant cactus in nature, it is slow-growing and perfectly suitable as a pot specimen; in a pot it can attain a diameter of 15cm (6in) or more, but takes years to do so. However, small plants do not usually flower.

Ferocacti are particularly sensitive to insufficient light and overwatering, so give this one all the direct sunshine you can, and add extra drainage material to a standard peat- or loam-based potting mixture (one part to two parts mixture). It is best to water only when the mixture has almost dried out. A top dressing of grit or gravel will keep the base dry.

Take care
Watch for drips in the greenhouse; they could be fatal! 394♦

Ferocactus horridus
- **Full sun**
- **Temp: 5-30°C (41-86°F)**
- **Keep dry in winter**

A fiercely armed cactus with an almost globular stem – which in cultivation is unlikely to exceed a diameter of 10cm (4in) – divided into about 12 ribs. Very strong, reddish spines occur in groups along the ribs, up to 5cm (2in) long; the longest spine in each group is flattened and hooked at the tip. Ideally designed to catch in the clothing and pull the plant off the staging! Although yellow flowers can be produced, they are unlikely on smaller plants, so it is best not to hope for them, but to be content with the plant itself.

Grow this ferocactus in a porous potting mixture, which you can make up by adding one part of sharp sand or perlite to two parts of a standard material, and mixing it thoroughly. It is best to water only on sunny days in summer, to avoid any risk of the potting mixture becoming too wet. If the plant should lose its roots, cut it back to clean tissue and allow to dry out for a few days before replanting.

Take care
To handle, wrap it in a thick fold of newspaper! 394◆

Ferocactus latispinus
- **Full sun**
- **Temp: 5-30°C (41-86°F)**
- **Keep dry in winter**

Probably the best-known of the ferocacti, and if you want only one from this group, this is the one to choose. Unlike most of the others, which usually need to reach massive proportions before flowering, this is a species that should burst into bloom when it reaches a diameter of about 10cm (4in). The flowers, 4cm (1.6in) across, are a beautiful purple-red in colour, and open in succession from autumn until early winter. But here lies the snag: unless the autumn is warm and sunny, the buds will probably not open at all! The deeply indented ribs of the bright green stem bear rows of strong, deep yellow spines, some flattened and tipped with red; the whole plant when in flower is a magnificent sight.

As with other ferocacti, a well-drained potting mixture is essential; one part of sharp sand or perlite mixed into two parts of a standard material will prevent any risk of waterlogging, often fatal.

Take care
Keep in the sunniest place. 395◆

Frailea castanea
- Full sun
- Temp: 5-30°C (41-86°F)
- Keep dry in winter

This one is a real dwarf cactus, a good-sized specimen being only about 4cm (1.6in) across and almost spherical in shape. Formerly known as *F. asteroides*, it is rather like a miniature version of the cactus *Astrophytum asterias* in appearance, though not in size or in colouring, as it is a greyish bronze. The slightly flattened plant body has a number of blunt ribs; the tiny clumps of spines are more a decoration than a menace. This little cactus flowers quite readily in spring and summer but fraileas exhibit an unusual phenomenon in that the flowers are mostly self-pollinated without opening. Occasionally, however, on a really sunny day the flowers open normally; they are yellowish.

Grow *Frailea castanea* in a mixture of standard material and sharp sand or perlite in proportions of about three to one. With such a small plant, you are never likely to need a pot larger than 5cm (2in). A top dressing of grit will protect the plant base.

Take care
Very small pots dry out easily.

Frailea knippeliana
- Full sun
- Temp: 5-30°C (41-86°F)
- Keep dry in winter

There are two types of fraileas; those with globular stems and those with more elongated stems. This little cactus is one of the latter. It is a true miniature with a bright green stem only about 4cm (1.6in) high and 2.5cm (1in) thick and it does not normally produce offsets. The flowers are prettily marked in red and yellow but are only likely to open in full sun; the plant is quite capable of pollinating itself.

You may come across other fraileas; they are all minute plants, needing very much the same method of cultivation, which is quite easy, and their size makes them ideal for the smallest space on a windowsill or greenhouse staging. Either peat- or loam-based potting mixture is suitable, but it is well to increase the drainage by mixing in one third to one quarter of sharp sand or perlite. Water all fraileas quite freely in spring and summer, but reduce watering towards the autumn, ready for the winter rest.

Take care
Avoid damp, cold conditions.

Gasteria batesiana

- Partial shade.
- Temp: 5-30°C (41-86°F)
- Keep slightly moist in winter

Among the most shade-loving of succulents, gasterias make ideal houseplants, or occupy that space under the greenhouse staging that is not always easy to make full use of. They are best kept out of full sun, or the usually cheerful green colouration may take on an unhealthy reddish tinge. *G. batesiana* has very thick, triangular-sectioned leaves arranged in a stout rosette. They are an olive-green colour spotted with raised white dots. Offsets are usually formed eventually, making propagation quite easy. Often these already have roots and it is merely necessary to pull one or more away and pot up straight away. Don't spoil a nice-looking clump, but you may have to remove some anyway to prevent the clump from becoming larger than you want. The pinkish-red tubular flowers are small and grouped along a stem.

Use a good, well-drained potting mixture, and water quite freely in spring and summer, reducing towards winter.

Take care
Mealy bugs hide between leaves.

Gasteria maculata

- Partial shade
- Temp: 5-30°C (41-86°F)
- Keep slightly moist in winter

Probably the most popular of the gasterias, this succulent is often to be seen in home and office windows, where its very existence is a tribute to its ability to survive adverse conditions! It is one of the easiest of succulents to grow, but so frequently ill-treated. Just water it freely in spring and summer and give it something nourishing to live in, and it will reward you with an appearance quite different from its ill-treated relatives. The flattened leaves are about 15cm (6in) long and 4cm (1.6in) wide, glossy green with white spots or bands. They form two rows, rather than a rosette, at least in younger plants. Offsets are freely produced, soon forming a clump, which will probably have to be split up eventually, unless it can be grown in a wide pan.

This gasteria will survive at 5°C (41°F) in winter if it is quite dry, but it is happier at a rather higher temperature and moister, in a living-room or kitchen. It may be outdoors in summer.

Take care
Avoid full sun and dark corners. 395♦

415

Glottiphyllum arrectum

- Full sun
- Temp: 5-30°C (41-86°F)
- Water with great caution

Glottiphyllums are pretty little South African plants that are easy to grow. But if overwatered, they lap the water up and turn into bloated monstrosities.

G. arrectum has two or three pairs of semi-cylindrical leaves, which are 5cm (2in) long and bright green. During summer, the leaves develop a pretty purplish colour. The shining golden-yellow flowers are about 7cm (2.8in) across and are formed in early winter; they open in the late afternoon and close at night, and they open for several days running, provided the sun shines. The side shoots may be used for propagation.

To prevent obesity, glottiphyllums should be grown in a mixture that is half grit; repot every three or four years. The growing period is from late summer to late autumn. During this period water the plant, allowing it to dry out between waterings. Otherwise, the plant should be kept dry. Keep it in a very light position.

Take care
Never overwater.

Glottiphyllum linguiforme

- Full sun
- Temp: 5-30°C (41-86°F)
- Water with great caution

Glottiphyllum linguiforme is an attractive plant, provided it is not overwatered. It will mop up any amount of water, becoming more and more distorted in the process. This glottiphyllum has two rows of thick tongue-like leaves, which are 5cm (2in) long, and bright shiny green in colour. The plant blooms on sunny days in late autumn or early winter. Like many South African succulents, its shining yellow flowers open on sunny days and close at night. The plant will form side shoots, which may be removed for propagation during the latter half of the summer.

A good potting mixture is half loam-based medium and half sharp sand or perlite. The plant should be repotted every third or fourth year. During late summer and autumn, water on sunny days, allowing it to dry out between waterings. Watch for mealy bugs, which are the main pest. Spraying with a proprietary insecticide will eliminate them.

Take care
Grow in a sunny position. 396♦

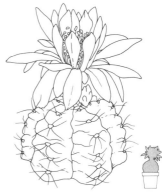

Gymnocalycium andreae

- **Full sun**
- **Temp: 5-30°C (41-86°F)**
- **Keep dry in winter**

Most gymnocalyciums are fairly small, compact cacti, very suitable for the average collection, but this one is particularly desirable as it only reaches a diameter of about 5cm (2in), although a small clump is eventually formed. The spines, some of which are curved, are quite short. This little plant is very free-flowering, producing its bright yellow blooms, about 3cm (1.2in) across, in spring and summer. The colour is unusual for a gymnocalycium, which mostly have white or greenish-white flowers. Offsets soon appear on the main plant; they can be removed for propagation, or left on to produce eventually a rounded mass of beautifully flowering heads.

Full sun is needed, and any good potting mixture may be used, either loam-based or loamless. But good drainage is essential and about one third of extra sharp sand or perlite should be added. During late spring and summer water freely but let the plant become almost dry first.

Take care
Watch out for the mealy bug pest. 396♦

Gymnocalycium baldianum

- **Full sun**
- **Temp: 5-30°C (41-86°F)**
- **Keep dry in winter**

Like *Gymnocalycium andreae* this cactus is different from the general run of gymnocalyciums in the colour of its flowers, in this case a brilliant red, although pink-flowered versions are to be found. It is sometimes met under its former name of *G. venturianum*, which may lead to some confusion when looking through nurserymen's lists. The stem is a bright green ball with a diameter of about 7cm (2.8in) and seldom produces offsets. The well-rounded ribs show the typical gymnocalycium notches or 'chins'. Well-treated plants produce beautiful flowers, about 4cm (1.6in) across, in spring and summer. Like most cacti, this one will give of its best in a greenhouse, but there is no reason why it should not be grown and flowered on a sunny windowsill.

Use a good, well-drained potting mixture, as for the preceding species, and feed every two weeks with a high-potassium fertilizer during spring and summer.

Take care
Avoid damp and cold conditions.

417

Gymnocalycium bruchii
- **Full sun**
- **Temp: 5-30°C (41-86°F)**
- **Keep dry in winter**

Another small-growing cactus, and if one had to choose a single beauty, easily obtainable, from among a lovely group, this could well be it. But it has a confusing alias; it is sometimes called *G. lafaldense*, so take care not to buy the same plant twice! A small compact clump of neatly spined, rounded heads is soon formed, which produces pinkish blooms very freely. Far better to leave this cactus as a clump, but often the heads become so crowded that a few can be removed to make room for the others. Carefully cut them away with a thin knife, allow them to dry off for a few days and just press them into fresh potting mix in late spring and summer.

Either loam- or peat-based potting mixture may be used, but increase the drainage by mixing in about one third of sharp sand or perlite. Watering can be quite free in spring and summer, and every two weeks or so give a dose of fertilizer.

Take care
Mealy bugs hide between heads. 396♦

Gymnocalycium denudatum
(Spider cactus)
- **Full sun**
- **Temp: 5-30°C (41-86°F)**
- **Keep dry in winter**

This is perhaps the best-known gymnocalycium and more or less typical of the whole group. It is an almost globular cactus reaching the size of about 15cm (6in) across and 10cm (4in) high. The deep green plant body or stem is furnished with broad ribs and the notches along them give the typical 'chin' effect, although this is less pronounced than in other similar plants. The popular name of 'Spider cactus' refers to the short spreading spines, somewhat resembling small spiders crawling over the plant. Beautiful greenish-white or pinkish flowers add to the attractiveness of this cactus during spring and summer. They are about 5cm (2in) across.

Grow this cactus in a potting mixture of about two thirds standard growing medium and one third sharp sand or perlite and feed occasionally with a high-potassium fertilizer during the bud and flower stage.

Take care
Make sure the winter dryness is not spoilt by greenhouse drips! 397♦

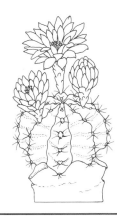

Gymnocalycium horridispinum

- Full sun
- Temp: 5-30°C (41-86°F)
- Keep dry in winter

One of the attractions of gymnocalyciums is their great variety of shape, spines and flowers, and this one is indeed a beauty among them. It is rather less typical of the group as a whole, being more elongated than globular; an average-sized plant is about 13cm (5in) tall and 8cm (3.2in) broad. Also it has delightful pink flowers up to 6cm (2.4in) across. In spite of their size, three or four flowers can be produced at a time, and they may last for up to a week. Unfortunately, they have no perfume! There are well-formed 'chins' along the ribs of the bright green stem and these bear stout, spreading spines, about 3cm (1.2in) long. Incidentally, its Latin name does not mean 'horrid', but 'prickly' or 'spiny'.

Grow this lovely plant in the usual well-drained standard potting mixture with extra sharp sand or perlite, and feed occasionally in spring and summer.

Take care
Avoid soggy potting mixture. 397♦

Gymnocalycium mihanovichii 'Hibotan'

- Partial shade
- Temp: 10-30°C (50-86°F)
- Keep dryish in winter

Looking something like a tomato on a stick, this cactus, sometimes also called 'Ruby Ball', is certainly unusual. It was first developed in Japan. Some cacti suppliers incorrectly call it the 'everlasting flower'. But the top is no flower, simply an abnormal version of *G. mihanovichii*, lacking chlorophyll. Consequently this novel cactus must always be grown grafted.

A tender jungle cactus, hylocereus, identified by its three-cornered stem, is most often used as a grafting stock; unless you can keep a winter temperature of at least 10°C (50°F), it is better to re-graft onto something tougher, such as a trichocereus. Otherwise treat 'Hibotan' as a houseplant, for which it is ideally suited. You may be rewarded with attractive white or pink flowers. Use a potting mixture of three parts of a standard material and one part of sharp sand or perlite, and be careful never to overwater.

Take care
Avoid full summer sun. 398♦

419

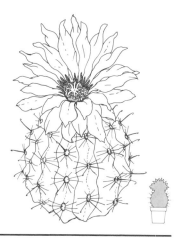

Gymnocalycium quehlianum
- **Full sun**
- **Temp: 2-30°C (36-86°F)**
- **Keep dry in winter**

Probably the most common gymnocalycium, and one of the hardiest. It is an ideal beginner's cactus. Large, lustrous flowers, up to 6cm (2.4in) across, white with pink centres, are abundantly produced, even on small plants. The plant is a flattened sphere, about 10cm (4in) across and 6cm (2.4in) high when fully grown, with deep rounded ribs and pronounced 'chins'. Offsets are rarely produced and the yellowish, curved spines are quite short. Although individual flowers last for only a day or two, a succession means that this fine cactus is in bloom for several weeks during spring and summer.

Water quite freely from spring until late summer, and use a high-potassium fertilizer about once every two weeks when the plant is in bud and flower. Add about one third of sharp sand or perlite to any good standard peat- or loam-based potting mixture.

Take care
Never let water collect in the depressed top of the plant.

Hamatocactus setispinus
- **Full sun**
- **Temp: 5-30°C (41-86°F)**
- **Water freely during summer**

This small cactus does particularly well in cultivation; plants only 2.5cm (1in) across will flower. The yellow blooms have a deep red throat and are borne on the top of the plant during summer. An adult plant is about 13cm (5in) across, with a dark green skin and white spines.

A suitable growing medium for this plant is two parts loam- or peat-based mixture to one part of sharp sand or perlite. Repot annually and inspect the roots for the grey ashy deposits that indicate the presence of root mealy bug. If found, wash the old soil off the roots and repot into a clean container. The plant should be watered freely during the summer months but allowed to dry out between waterings; keep it dry during the winter. Full sun is necessary to stimulate flowering and to encourage the growth of long stout spines. Feed every two weeks with a high-potassium fertilizer when flower buds start to appear.

Take care
Make sure drips in the greenhouse do not spoil winter dryness.

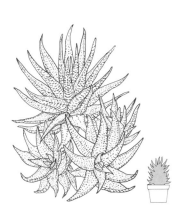

Haworthia attenuata

- Partial shade
- Temp: 5-30°C (41-86°F)
- Keep slightly moist in winter

In their native Africa, haworthias receive shade from the larger plants among which they are growing. If exposed to very strong light, the leaves become unattractively bronzed. In a greenhouse they thrive in shady corners or under the staging – places where most succulent plants become distorted because of the poor light. They also do very well as room plants; their tolerance of partial shade and their small size make them ideal.

Haworthia attenuata forms a stemless rosette of tough, dark green leaves. These have bands of white tubercles, which glisten attractively. Haworthias are all grown for the beauty of their form, not for their flowers; the tiny white bells are carried on the end of long straggly stems.

Grow this species in half-pots, in a loam-based potting mixture, and repot annually. With age H. attenuata will form offsets, which can be removed and used for propagation.

Take care
Avoid strong sunshine. 398♦

Haworthia margaritifera

- Partial shade
- Temp: 5-30°C (41-86°F)
- Keep slightly moist in winter

Haworthia margaritifera is a stemless rosette about 15cm (6in) in diameter, consisting of dark green curved leaves, frosted with prominent pearly tubercles. Some plants are more prettily marked than others; if possible, choose your plant personally. The flowers are small white bells, carried on the end of long wiry stems.

This plant grows best in partial shade. It does well as a houseplant, or it will fill in a shady corner of the greenhouse. If grown indoors, occasionally wash the leaves to remove any dust.

Use a loam-based potting mixture and grow in a half-pot. Haworthias have thick, shiny white roots. During the resting period these shrivel and the plant grows a new set of roots. If you repot in the early summer you may well find that the plant has little root, but this is quite natural. Haworthias tend to grow and flower well into the winter, and rest during the spring.

Take care
Do not let it dry out completely.

Haworthia maughanii
- ● **Diffuse sunlight**
- ● **Temp: 5-30°C (41-86°F)**
- ● **Water with caution**

Huernia aspera
- ● **Full sun**
- ● **Temp: 5-30°C (41-86°F)**
- ● **Keep almost dry in winter**

This is one of the choicest haworthias. The semi-cylindrical leaves are arranged in rosettes. The leaves are about 2.5cm (1in) long, and look as if someone had sliced the tip of the leaf off. The leaves have 'windows' at the ends. In their native desert the leaves are buried with only the tips showing, and light is filtered into the plant through the exposed 'windows'. However, in cultivation the plant is grown completely above the soil, to prevent rotting. The leaves are dark green, and the plant flowers during early winter, producing small white bells.

A growing medium consisting of one half loam-based potting mixture and one half sharp sand or perlite will ensure that the plant does not become too wet. Always allow it to dry out between waterings. This is a very slow-growing plant and will live in a 7.5cm (3in) pot for many years. During the resting period, the thick contractile roots will shrivel and be replaced by new ones.

Take care
Never overwater. 399♦

Huernia aspera is a neat little succulent plant, related to the much larger stapelias. The freely branching, bright green stems are only about 8cm (3.2in) long and 1.5cm (0.6in) in thickness. They are angled with soft teeth, but no leaves. The purple-red flowers are five pointed and very fleshy, 2cm (0.8in) across, with little or no odour.

All stapelia-type succulents tend to be rather touchy with regard to watering and temperature, but this is one of the easiest and most hardy, surviving quite happily in a cool greenhouse in winter, with only enough dampness in the potting mixture to prevent it from shrivelling unduly. It also makes a good little specimen for the living-room windowsill. But it cannot tolerate overwatering; ensure a well-drained potting mixture by adding one part of sharp sand or perlite to two parts of a standard material. To water, dip the pot, remove it, and allow it to drain.

Take care
Watch for black marks in winter – a sign of rot, or infection.

Huernia zebrina
- **Full sun**
- **Temp: 5-30°C (41-86°F)**
- **Keep almost dry in winter**

The name refers to the zebra-like stripes on the flowers of this miniature succulent — if a zebra could have purple-brown stripes on a yellow background! But, accurate or not, this flower is delightfully attractive and unusual. The five striped lobes surround a thick purple central ring, the whole flower being about 4cm (1.6in) across. There is almost no smell, but what little there is is unpleasant, characteristic of most of the stapelia-type succulents! The plant itself consists of sharply toothed, angled stems, bright green in colour and around 8cm (3.2in) long and 2cm (0.8in) thick.

Grow this huernia in a mixture of two parts of a standard material and one part of sharp sand or perlite. Never allow the potting mixture to become too wet, or rot or infection can set in. This is indicated by black marks, or black tips to the stems. In winter, give only enough water to prevent severe shrivelling, but in spring and summer water freely.

Take care
Treat black marks with fungicide. 399♦

Kalanchoe blossfeldiana
- **Good light**
- **Temp: 10-27°C (50-81°F)**
- **Keep slightly moist in winter**

This succulent is undoubtedly a houseplant, although it can certainly be grown in a greenhouse. Many horticultural hybrids are on the market, as they are popular florists' plants, usually being available in autumn and winter in full bloom. A typical specimen would be up to 30cm (12in) high with wide, thick bright green leaves, but the plants offered for sale are usually smaller. This is predominantly a flowering plant, producing masses of bright red flowers from autumn until spring. The flowers are individually small, but they are clustered in tight heads, giving a brilliant display of colour. There is a yellow-flowered variety.

Never overwater this plant, as the stems are prone to rot off, but never let it dry out completely either. However, in a good, well-drained potting mixture it is easy to cultivate; mix some extra sharp sand or perlite with a standard material to improve the drainage. Take stem cuttings in spring; pot them straight away.

Take care
Full summer sun can scorch. 401♦

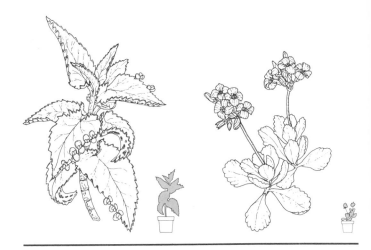

Kalanchoe daigremontiana
- Full sun
- Temp: 10-27°C (50-81°F)
- Keep slightly moist in winter

Kalanchoes are a very varied group and this one, once known as *Bryophyllum daigremontianum*, is totally different from the previous plant, as it is grown for its attractive leaves rather than the somewhat insignificant flowers. These leaves, green marbled with brown, are arrow-shaped and may be up to 10cm (4in) long. But the great curiosity is the tiny plantlets that appear within the leaf notches. When these fall off, they will take root (actually they mostly have minute roots already!) in any patch of soil they touch, giving rise to further plants; any nearby pot will soon have a kalanchoe growing beside the rightful owner! It would not be possible to have an easier plant to propagate, since it requires no effort on the part of the grower at all. The parent plant can reach a height of 60cm (24in).

Grow this novelty in any good potting mixture, and water quite freely in spring and summer.

Take care
It can become a weed! 400♦

Kalanchoe pumila
- Full sun
- Temp: 5-27°C (41-81°F)
- Keep slightly moist in winter

This pretty little plant is ideal for a hanging basket indoors, where it will grow and flower freely in a light window. Of course, it can also be grown in a greenhouse, where its relative hardiness will enable it to survive the lower winter temperature. The slightly thickened leaves are basically pale pinkish-green in colour, but this is almost completely masked by a grey mealy coating, giving the whole plant a delightful pearly-grey appearance. It is very free-flowering, producing masses of dark pink blooms in spring. Although these are individually only about 2cm (0.8in) across, they appear in small groups at the end of quite short stems. The plant is only about 15cm (6in) high.

To grow it in a hanging basket, line a small one with sphagnum moss or coarse peat, well damped, fill with any good potting mixture, and plant the kalanchoe in this. To propagate this succulent, cut off a few stems in spring or summer and pot them up.

Take care
Sprays can mark the leaves. 400♦

Above: **Notocactus haselbergii**
*Flowers are produced on a neatly
spined white ball and the contrast*
*between the plant and flower colour
is most striking. This cactus does not
usually flower when young.* 449♦

Above: **Notocactus leninghausii**
This golden-spined cactus is grown for itself rather than for the flowers, which, although attractive, are produced only on older, larger plants. Nevertheless they are well worth waiting for, and they certainly add to the beauty of the plant. 450♦

Above right:
Notocactus mammulosus
This is a particularly striking notocactus, with long, stout spines. This free-flowering plant will set seed quite readily. This species is hardy even in temperate countries and – if kept quite dry in winter – can withstand temperatures down to freezing. As in most freely flowering cacti, a cold winter rest is vital. 451♦

Right: **Notocactus herteri**
The flower colour of this notocactus makes it different from the others illustrated here. The plant itself is neatly rounded and has delightfully compact spines, contrasting with its brilliant blooms. It is reasonably hardy and is easy to cultivate in a well-drained potting mixture. 450♦

Above: **Notocactus ottonis**
This small, globular cactus clusters freely and produces large brilliant flowers with red centres. Propagation by offsets is easy. 451♦

Far left: **Opuntia basilaris**
Most of the opuntias, or 'Prickly Pears', do not flower as reasonably small pot plants, but this one will usually do so quite readily and is not too large for a collection. 452♦

Left: **Opuntia robusta**
This is a natural giant, but small specimens are attractive in a collection. However, they are not likely to flower. 453♦

Above: **Opuntia microdasys**
This is the usual colour for the bunches of barbed bristles, or 'glochids', of this well-known opuntia. Large specimens may become sprawling. 452♦

Left: **Opuntia microdasys**
var. **albispina**
This variety with white glochids is particularly attractive, especially if space permits a large clump. 452♦

Below:
Opuntia microdasys var. **rufida**
A third variety, with shorter and thicker joints, and reddish-brown glochids contrasting beautifully with the dark green stems. 452♦

Above: **Opuntia scheeri**
As well as the typical glochids, or barbed bristles, this opuntia has a network of golden spines covering the joints. With its compact habit of growth and freely formed branches it is ideal for the average collection, and it is unlikely to become too large for many years. If and when it does, it is a simple matter to re-start by removing a few joints and treating them as cuttings. They can be potted up after a few days' drying to seal the cut surface. The best time to do this is from late spring to summer, when they should soon root. 454♦

Right: **Opuntia spegazzinii**
This is one of the cylindrical-jointed opuntias, which are less familiar than the 'Prickly Pear' shape. Its outstanding characteristic is that it can be expected to flower easily in a small pot, which is unlikely in the case of the larger-growing opuntias. The cylindrical stems tend to trail, and this cactus needs to be supported in some way, possibly on a plastic trellis as used for some houseplants. Otherwise it could be planted in a hanging basket, but be careful that it does not get tangled in anyone's hair! 454♦

Far right: Opuntia pycnantha
Do not expect flowers on this opuntia; only large old plants are likely to produce them. But the beauty of this cactus does not depend on flowers; the shape and spine colour are enough. 453♦

Right: Oreocereus celsianus
An impressive cactus by any standards, with its contrasting hair and sharp, stout spines. It is comparatively slow-growing; although it can eventually become very large, it will take years. 455♦

Below: Oroya subocculta
This may not be the easiest plant to obtain but it is worth the effort. Fortunately it is most attractive in itself, because flowers are unlikely to be produced except on large specimens. 455♦

Above: **Pachypodium lamerei**
Long, non-succulent leaves are formed at the top of a very succulent stem, well equipped with stiff spines. As the stem elongates, the lower leaves fall and are replaced by new ones, so that there is always a tuft at the top. But if this succulent is allowed to get too cold in winter it is likely to lose all its leaves and may rot as well. So keep it warm in winter. Indoors it needs a sunny window and occasional turning. 456♦

Right: **Pachyphytum oviferum**
An excellent example of a leaf succulent, like sugared almonds on a stem. The leaves are covered with a whitish mealy coating, which makes them very easily marked, so it is particularly important not to finger them or the pristine beauty of this attractive succulent will be spoilt. Clumps of rather unusual flowers are produced in spring. Like many shrubby succulents, it may become too straggly with age, when it is probably best to cut and restart. 456♦

Above: **Parodia aureispina**
This is a neat golden ball freely producing bright yellow flowers. Care with watering is necessary to avoid root loss. 473♦

Left: **Parodia microsperma** var. **gigantea**
Typical P. microsperma has yellow flowers. This red variety is possibly even more attractive. 473♦

Right: **Parodia microsperma**
The typically yellow flower almost obscures the elegantly spined plant body. Water with care. 473♦

Above: **Pereskia aculeata**
Almost like a wild rose, this is a
strange non-succulent cactus. It
definitely needs some support. 474▶

Leuchtenbergia principis

- **Full sun**
- **Temp: 5-30°C (41-86°F)**
- **Keep dry in winter**

A true cactus that bears a remarkable resemblance to an agave or aloe, this strange-looking plant is the sole representative of its group. Unlike agaves or aloes, the long tubercles are part of the stem, not leaves. These tubercles can be up to 10cm (4in) long and they are tipped with groups of soft, rather papery spines. This cactus does not appear to be very free-flowering, and to give it the best chance to produce its beautiful perfumed yellow flowers, 8cm (3.2in) across, it needs as much full sunlight as possible. It is unlikely to flower as a houseplant. Propagation is said to be possible from removed tubercles, dried for a while and potted up. This is a very easy plant to raise from seed.

Water this unique cactus freely in spring and summer; the tubercles tend to spread when the plant is moist and to close in with dryness. Use three parts of a standard potting mixture added to one part of sharp sand or perlite.

Take care
Use a deep pot.

Lithops aucampiae

(Living stone)
- **Full sun**
- **Temp: 5-30°C (41-86°F)**
- **Keep dry in rest period**

These little stone-like plants are perhaps the most delightful of all the South African succulents. A large collection of them can be grown in a pan 30cm (12in) square, which makes them ideal for a small greenhouse. Lithops consist of one pair of flat-topped fleshy leaves; the stem is so short as to be invisible when the plant is potted up, and they are often described as stemless. *L. aucampiae* is one of the larger species, with leaves 2.5cm (1in) across; they are a lovely rich brown colour with darker brown dots. The golden flowers appear from between the two leaves in early autumn.

Grow this species in a mixture of half loam-based medium and half sharp sand or perlite. Keep dry all winter. Do not water until the old leaves have completely shrivelled away; this will probably be in late spring. Water on sunny days, and gradually tail off in autumn.

Take care
When watering, do not splash the leaves, as the water will leave 'chalk' marks. 402♦

441

Lithops bella

(Living stone)
- **Full sun**
- **Temp: 5-30°C (41-86°F)**
- **Keep dry in rest period**

Lithops bella has a pair of pale grey leaves with darker markings. The white flowers appear between the leaves in early autumn. This is one of the lithops that will form an attractive clump. In spring, when the old head has shrivelled away, two new heads will be found inside the old skin. The plant does not double its size every year; some years no new heads are formed, or perhaps only one head in a clump will double. Overlarge clumps can be split up. The summer growing period is the best time to do this.

No water should be given until the old leaves have completely shrivelled away, usually in late spring. Grow in a mixture of equal parts of loam-based material and grit. Do not repot annually; once every three years is sufficient. It is important to give the plant the maximum light available. The flowers open in the afternoon on sunny days, and close at night. They last for about a week.

Take care
Avoid drips from the greenhouse roof during dry rest period. 402♦

Lithops helmutii

(Living stone)
- **Full sun**
- **Temp: 5-30°C (41-86°F)**
- **Water only during summer**

Lithops helmutii has a pair of plump, apparently stemless leaves, which are bright green marked with grey and have a large 'window'. This is one of the lithops that cluster freely. Each head is about 3cm (1.2in) across. The golden-yellow flowers are also 3cm in diameter, and completely hide the leaves. The plant flowers in early autumn. The blooms open in the afternoons of sunny days and close again at night; they last for about a week.

Lithops have a definite winter resting period, when no water should be given. The new leaves grow at the expense of the old. In spring the old leaves will be partly shrivelled and the new head or heads will be seen emerging. When the old leaves are completely shrivelled away, water the plant. Water frequently until the autumn, but allow to dry out between waterings. Grow the plant in a mixture consisting of one part loam-based material and one part sharp sand or perlite. Repot every three years.

Take care
Avoid a damp atmosphere in winter.

Lithops marmorata
(Living stone)
● **Full sun**
● **Temp: 5-30°C (41-86°F)**
● **Water only during summer**

Lithops marmorata consists of a pair of almost stemless succulent leaves. The leaves are greyish-green, marbled with grey or yellowish lines. The white flower appears from the cleft between the leaves and is large enough to hide the plant body completely. The flowering period is early autumn.

An open potting mixture consisting of half loam-based potting medium and half sharp sand or perlite will ensure that the plant does not take up too much water and become overlarge. Allow it to dry out between waterings. It is essential to grow this plant in full sun, as the flowers open only when exposed to sunlight: they open in the afternoon and close at night. Lithops look their best when grown in pans surrounded by small pebbles with similar markings to themselves. It is not necessary to repot yearly. The main pests that attack lithops are mealy bug and root mealy bug. Water with insecticide.

Take care
The leaves will be marked if splashed during watering. 403♦

Lobivia backebergii
● **Full sun**
● **Temp: 5-30°C (41-86°F)**
● **Keep dry in winter**

The lobivias are a large group of cacti closely related to the genus *Echinopsis*, and many hybrids exist between them. *L. backebergii* starts by being an almost globular plant and gradually becomes more oval. It will not create much of a space problem, as it reaches a diameter of only 5cm (2in). The bright green ribbed stem will sometimes form offsets from the base. Curved dark spines spread over the ribs, about 1.5cm (0.6in) long, but may be larger if the plant is grown in strong sunlight. The beautiful flowers are carmine with a bluish sheen, and are about 4cm (1.6in) across.

This cactus is quite tolerant with regard to the potting mixture. If your standard mix looks at all compacted, add some extra sharp sand or perlite. Water it freely during spring and summer, and to encourage continued flowering add a high-potassium, tomato-type fertilizer to the water about once every two weeks during this time.

Take care
Good flowering demands a cold winter rest. 404♦

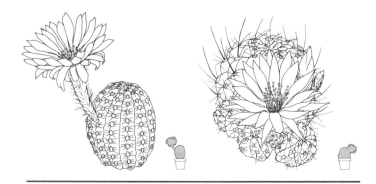

Lobivia famatimensis

- Full sun
- Temp: 5-30°C (41-86°F)
- Keep dry in winter

A small, particularly beautiful lobivia, this cactus is clump-forming, with individual 'heads' about 6cm (2.4in) long and 2.5cm (1in) thick. The yellowish spines on the 20 or so small ribs are so numerous and interlocking that they almost cover the stem. Flowers are normally yellow, around 5cm (2in) across, and occur in clusters at the top of the stems. Quite often they will open for several days in succession, closing at night. Don't be perturbed if your specimen produces flowers of another colour: there are varieties with orange, pink or red flowers.

This pretty lobivia is rather more moisture- and temperature-sensitive than many, so make sure that the potting mixture is very well drained by adding one part of sharp sand or perlite to three parts of a standard material. Water quite freely on sunny days during spring and summer. Stems can be removed for propagation in spring, but let them dry for a few days before potting.

Take care
Spines can hide mealy bugs. 405♦

Lobivia hertrichiana

- Full sun
- Temp: 5-30°C (41-86°F)
- Keep dry in winter

One of the most popular and widely grown of the lobivias, this small cactus flowers very freely, even when quite young. Stems are more or less globular, ribbed, with fairly short, bristly, spreading spines. Individual heads are about 2.5-4cm (1-1.6in) thick, and the plant rapidly forms quite a large clump. But there is no need to let it become any larger than required; heads are easily removed for propagation in spring. Merely let them dry for a few days before potting up. Brilliant scarlet flowers, produced in masses in spring and summer, may be up to 5cm (2in) across.

To get the best from this attractive cactus, let it form a reasonably large clump if space permits, preferably growing it in a pan or half-pot. Use a good standard potting mixture but make sure that it is well drained. A cold winter rest is desirable to promote good flowering, as is feeding in spring and summer.

Take care
A top dressing of gravel will protect the clump from excess water.

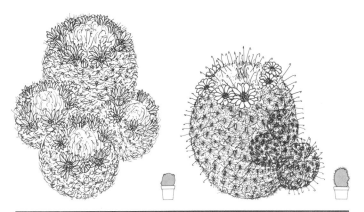

Mammillaria bocasana

- Full sun
- Temp: 5-30°C (41-86°F)
- Keep dry in winter

Mammillarias are the most popular of the cacti: they are small, flower freely, and have beautiful spines. *M. bocasana* is a many-headed plant that forms a cushion. The plant is blue-green and covered with silky white spines. Appearances are deceptive: underneath the soft spines are spines with hooks, which cling to the hands, clothing or anything else that touches them. The small creamy flowers form circlets around each head in spring. This is a very free-flowering plant.

This cactus needs a sunny position and ample water plus a dose of high-potassium (tomato-type) fertilizer every two weeks or so during the growing period. During winter, keep it dry. A suitable mixture is two parts of a loam-based potting medium to one part of sharp sand or perlite. Repot annually. If the plant is becoming too large, remove one of the heads, dry it for two days, and then pot it up. If the cutting is taken in spring, it will soon root.

Take care

Avoid the hooked spines. 404♦

Mammillaria bombycina

- Full sun
- Temp: 5-30°C (41-86°F)
- Keep dry in winter

Mammillaria bombycina is one of the beautiful white-spined mammillarias. It is a cylindrical plant that clusters from the base with age. The stems are densely clad in white spines. The reddish-purple flowers form circlets around the tops of the stems in late spring to early summer. Young plants do not flower. It seems to be characteristic of mammillarias that cream-flowered species bloom easily, even as young plants, but most of the red-flowered ones bloom only as mature plants.

An open growing medium, two parts loam- or peat-based potting mixture to one part grit, is necessary for this cactus. Since it spreads outwards, it looks well grown in a half-pot. Repot annually and examine the roots for signs of root mealy bug. Water generously during summer, but allow it to dry out before watering again. Feed every two weeks with a high-potassium fertilizer when the plant is flowering. Keep dry in winter.

Take care

Avoid a damp, cold atmosphere. 406♦

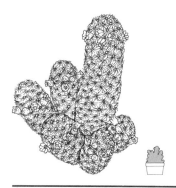

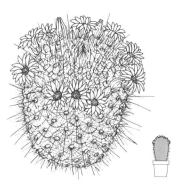

Mammillaria elongata
- ● Full sun
- ● Temp: 5-30°C (41-86°F)
- ● Keep dry in winter

Mammillaria perbella
- ● Full sun
- ● Temp: 5-30°C (41-86°F)
- ● Keep dry in winter

Mammillaria elongata is a clustering plant that consists of long finger-shaped shoots. The spines are prettily arranged in a star, and are variable in colour; plants exist with white, yellow, brown or deep red spines. The cream flowers are freely produced, even on small plants, in early spring.

This cactus needs an open mixture, two parts loam- or peat-based potting medium to one part grit. It looks at its best if grown in a half-pot. If the cluster becomes too large, remove a shoot, dry it for two or three days, and pot it up separately. The late spring is a good time to take cuttings. The plant may be watered generously during summer, but keep it dry during winter. Feed every two weeks with a high-potassium fertilizer during the flowering period. Full sunlight is necessary to maintain the rich colour of the spines.

Take care
To avoid weak spines, grow in good sunlight.

Mammillaria perbella is a silvery-white cylindrical cactus, about 6cm (2.4in) in diameter, and does not usually branch. The stem is covered in short white spines. The flowering period is early summer, when a ring of flowers appears near the top of the plant. The petals are pale pink with a darker stripe down the middle.

Grow in a mixture of one part loam- or peat-based potting medium and one part sharp sand or perlite. Repot every year and examine the roots for signs of root mealy bug. During spring and summer, water on sunny days, allowing it to dry out between waterings. During the flowering period feed every two weeks with a high-potassium fertilizer. Taper off the watering in autumn and allow the plant to remain dry in winter. Keep this cactus in the sunniest part of your greenhouse; sun stimulates bud formation and spines.

Take care
Do not allow the potting mixture to become hard and compacted.

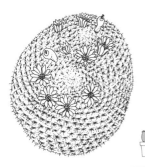

Mammillaria spinosissima var. sanguinea

- **Full sun**
- **Temp: 5-30°C (41-86°F)**
- **Keep dry in winter**

Mammillaria spinosissima var. *sanguinea* has a dark green cylindrical stem and long white spines, the central spines having red tips. The purplish-red flowers are quite large for a mammillaria and form a ring in summer.

This cactus is easy to cultivate. A porous mixture consisting of two parts loam- or peat-based material to one part sharp sand or perlite is needed, and a sunny position. Repot annually. Water generously during spring and summer, but allow it to dry out between waterings. When the flower buds appear, feed every two weeks with a high-potassium (tomato) fertilizer until flowering is over. Keep it dry in late autumn and winter. When repotting, inspect the roots for any ashy deposit, which indicates the presence of root mealy bug. If found, wash the soil off the roots and replant into a clean pot; treat with a systemic insecticide.

Take care
Avoid drips from the greenhouse roof during the rest period.

Mammillaria zeilmanniana

- **Full sun**
- **Temp: 5-30°C (41-86°F)**
- **Keep almost dry in winter**

This is a very free-flowering mammillaria and the blooms are a beautiful reddish-violet colour; it is one of the few mammillarias of this colour to flower as a young plant. Occasionally a plant has flowers with a double row of petals, and there is also a form with white blooms. The flowering period is early summer.

The stems of this plant are cylindrical, and branch to form multi-headed clumps. Heads can be detached during summer, and used to propagate the plant. Grow in half-pots; a suitable potting mixture is two parts loam- or peat-based medium and one part grit. Water freely and feed every two weeks with a high-potassium fertilizer during spring and summer, allowing it to dry out between waterings. Let it become almost dry during winter. Keep in a sunny part of the greenhouse and inspect for mealy bug; water with insecticide.

Take care
Do not allow water to accumulate between the heads. 407♦

Neoporteria napina
- **Moderate light**
- **Temp: 5-30°C (41-86°F)**
- **Keep dry in winter**

Neoporteria nidus
- **Full sun**
- **Temp: 5-30°C (41-86°F)**
- **Keep dry in winter**

Neoporterias are somewhat uncommon cacti, but they are fairly readily available nowadays and well worth growing. They have suffered in the past from the common trouble of name changing, and have been switched from one group to another. However, that need not bother those of us who merely want to grow an attractive cactus. *N. napina* is quite small, up to 8cm (3.2in) high and 2.5cm (1in) thick, although most specimens are not as large as this. The brownish-green stem is divided into many narrow ribs, arranged in a spiral and with tiny spines. Flowers are large for such a small plant, often 5cm (2in) across, and bright yellow in colour. The root is distinctly odd, something like a small turnip, and easily troubled by any excess water. Use a very well-drained potting mixture made up from one part sharp sand or perlite and two parts of a standard peat or loam material. Best to avoid full sun, and water freely on sunny days in spring and summer.

The cultivation of this little cactus is rather a challenge; it is not one of the easiest, but should not be spurned on that account, as it only needs a good, loving owner! It is a small plant consisting of a solitary, ribbed stem 5-8cm (2-3.2in) in diameter, at first more or less spherical but usually elongating with age. This stem is beautifully clothed with a mass of spines, some long and curved, others slender and almost hair-like. The reddish flowers are fairly easily produced; up to 4cm (1.6in) across.

Cultivation is not really a problem; it merely needs care. Never overwater this cactus, as damp, airless conditions at the root can cause it to disappear. If this happens in spring or summer, cut away all dark tissue, allow to dry for a week, and repot. At any other time of the year leave the repotting until the following spring. Use a particularly well-drained potting mixture made by adding one part of sharp sand or perlite to two parts of a standard mix.

Take care
Use a deep pot for the long root.

Take care
Give full sun whenever possible.

Neoporteria mammillarioides

- **Full sun**
- **Temp: 5-30°C (41-86°F)**
- **Keep dry in winter**

Although probably one of the less well-known neoporterias, this beautiful cactus, previously a pyrrocactus, is certainly one of the most attractive. The almost globular stem, perhaps up to a diameter of 8cm (3.2in), is bright green in colour, with many acute ribs furnished with tufts of straight, stiff spines. Although it is a neat, compact little plant, it is the flowers that make it out of the ordinary. They are of a deep rose-pink or red colour, yellowish towards the base of the petals, and are produced very freely at the top of the plant, usually several opening at one time and lasting for several days.

Grow this neoporteria in a good potting mixture. Mix one part of sharp sand or perlite with three parts of a standard peat- or loam-based material. A top dressing of gravel will help to reduce the risk of rotting off at the base, and with this protection you can water reasonably freely during spring and summer, but remember to reduce watering in the autumn.

Take care
Watch for any signs of rot. 408♦

Notocactus haselbergii

- **Full sun**
- **Temp: 5-30°C (41-86°F)**
- **Water with caution**

Notocacti are found growing in the grasslands of South America, and they need full sun. *N. haselbergii* is one of the most beautiful of these cacti. It is a silver ball: the numerous ribs are densely clad in soft white spines, which gleam in the sunshine. It does not form offsets. The flowers are carried on top of the plant in late summer; they are tomato red, an unusual colour in this group of plants. Very young plants do not flower.

N. haselbergii should not be allowed to become too wet, or it may lose its roots. A mixture consisting of one part loam-based potting medium to one part sharp sand or perlite will ensure good drainage. Water freely during summer, but allow it to dry out between waterings. Feed every two weeks with a high-potassium fertilizer during the flowering period. Keep it dry during winter. The only pests likely to be found on this plant are mealy bug and root mealy bug; water with a proprietary insecticide.

Take care
Avoid a wet, soggy potting mix. 425♦

449

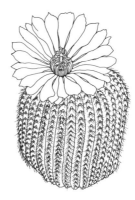

Notocactus herteri
- **Full sun**
- **Temp: 5-30°C (41-86°F)**
- **Water with care**

All the notocacti that have been in cultivation for many years have yellow flowers, but some recently discovered species have beautiful purple flowers, and one of the best of these is *N. herteri*. It is a large globular plant with reddish-brown spines. Although seedlings do not flower, the plant grows quickly and will eventually reach a diameter of at least 15cm (6in). The deep magenta flowers are formed at the top, and open in late summer.

A porous growing mixture consisting of one part loam-based material and one part sharp sand or perlite is suitable. Water freely during the summer, allowing the plant to dry out between waterings. When the buds start to form, feed every two weeks with a high-potassium fertilizer. During winter keep the plant completely dry. It is always advisable to look plants over regularly for the presence of mealy bug: treat with a proprietary insecticide if found.

Take care
Repot annually. 427♦

Notocactus leninghausii
- **Full sun**
- **Temp: 5-30°C (41-86°F)**
- **Keep dry in winter**

Notocactus leninghausii is a golden plant that branches and becomes columnar with age. The many close ribs carry soft yellow spines. It is characteristic that the growing centre of this plant tends to be on one side of the stem. The large yellow flowers appear on top of the plant in late summer. Young plants do not flower.

This cactus is not difficult to cultivate; a growing medium consisting of two parts peat-based potting mixture to one part grit, and a sunny position, will ensure a healthy plant. Repot annually. If the plant gets too large or the base of the stem becomes corky, branches may be removed in summer and used for propagation. Water freely during summer, allowing it to dry out between waterings. During flowering, feed every two weeks with a high-potassium fertilizer. Gradually taper the water off in autumn and keep the plant dry during the winter. Watch out for root mealy bug and mealy bug.

Take care
Avoid damp winter conditions. 426♦

Notocactus mammulosus
- Full sun
- Temp: 5-30°C (41-86°F)
- Keep dry in winter

Notocactus mammulosus is a trouble-free plant that flowers freely while quite small. It is a globular cactus that remains solitary. The ribs carry long, stout spines, brownish in colour. The flowers, borne on top of the plant in late summer, are yellow with purplish stigmas. They are also self-fertile; the furry seed pods contain hundreds of seeds, which germinate easily if sown in the following spring.

Grow this notocactus in a mixture of two parts loam- or peat-based material plus one part sharp sand or perlite. Repot annually. Water freely during the spring and summer growing period, but keep it dry during the winter. When flower buds form, feed every two weeks with a high-potassium fertilizer. If really dry this cactus will withstand temperatures around freezing point. Keep in full sunlight, which ensures not only good flowering but also long, stout spines. A beautifully spined plant is attractive all year.

Take care
Give a dry, cool winter rest. 427♦

Notocactus ottonis
- Full sun
- Temp: 5-30°C (41-86°F)
- Never overwater

Notocactus ottonis is quite different from other notocacti; it is much smaller, and clusters freely from the base. It is deep green, and the ribs carry slender yellowish spines. Individual heads are about 7.5cm (3in) across. The yellow flowers are about 6cm (2.4in) across.

This notocactus is touchy about watering; to prevent it losing its roots, grow in an open mixture consisting of one part loam-based potting medium to one part grit. Grow it in a half-pot: the cluster looks better, and the roots are not surrounded by large quantities of cold, damp soil. Water freely during spring and summer, always allowing it to dry out between waterings. Feed every two weeks during the flowering period using a high-potassium (tomato) fertilizer. Keep it dry in winter. Place this plant where it will get plenty of light. The main pests are mealy bug and root mealy bug; treat with a proprietary insecticide.

Take care
Avoid damp winter conditions. 428♦

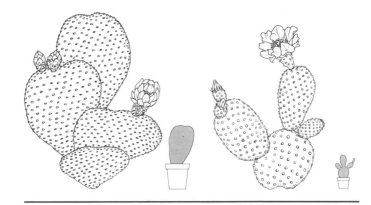

Opuntia basilaris
(Beaver-tail cactus)
- Full sun
- Temp: 5-30°C (41-86°F)
- Keep dry in winter

If there is any typical cactus, it must surely be the opuntia, or prickly pear, although the latter name was originally applied to the spiny fruit of a desert giant. But *O. basilaris* is not a giant and is ideal for the collection as it rarely becomes more than two segments, or pads, high, sometimes branching from the base. The pads are flattened stems (beaver-tail shape), and although almost spineless, they are dotted with clusters of dark red barbed bristles (glochids), characteristic of all opuntias, spined or not. Most opuntias do not flower readily in a collection, needing to be very large before they do so. But this one, being smaller, will often produce red blooms up to 5cm (2in) across on its second segment, when about 20cm (8in) high.

   Grow this opuntia in a good porous potting mixture; extra drainage material is probably not necessary. If you winter it indoors, give just enough water to prevent shrivelling. Best kept dry if in a greenhouse.

Take care
Glochids can penetrate skin. 428♦

Opuntia microdasys
- Full sun
- Temp: 10-30°C (50-86°F)
- Keep slightly moist in winter

Probably the most common cactus of all, and certainly the most popular opuntia; but also the most ill-treated cactus. Witness the poor, spotted, dried-up plants so common in windows. Although it spreads over a wide area in the wild, cultivated specimens form small branched bushes, consisting of many beautiful bright green pads, or flattened stem segments, closely dotted with clumps of yellow glochids (barbed bristles) but no other spines. There are also varieties with reddish and white glochids. All are beautiful but need careful handling, because the pads are not as innocent as they look; the glochids stick into the skin at the slightest opportunity. Rarely, yellow flowers are produced.

   A well-drained potting mixture is needed, and free watering in spring and summer. Give sufficient water in winter to prevent undue shrivelling and keep this cactus rather warmer than it would be in the average cool greenhouse.

Take care
Cold winter conditions cause brown spots. 430/1♦

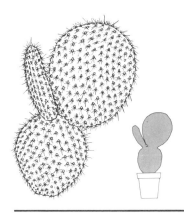
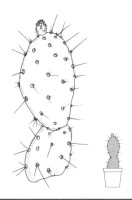

Opuntia pycnantha
- **Full sun**
- **Temp: 5-30°C (41-86°F)**
- **Keep dry in winter**

The fact that the name is sometimes mis-spelt as *pycnacantha* detracts in no way from the beauty of this most handsome opuntia of all, with its bright green stem and contrasting groups of reddish-brown bristly spines (glochids), in addition to the lighter-coloured, longer spines. Individual flattened stem segments or pads are about 8cm (3.2in) across, each being right-angled to the one below. Fortunately this delightful cactus does not depend upon flowers for its beauty, as they are most unlikely on cultivated specimens. Tiny cylindrical leaves appear at the ends of young pads, but soon shrivel and fall off; this is quite natural.

This species is somewhat more susceptible than many opuntias to over-wet potting mixture, which results in root loss; it is best to add about one third of sharp sand or perlite to your usual good standard material. Give water generously in spring and summer; even opuntias can wilt!

Take care
Turn indoor plants regularly.

Opuntia robusta
- **Full sun**
- **Temp: 0-30°C (32-86°F)**
- **Keep dry in winter**

Although this cactus is one of the giant opuntias in its native state, where it can reach a height of 5m (16ft) with bluish-green pads the size of dinner plates, it can be tamed as a pot plant and makes a good, tough specimen for the average collection. This species grows quite quickly for a cactus, and soon makes a nice plant, but without the glorious yellow flowers of desert specimens, as you will not want it to get large enough for that!

It is easy to prevent it from becoming too big: just remove one or more pads when there is any danger of this, let them dry for a few days, and start another specimen. The old plant will send out further shoots, if you want them; otherwise, throw it away! Living up to its name, *O. robusta* is hardy enough to be grown out of doors throughout the year, if it can be protected from winter rain, but it must be dry to survive. Ordinary, good potting mixture will suffice.

Take care
Protect from slugs outdoors. 429♦

453

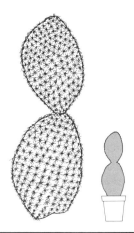

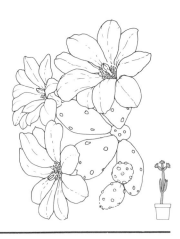

Opuntia scheeri
- Full sun
- Temp: 5-30°C (41-86°F)
- Keep dry in winter

By contrast with the previous opuntia, this one is ideal for the collection without any size-reducing manipulations. The flattened pads or stem segments are usually around 15cm (6in) long and 5cm (2in) broad, but older plants produce larger ones. A decorative, bushy plant results from branches off the main segment. The whole surface of each pad is covered with a network of golden spines, in addition to the inevitable barbed bristles (glochids). Flowers are yellow, but unlikely in cultivation.

Grow this cactus in a standard potting mixture, either peat- or loam-based, preferably with the addition of one third of sharp sand or perlite. Slight shrivelling of the stems may occur if the plant is quite dry in winter, as it should be if in a cool greenhouse; but in a warmer room give it just enough water to prevent this happening. You can water quite freely in spring and summer. Pads can be removed for propagation.

Take care
Mealy bugs tend to collect at the base of joints. 432♦

Opuntia spegazzinii
- Full sun
- Temp: 5-30°C (41-86°F)
- Keep dry in winter

There should be no trouble whatsoever in flowering this opuntia, even in a 5cm (2in) pot. It is quite different from the others mentioned: it does not have flattened 'pads' but long, slender cylindrical stems, freely branching; which in pot-grown specimens usually reach a length of about 30cm (12in) with a thickness of only 1cm (0.4in). Patches of barbed bristles (glochids) and very short spines are distributed over the stems. Large or small branches drop off at the slightest touch, usually rooting where they fall.

Grow this particularly easy opuntia in any good standard potting mixture and it should delight you every summer with its show of snow-white flowers, up to 4cm (1.6in) across, freely produced along the stems. The long, slender stems will need staking, or supporting in some way; a miniature pot plant trellis is ideal and the stems can be gently tied to this. Water freely in spring and summer; plants indoors may need a little water in winter to prevent shedding.

Take care
Handle gently. 433♦

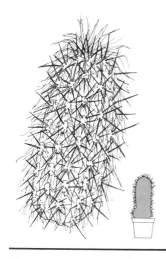

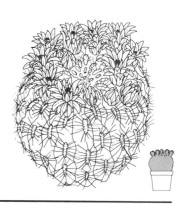

Oreocereus celsianus

- **Full sun**
- **Temp: 5-30°C (41-86°F)**
- **Keep dry in winter**

Although wild specimens of this cactus can reach a large size, it is relatively slow-growing, and in the collection it makes a majestic plant, probably eventually reaching a height of around 40cm (16in) and a diameter of 10cm (4in) but taking a number of years to do so from the usual small bought specimens. The cylindrical stem has a number of rounded ribs, and rows of stout, sharp, brownish spines up to 3cm (1.2in) long in larger specimens, and appearing through a mass of silky white hairs. In cultivation this beautiful cactus does not appear to form offsets or branches, so propagation is not practicable; nor is it likely to flower. Enjoy it for itself!

Grow in a standard potting mixture; and although this is not a demanding plant, it is advisable to mix in about one third of sharp sand or perlite, to be on the safe side. Water in spring and summer whenever the potting mixture appears to be drying out.

Take care

In light potting mixtures this plant can become top-heavy. 434♦

Oroya subocculta

- **Full sun**
- **Temp: 5-30°C (41-86°F)**
- **Keep dry in winter**

Oroyas are somewhat problem plants among botanists, because they do not always fit into pre-conceived groups. *O. subocculta* is a very neat plant and its arrangement of ribs and spines makes it a rather unusual-looking cactus. The many blunt ribs are divided into oval segments, each with a cluster of spreading spines, also arranged in an oval pattern. These are pale brown in colour, up to 1cm (0.4in) long, thin but very sharp. The roughly globular stem will probably reach a diameter of 13cm (5in). Small specimens do not usually flower readily but when the blooms do appear they are of a beautiful orange-reddish colour, yellowish underneath. Unfortunately, they are not very large, only about 2.5cm (1in) across, and unscented.

Grow this cactus in a potting mixture consisting of one part of sharp sand or perlite added to three parts of a good standard material. Water freely in summer.

Take care

Sun will encourage flowering. 435♦

Pachyphytum oviferum

(The sugared-almond plant)
- **Full sun**
- **Temp: 5-30°C (41-86°F)**
- **Keep slightly moist in winter**

Pachyphytum oviferum forms a small shrub about 20cm (8in) high. The fat leaves, arranged in rosettes on the stems, are bluish to lavender in colour and heavily covered with white 'meal'. The white bell-shaped flowers open in spring.

This succulent is not difficult to grow. During the winter months the lower leaves will shrivel; remove dead leaves regularly, or fungus will grow on them and spread to the living plant. If the plant looks leggy in spring, cut the rosettes off, dry them for two days, and repot. If the base of the plant is kept, new rosettes will form at the leaf scars.

Grow in a loam- or peat-based potting medium. Water freely during spring and summer. Be careful not to splash the white leaves. In the winter, give a little water to prevent excessive shrivelling of the plant. To keep a thick white coating of 'meal' grow in a strong light.

Take care
Do not finger the leaves, or they will permanently mark. 437♦

Pachypodium lamerei

- **Full sun**
- **Temp: 12-30°C (54-86°F)**
- **Keep slightly moist in winter**

On the whole pachypodiums are not easy succulents and are something of a challenge, but *P. lamerei* is the least difficult and should be quite within the capability of a careful grower. The greyish succulent stem bears many thorny spines, neatly arranged in groups of three and up to 2.5cm (1in) long. Although sharp, they are not as vicious as those of many cacti. It is difficult to state an exact size, but a good cultivated specimen could be 20cm (8in) high with a thickness of about 5cm (2in). The top of the plant bears a tuft of leaves; as the stem grows they fall, to be replaced by others higher up.

Grow this pachypodium in a mix made by adding one part of sharp sand or perlite to two parts of a standard mix, and never overwater. Definitely a plant for indoors rather than the cool greenhouse in winter, but it will appreciate the extra light there in summer; indoors give maximum light and turn regularly.

Take care
Avoid cold at all times. 436♦

Above: **Pleiospilos bolusii**
Looking more like a piece of rock with a flower in the cleft, this is an extreme succulent. The flower often has a delicate perfume, somewhat almond-like. 475♦

Above: **Rebutia albiflora**
*One of the smallest rebutias, this has
tiny clustering heads and an all-white
appearance, with white spines and
unusual white flowers.* 475♦

Left:
Rebutia calliantha var. **krainziana**
*All rebutias are small cacti, ideal for
the collection on the windowsill, if
given plenty of light.* 476♦

Below: **Rebutia muscula**
*Another little gem, with many offsets
and beautifully coloured flowers
peeping out from silky white spines.
Thrives in the sun.* 476♦

Above: **Rebutia senilis**
Rebutias are the most floriferous of all cacti; some can almost flower themselves to death. Fortunately most produce offsets readily and are easy to propagate. This rebutia has a number of varieties with differing flower colours: pink, orange and yellow. Seed pods follow the flowers. 477♦

Above right: **Rhipsalis pilocarpa**
Rhipsalis come from tropical rain forests; they are true cacti but quite different from the more typical desert types. Many are not particularly interesting for the collector, but this one is ideal for a hanging basket. Full sunlight should be avoided in summer. 478♦

Right: **Rhipsalidopsis rosea**
This is another cactus originating from the tropical rain forests; it needs some moisture at all times, and more winter warmth than the desert cacti. Flowers are very freely produced on flattened stem segments. If you want only one cactus in a hanging basket, this is worth considering. 477♦

Left: Schlumbergera 'Buckleyi'
This must be the best-known cactus of all and possibly also the best-known houseplant. Whatever may be said to the contrary, it is a true cactus – one of the jungle or tropical rain forest types. Unfortunately, like many popular plants, it is not always well grown. Although watering may be reduced after flowering, this plant should never be completely dry. 478♦

Below left: Sedum morganianum
One of the attractions of succulent plants is their great variety and the so-called 'Donkey's Tail' is certainly different. With its long trailing stems, clad in small succulent leaves, it does well in a hanging basket. It is difficult to handle without damage as the leaves fall off easily. Attractive flowers are produced but usually on large plants only. 479♦

Below: Sedum hintonii
There is a vast number of sedums, including many well-known garden plants and also many rather dull species, scarcely worth growing. This, however, is a beauty, with its tiny rounded leaves clad in white glistening hairs. It is winter-flowering, which makes a pleasant change but can create difficulties with watering. Do so sparingly in winter time. 479♦

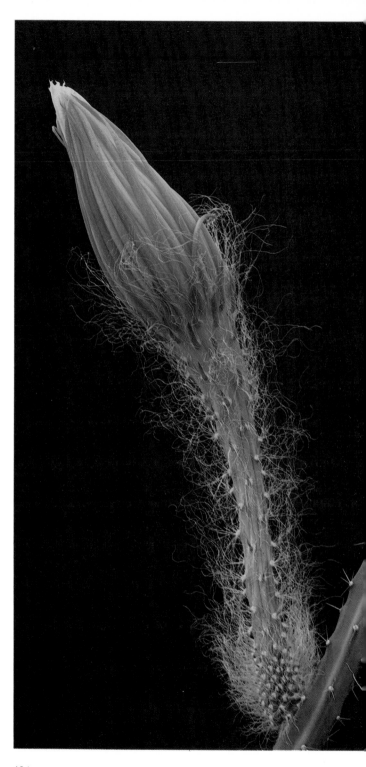

Left: Selenicereus grandiflorus
For those who have sufficient room this majestic cactus really deserves a place. The long trailing stems need some support – hardly possible in the living-room! This shows one of the immense buds, which will open during the night to a huge flower. 480♦

Right: Sedum rubrotinctum
The tiny, succulent leaves of this sedum are nicely tinted red. It is easy to propagate, as the stems tend to take root wherever they touch soil. It is usually necessary to trim the plant in order to keep it neat. This succulent is grown for its leaf colour, not its flowers. 480♦

Below: Senecio rowleyianus
Senecios show a vast difference in size; this is one of the miniature succulent ones. The photograph shows why it is known as the 'String of Beads' and also why it really has to be grown in a hanging basket. The stems take root easily on contact with the soil. 481♦

Far left: **Stapelia revoluta**
Stapelias are known as 'carrion flowers' because of their smell and appearance. This one has a fringe of hairs along the reflexed petals. 482♦

Left: **Stapelia hirsuta**
The large flowers of this stapelia are covered with fine hairs, hence the name 'hirsuta', or hairy. Stems are velvety. Sometimes flies lay eggs in the flower. 481♦

Below: **Stapelia variegata**
Probably the commonest stapelia in cultivation and one of the easiest to grow and flower. Also, it seems to be the one that smells worst. 482♦

Above: **Sulcorebutia totorensis**
*Sulcorebutias (not to be confused
with rebutias) are not the
commonest of cacti, and are not easy
to obtain, but they are well worth
seeking out. These delightful little
plants have strikingly coloured
flowers. This is one of the larger
sulcorebutias, but still small and
forming a cluster of compact heads.
The flowers open in succession,
which gives a prolonged flowering
period. Because of the long roots, a
deep pot is necessary; and particular
care is needed with watering.* 483♦

Left: **Trichocereus chilensis**
*All trichocerei are potentially large
cacti. They are only suitable for the
average collector because they are
slow-growing, and they make good
pot plants in their early years. Many
are somewhat dull columns, hardly
worth the space they take; but this is
one of the exceptions. It is a beautiful
plant, with stout, sharp spines of an
attractive colour. However, since
flowering is related to maturity, this
cactus must be grown for its
appearance.* 485♦

Above: **Trichocereus spachianus**
*This trichocereus will make a good
pot specimen; and if it can be given
enough space, it may well flower.
Very easy to propagate.* 485♦

Right: **Weingartia cumingii**
*A particularly free-flowering small
cactus, producing masses of blooms
in spring and summer. The spines
are quite soft.* 486♦

Below: **Weingartia lanata**
*The tufts of white wool give this
cactus its name. Very freely
produced flowers appear over a long
period. They have no perfume.* 486♦

Above: *A striking display of cacti and other succulent plants, all from the Americas. Notable among the specimens on show here are the beautifully varied shapes and colours of the echeveria rosettes.*

Parodia aureispina
- **Full sun**
- **Temp: 5-30°C (41-86°F)**
- **Water with great care**

Parodias are among the most beautiful of the South American cacti, but not the easiest to cultivate. They have a nasty habit of losing their roots for no apparent reason. They will regrow them but the cessation of growth can leave a scar.

Parodia aureispina is a beautiful golden ball; the spirally arranged ribs are densely covered with short yellow spines, at least one of which in each group is hooked. The large buttercup-yellow flowers are borne on top of the plant, and open during the summer. With age the plant becomes cylindrical and reaches a height of about 20cm (8in); some offsets will form.

A porous soil consisting of half loam-based potting mixture and half grit will ensure good drainage. Always allow the soil to dry out between waterings, and keep the plant dry during winter. Feed every two weeks with a high-potassium fertilizer when the buds form. Repot annually. Grow in a half-pot so that the roots are not surrounded by too much cold, wet soil.

Take care
Never overwater. 438♦

Parodia microsperma
- **Full sun**
- **Temp: 5-30°C (41-86°F)**
- **Water with care**

Parodia microsperma is globular when young, but with age it becomes elongated. It is a pale green plant with numerous spirally arranged ribs carrying many whitish spines. It will form some offsets, which may be used for propagating the plant. The golden-yellow flowers are about 5cm (2in) across and are carried on the top of the plant during the summer months.

Keep this plant in a sunny position and water it with care during the summer, allowing the soil to dry out before watering again. When buds form feed with a high-potassium fertilizer about every two weeks. Keep dry in winter. Grow in a half-pot in a mixture of one part loam-based mixture to one part grit. Repot annually. The only pests likely to attack parodias are mealy bug and root mealy bug. The odd mealy bug may be picked off with forceps but a bad infestation of either of these pests should be treated with a proprietary insecticide. A systemic one will deal more effectively with root mealy bug.

Take care
Avoid the hooked spines. 439♦

473

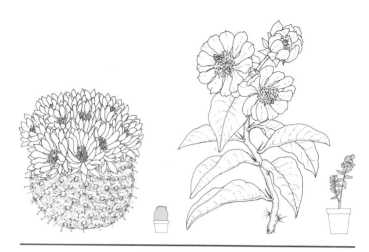

Parodia sanguiniflora
- **Full sun**
- **Temp: 5-30°C (41-86°F)**
- **Water with care**

Parodia sanguiniflora, true to its name, has large blood-red flowers. These open in summer, and make a change from the yellow flowers usual in parodias. As a young plant this cactus is globular, but it tends to become cylindrical with age. The numerous spirally arranged ribs carry many brownish spines, some of which are hooked. Some specimens form excessive numbers of offsets to the detriment of flowering. If this happens, restart the plant from an offset. For several years it will flower freely before starting to offset again.

Grow in an open potting mixture, one part loam-based medium to one part grit. Repot annually and inspect the roots for ashy deposits, which indicate root mealy bug; if found, wash off old soil and repot in a clean container. Always water parodias carefully, as they have a tendency to lose their roots if their growing medium becomes excessively wet. Feed with a high-potassium liquid fertilizer every two weeks when in flower. Keep dry during the winter.

Take care
Avoid damp conditions.

Pereskia aculeata
- **Full sun**
- **Temp: 10-30°C (50-86°F)**
- **Keep slightly moist in winter**

With this plant you will have difficulty in persuading your friends that it is a cactus at all. Pereskias are the most un-cactus-like of all cacti, but their spine formation and flower structure prove their identity. This plant is scarcely succulent at all; with its large privet-like leaves and slightly spiny long trailing stems, it somewhat resembles a wild rose. The leaves are bright green, but the variety *godseffiana* (often called *Pereskia godseffiana*) has reddish tinged leaves. The stems will need supporting in some way, with sticks or a plant trellis. In a greenhouse it can be trained up and along the roof, but the rather higher winter temperature needed makes it difficult for the cool greenhouse. Indoors, it should thrive in a light window, large enough to accommodate its stems.

Pinkish flowers, rather like those of a wild rose and about 4.5cm (1.8in) across, appear in autumn, but only on large plants. Water freely in spring and summer and feed occasionally.

Take care
Cold conditions cause leaf fall. 440♦

Pleiospilos bolusii
- **Full sun**
- **Temp: 5-30°C (41-86°F)**
- **Keep dry during rest period**

Pleiospilos bolusii is one of the stone-like plants, its speckled leaves resembling a small chunk of granite. The plant consists of one pair of very succulent leaves with flattened tops; the leaves are about 2.5cm (1in) long and almost as broad. The stem is so short that the plant is often described as 'stemless'. The heads may be split off in late summer to propagate the plant. Try to include a piece of 'stem' or leaf base.

P. bolusii flowers in autumn; the flowers open in the late afternoon to early evening, but only on sunny days. They are golden-yellow in colour and 7.5cm (3in) across.

When the previous season's leaves have completely shrivelled, the current season's leaves will be well formed. This will be late summer. Start watering at this stage and continue into the autumn, when the next season's pair of leaves will be appearing. Stop watering when they are about 1cm (0.4in) high. Grow in an open mixture, half loam-based medium and half grit.

Take care
Do not overwater. 457♦

Rebutia albiflora
- **Full sun**
- **Temp: 5-30°C (41-86°F)**
- **Water with care**

Rebutia albiflora is one of the very few rebutias with white flowers. This is a very desirable plant if space is limited; it will flower when only 1cm (0.4in) across. The flowering period is spring. The plant consists of a cluster of small heads, covered in short white spines. Individual heads can be split off and used to start new plants.

This cactus has a weak root system and should be grown in a shallow pan so that the roots are not surrounded by large quantities of cold, wet soil. A loam-based mixture or a soilless medium, to which one third sharp sand or perlite has been added, is suitable for this cactus. During spring and summer water freely, allowing it to dry out between waterings. Feed every two weeks with a tomato fertilizer when the buds appear. During the winter months keep it dry.

Mealy bug and root mealy bug are the pests most likely to attack this rebutia. A proprietary insecticide spray will deal with these.

Take care
Do not overwater. 459♦

Rebutia calliantha var. krainziana
- Full sun
- Temp: 5-30°C (41-86°F)
- Avoid overwatering

All rebutias are beautiful in the spring flowering period, but this species is outstanding. Each head is surrounded by a complete ring of orange-red flowers. The flower colour in this plant can vary from an almost true red through to a pure orange. The buds are purple.

The individual heads of this clustering cactus are cylindrical, and reach a height of about 10cm (4in). The very short white spines form a neat pattern against the green stem.

This rebutia needs a sunny position to keep it a bright colour and to ensure flowering. Any good potting mixture may be used, either loam- or peat-based. During spring and summer water freely, letting it get almost dry before watering again. When the buds form feed every two weeks with a tomato fertilizer.

Watch carefully for any signs of mealy bug, particularly around the growing point of the stems, where these woolly white pests can fade into the white wool on new growth.

Take care
Give plenty of light. 458♦

Rebutia muscula
- Full sun
- Temp: 5-30°C (41-86°F)
- Avoid overwatering

Rebutia muscula is one of the more recently discovered rebutias, and should not be confused with the less attractive *R. minuscula*. With its clear orange flowers, *R. muscula* is a beautiful addition to any cactus collection. The flowers open in late spring. The plant body is densely covered with soft white spines. It is a clustering plant and in the sun looks like a silvery cushion. The offsets may be used for propagation.

Like most cacti, *R. muscula* needs to be grown in strong light. Any loam-based mixture may be used for this plant; to improve the drainage, add one third sharp sand or perlite. During spring and summer water freely, allowing the plant to dry out between waterings. Feed with a high-potassium (tomato) fertilizer every two weeks when buds form.

Mealy bug hide between the clustering heads and suck the sap from the plant. Their white bodies blend with the plant and make discovery difficult.

Take care
Grow in a strong light. 459♦

Rebutia senilis
- **Full sun**
- **Temp: 5-30°C (41-86°F)**
- **Water with care**

Rebutias are ideal cacti for the collector without a greenhouse. They are small and will flower freely every spring if kept on a sunny windowsill. One of the prettiest is *R. senilis*: the rings of red flowers show up well against the silvery white spines. The flowers are followed by seed pods, and in autumn dozens of seedling rebutias will be found nestling around the parent plant. With age *R. senilis* clusters, forming a cushion about 30cm (12in) across. Individual heads may be removed and used for propagation.

Rebutias are not fussy about their soil, and either a loam-based or a soilless mixture may be used. In spring and summer water freely, allowing the compost to dry out between waterings. When the buds form feed every two weeks with a high-potassium fertilizer.

Carefully watch for signs of mealy bug. It is easy to miss these white pests on a white-spined plant. A systemic insecticide will be ideal.

Take care
Check for mealy bug. 460♦

Rhipsalidopsis rosea
(Easter cactus)
- **Partial shade**
- **Temp: 10-30°C (50-86°F)**
- **Keep slightly moist all year**

This is one of the jungle cacti, related to the well-known Christmas cactus, but producing its rose-pink flowers in early spring; they are about 2.5cm (1in) across. The plant itself consists of very small flattened segments, each around 2cm (0.8in) long, which, joined end to end and branching freely, eventually form a little bush. The segments carry small bushy spines along the edges and tips; they are quite harmless. Propagation is simplicity itself; just remove a small branch in spring or summer and pot it up.

Although this delightful little cactus and its many hybrids can be grown as an ordinary pot plant, it is ideal for a hanging basket. A rich growing medium is appreciated, so add about one third of peat (or leaf mould, if you can get it) to your standard potting mixture. Give a dose of high-potassium fertilizer every two weeks in spring, when buds are forming, and water freely.

Take care
Spray indoor plants occasionally with clean water. 461♦

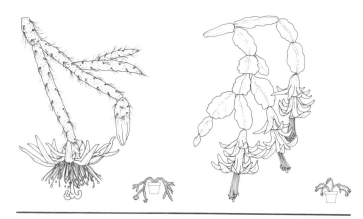

Rhipsalis pilocarpa
- **Partial shade**
- **Temp: 10-30°C (50-86°F)**
- **Keep slightly moist in winter**

At least one rhipsalis makes an interesting addition to the collection, as these are unusual cacti with an appearance quite at variance with the popular conception of a cactus. There are many species, but *R. pilocarpa* is one of the most attractive. A mass of dark green, cylindrical trailing stems, up to 40cm (16in) long and only 3-6mm (0.125-0.25in) thick, with small bushy spines make this an ideal subject for a hanging basket. White or cream flowers, about 2cm (0.8in) across, are borne on the tips of the branches; they are not very spectacular, but they do appear in winter, and they are perfumed.

Grow this rhipsalis in a good porous potting mixture, and preferably add some extra peat (sterile leaf mould is better, if available) as it needs a rich soil. Feed from time to time and water freely in spring and summer.

Take care
Best kept quite dry if wintered in a cool greenhouse. 461♦

Schlumbergera 'Buckleyi'
(Christmas cactus)
- **Partial shade**
- **Temp: 10-30°C (50-86°F)**
- **Keep slightly moist all year**

There is no doubt that this is the most popular cactus of all and the one most commonly grown, in spite of the fact that many people do not consider it to be a 'true' cactus at all, whatever that means! But it *is* a cactus, a jungle type, needing more warmth and moisture than the desert cacti. The many segments, joined end to end, are true stems (there are no leaves) and the whole plant forms a densely branched bush.
Unscented flowers of an unusual shape and about 3cm (1.2in) across, are freely produced in winter at the end of segments; the typical colour is carmine but varieties exist with flowers of various shades of red, pink or even white (never blue).

Use a rich potting mixture with added peat or leaf mould, and water the plant freely when in bud and flower, feeding every two weeks at this time. Reduce the water somewhat after flowering. Propagation from segments is easy.

Take care
Buds drop if the plant is moved. 462♦

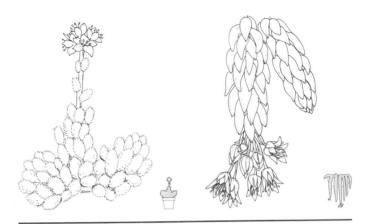

Sedum hintonii
- **Full sun**
- **Temp: 10-30°C (50-86°F)**
- **Keep almost dry in winter**

Many of the large number of sedums are somewhat uninteresting plants, but there are also some delightful little succulents, ideal for any collection. *Sedum hintonii* is one of the most beautiful of all. It consists of a mass of short stems bearing tiny egg-shaped leaves, densely covered with white hairs. Little white flowers appear in winter, always a welcome time. At flowering time the plant should be very sparingly watered, because it is very prone to rot if water becomes trapped within the leaves.

Grow this little gem in a well-drained potting mixture; add about one third of sharp sand or perlite to a good standard material, either loam- or peat-based. Although it will withstand quite low temperatures if kept dry, *S. hintonii* is better if kept rather warmer than in the average greenhouse in winter, and it makes a good houseplant.

Take care
Watch for rotting between the tightly packed stems. 463♦

Sedum morganianum
(Donkey's tail)
- **Full sun**
- **Temp: 10-30°C (50-86°F)**
- **Keep slightly moist in winter**

One glance at this unusual succulent will explain the popular name, although whether the tail-like stems resemble the tail of a donkey is a matter of opinion! Stems can be up to 90cm (36in) long, branching freely from the base, and are completely clad with small succulent leaves about 2cm (0.8in) long and 1cm (0.4in) thick. Their pale green colour is masked with a whitish bloom. The only practicable way to grow this plant is in a hanging basket. Line it with sphagnum moss and pack with a good standard potting mixture.

Any pot plants beneath the basket will soon have little sedums growing in them, as *S. morganianum* sheds its leaves easily and they take root where they fall. Very attractive rose-pink flowers are borne on the ends of shoots, but only on large mature ones. Water this unusual succulent freely in spring and summer, and never let it dry out completley or leaves will be shed.

Take care
Always handle carefully. 462♦

479

Sedum rubrotinctum
- **Full sun**
- **Temp: 5-30°C (41-86°F)**
- **Keep slightly moist in winter**

Another very attractive little sedum, this colourful succulent consists of branched stems covered with small, oval, very fleshy leaves. These are about 2cm (0.8in) long and 7mm (0.3in) thick. The basic colour is bright green but a delightful red coloration extends downwards from the tips. As the stems become longer they are likely to bend over and take root in any soil they touch. To keep a small bushy plant, remove any over-long shoots; you can always use them as cuttings. Flowers are small and yellow, but are by no means freely produced.

Any good potting mixture is satisfactory; it can be either peat- or loam-based. The plant is reasonably hardy and in winter needs only sufficient water to prevent shrivelling and leaf fall. When it is actively growing in spring and summer, you can water it quite generously, but never let the mix become soggy.

Take care
With insufficient light the red colouring is not produced. 464♦

Selenicereus grandiflorus
(Queen of the night)
- **Diffuse sunlight**
- **Temp: 7-30°C (45-86°F)**
- **Keep moist all year**

Selenicereus grandiflorus is only suitable for greenhouse cultivation; its long straggly stems are up to 5m (16ft) long and need to be trained along the roof of a greenhouse. The stems are 2.5cm (1in) thick, greyish-green in colour, and the ribs have needle-like spines.

This cactus is grown for its glorious flowers rather than the beauty of its form. The bell-shaped white flowers are about 30cm (12in) long and have a sweet scent. They open in the late evening and fade the following morning.

Grow this plant in a loam-based mixture to which bone meal has been added. Feed during the growing period with a liquid fertilizer, of the type sold for tomatoes. Repot annually. Water generously during spring and summer. Give it a little moisture during winter. When the plant becomes too large, it may be propagated by stem cuttings about 15cm (6in) long.

Take care
Protect from strong sunlight. 465♦

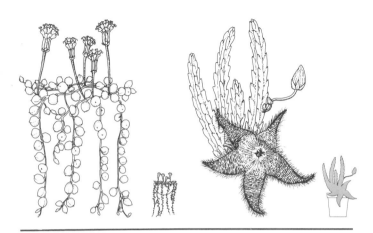

Senecio rowleyianus
(String-of-beads senecio)
- **Full sun**
- **Temp: 5-30°C (41-86°F)**
- **Keep slightly moist in winter**

Senecios are a very large group of plants; some are succulent, others are garden bushes, and they show a wide variety of shape and size. This is one of the small succulent types and a most unusual plant, with its long thin stems along which appear to be strung 'beads' in the form of spherical leaves 7mm (0.3in) in diameter. These beady stems trail and root when they make contact with the soil, so that a dense mat is eventually formed. The main interest of this little succulent is its fascinating leaf formation; the white flowers may or may not appear.

You can easily grow this senecio in a hanging basket if you persuade the stems to hang over the edge rather than rooting on the surface. To propagate, just remove a few pieces and pot them up at once. Any good potting mixture may be used; the plant is quite undemanding. Water it freely in spring and summer; feeding is not usually necessary.

Take care
Aphids can appear on the stems. 465♦

Stapelia hirsuta
(Carrion flower)
- **Full sun**
- **Temp: 10-30°C (50-86°F)**
- **Keep dry in winter**

This is a very succulent plant with four-angled velvety stems branching from the base. Although there are no spines, small teeth are borne along the angles of the stems; the stems can be up to about 20cm (8in) high and 2.5cm (1in) thick, but the plant may flower when only half this size. Of course, the most notable feature of any stapelia is its flower, with a supposed resemblance to carrion in appearance and colour. The flowers of *S. hirsuta* are up to 10cm (4in) across and of a starfish shape, the five 'arms' being purple-brown, striped with yellow; the whole is covered with purple hairs. The plant is less offensive to our noses than some other stapelias and you need not fear to keep it in the living-room.

Use a very well-drained potting mixture; add one part of sharp sand or perlite to two parts of a standard material, and top dress with gravel to prevent base rot.

Take care
Winter cold can cause black fungus spots. 467♦

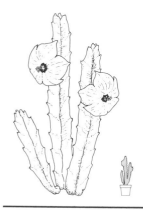

Stapelia revoluta

(Carrion flower)
- **Full sun**
- **Temp: 10-30°C (50-86°F)**
- **Keep dry in winter**

The popular name of 'Carrion flower' applies to all the large-flowered stapelias, as they are pollinated in nature by flies. This unusual succulent plant has four-angled smooth stems with soft 'teeth' along the edges. The colour is bluish-green, brown towards the growing tips. Cultivated specimens reach a length of about 20cm (8in), with a stem thickness of 2cm (0.8in). Flowers of the typical starfish shape and reddish-brown in colour have the five lobes strongly reflexed backwards (hence the name 'revoluta') making the diameter of 3cm (1.2in) much less than the opened out size. Hairs on the flowers form a fringe around the edge.

Use an open potting mixture, consisting of one part sharp sand or perlite added to two parts of a standard material. Water in spring and summer, when the soil has almost completely dried out.

Take care

Avoid base rot by a top dressing of gravel. 466♦

Stapelia (Orbea) variegata

(Carrion flower)
- **Full sun**
- **Temp: 10-30°C (50-86°F)**
- **Keep dry in winter**

This is undoubtedly the commonest stapelia in cultivation and deservedly popular for the ease with which it produces its fascinating flowers. These are 5cm (2in) or more across with blunt lobes, very starfish-like, attractively patterned with chocolate blotches on a yellow background, and with a yellow central disc.

Stems are quite small; a large specimen would be only 10cm (4in) high but freely branching.

You can easily propagate this and other stapelias by removing a stem, sometimes with roots attached, in spring or summer. *S. variegata* is one of the less demanding stapelias, but nevertheless use a well-drained potting mixture; add about one third sharp sand or perlite to a good standard material. Although this stapelia will tolerate a winter temperature below 10°C (50°F), it does better if kept rather warmer. A living-room is ideal; there is no smell in winter!

Take care

Water freely in warm weather. 466♦

Stomatium geoffreyii
- **Full sun**
- **Temp: 5-30°C (41-86°F)**
- **Keep dry during winter**

This attractive little plant will flourish either in a greenhouse or on a sunny windowsill. The many-headed plant has very short stems so that it appears to be almost 'stemless' at first glance. Each head consists of about six fleshy, triangular leaves with white 'teeth' along the edges. Each head is about 4cm (1.6in) across. The yellow flowers are produced continuously throughout the summer, opening on sunny days and closing at night.

Grow this plant in a 10cm (4in) half-pot. When the plant fills its pot, the stems will be noticeable and woody. Restart the plant by removing the heads with about 5mm (0.2in) of stem attached, and potting up in a mixture of one part loam-based medium and one part sharp sand or perlite. This is best done in early summer. Water generously during the summer, but keep completely dry during the winter.

Take care
Repot every two or three years.

Sulcorebutia totorensis
- **Full sun**
- **Temp: 5-30°C (41-86°F)**
- **Keep dry in winter**

Sulcorebutias are small, clump-forming, low-growing cacti with large tap-roots; often there is more plant below the soil than above. They are particularly outstanding for their brightly coloured and distinctive flowers. Many have very small individual heads, but this is one of the larger growing types with heads up to 6cm (2.4in) across and almost as high. By the time the plant has reached this size there will usually be a number of offsets around the base. The deep reddish-purple flowers last for about five days, but because they open in succession, the flowering period may be four weeks.

Use a deep pot to accommodate the long root. Like all sulcorebutias, this plant needs a particularly well-drained potting mixture: up to half its volume of sharp sand or perlite.

Water quite freely in spring and summer, and when it is in full bloom feed every two weeks with a high-potassium fertilizer.

Take care
Waterlogged soil can cause rot. 469♦

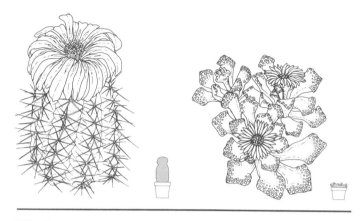

Thelocactus bicolor
- **Full sun**
- **Temp: 5-30°C (41-86°F)**
- **Keep dry in winter**

Although this is not a very large cactus in nature, it does not appear to flower readily in a collection, where the globular stem could reach a diameter of 10cm (4in). Some specimens produce offsets, but others spend solitary lives. Ribs on the stem are divided into notches, giving the effect of low tubercles, carrying the spines that give this cactus its beauty. On each tubercle there is a group of spreading spines up to 2.5cm (1in) long, and four stouter ones somewhat longer. All have the most attractive coloration, red with amber tips (whence the 'bicolor' in its name).

Thelocactus is quite an easy plant to cultivate. Use a good standard potting mixture; and add some extra sharp sand or perlite if you have any doubts about its porosity. With such beautiful spines one hardly needs flowers, but if they *do* come they are violet-red in colour. A cold winter rest will encourage them.

Take care
See that no water collects in the crown of this plant.

Titanopsis calcarea
- **Full sun**
- **Temp: 5-30°C (41-86°F)**
- **Keep dry during rest period**

'Titanopsis' means 'chalk-appearance' in Greek and describes the chalky appearance of the leaves, which closely resemble the limestone on which they grow. *T. calcarea* consists of 'stemless' rosettes 7.5cm (3in) across. Each rosette consists of two or three pairs of leaves. The grey-green leaves are wider at the tip, which is covered with whitish warts. The deep golden-yellow flowers appear during the winter months. If it is a sunny winter the buds will open during the afternoon and close again at night. In cloudy weather the buds may abort.

The growing period of this plant is winter, when it should be watered on sunny days. Keep fairly dry in summer. Grow in a half-pot in a mixture of one part loam-based medium to one part grit. The plant may be propagated by splitting the cluster. Always include a short length of stem on the heads that are removed for propagation.

Take care
Grow in the sunniest part of the greenhouse, near the glass.

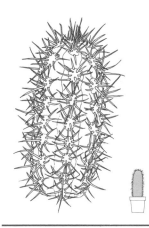

Trichocereus chilensis

- **Full sun**
- **Temp: 5-30°C (41-86°F)**
- **Keep dry in winter**

Trichocerei are pretty when small, but this cactus will not grow too large during the lifetime of its owner. This one is sometimes offered for sale and is well worth acquiring. With naturally large-growing cacti it is difficult to state a definite size but a good cultivated specimen would be about 20cm (8in) high and 5-8cm (2-3.2in) across after many years. But you are likely to buy this one at around 5cm (2in) high. The long golden-brown, stout spines arranged along the many-ribbed bright green stems make this a most attractive cactus, which is just as well, because it is of no use to expect flowers except on very large specimens. But the white flowers, when produced, are beautiful and pleasantly perfumed. Because the stem is unbranched, propagation from cuttings is not possible.

Any good standard peat- or loam-based potting mixture will do for this very tolerant cactus and you can water it freely in spring and summer.

Take care
The spines are needle-sharp! 468♦

Trichocereus spachianus

- **Full sun**
- **Temp: 5-30°C (41-86°F)**
- **Keep dry in winter**

This trichocereus is another naturally large cactus that makes a good smaller specimen for a collection. It could easily reach a height of 30cm (12in), with bright green stems eventually branching from the base. The blunt ribs bear only quite short spines, and the plant is reasonably easy to handle. If allowed to become large enough it may well respond by producing large greenish-white flowers from the top, opening at night. But the main use for this plant is as a grafting stock for other cacti, and unless you want a large specimen, it is simplicity itself to produce many small ones. If any branch is cut off, not only will it root if given the usual few days' drying-off period, but the stump will send out a ring of offsets, which can be removed and potted up in their turn.

With a good standard porous potting mixture, peat- or loam-based, it is not necessary to add extra drainage material. Water freely in spring and summer.

Take care
Tall plants become top-heavy. 470♦

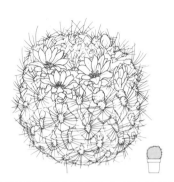

Weingartia cumingii
- Full sun
- Temp: 5-30°C (41-86°F)
- Keep dry in winter

This free-flowering small cactus is sometimes included with *Gymnocalycium*, because of also having hairless flower buds. But, apart from this, the resemblance is not very great. *W. cumingii* is a bright green, spherical plant with a maximum diameter of about 10cm (4in), and divided into a number of spiral, notched ribs. The golden spines are usually less than 1cm (0.4in) long and quite soft and bristly. Deep yellow flowers are freely produced around the top of the stem in spring and summer, about 3cm (1.2in) across.

If you keep this plant indoors, be sure to put it in the coldest room in winter (but with good light) in order to encourage flowering the following year. In a greenhouse there should be no problem. Grow this weingartia in a mixture of a good standard material and sharp sand or perlite in the proportion of three to one. Water freely in spring and summer, and give a feed every two weeks with a high-potassium fertilizer.

Take care
Watch for mealy bugs at the base of the flowers. 470♦

Weingartia lanata
- Full sun
- Temp: 5-30°C (41-86°F)
- Keep dry in winter

The 'lanata' in the name of this delightful cactus is derived from the clumps of white wool scattered over the stem, which is roughly spherical and reaches a diameter of about 10cm (4in). The spiral ribs are deeply notched so that the appearance is of a mass of large tubercles rather than ribs. It is on the ends of these tubercles that the woolly hair appears, more towards the top of the plant, and also clumps of stiff but not very stout pale brown spines, about 2cm (0.8in) long. For sheer beauty the golden yellow flowers are unsurpassed. Although only about 3cm (1.2in) across, they are produced in profusion around the top of the stem, and in a good year spring or summer flowering is often followed by one in the autumn. The flowers last for several days, but unfortunately they are scentless.

This is not a demanding cactus, but to be on the safe side add about one third of extra sharp sand or perlite to a good standard mixture. Feed during the flowering period with a high-potassium fertilizer.

Take care
Water freely spring and summer. 471♦

Picture Credits

The publishers wish to thank the following photographers and agencies who have supplied photographs for this book. Photographs have been credited by page number and position on the page: (B) Bottom, (T) Top, (C) Centre, (BL) Bottom Left, etc.

A-Z Botanical Collection: 18(T), 21(B), 42(BL), 87(TR), 146(L), 136-7(B), 149(B)

Pat Brindley: 50(BL), 52(BL), 87(B), 118(B), 119

Peter Chapman and Margaret Martin: Contents page, 329, 336(B), 337, 339(T), 340(B), 342(C), 343, 344(T), 361, 362(B), 365, 366, 367(T), 368(T), 369(CR, B), 370(T), 372, 373(T), 374(TR,BR), 375(B), 376(T), 393(T), 394(T), 395(B), 396(BL), 397, 398(T), 399(T), 403(BR), 404(T), 407(T), 408, 426(T), 427(B), 428-9(T), 432, 433, 434(TR), 434-5(B), 436(TL), 457, 458, 459(BR), 460(T), 461(B), 462, 466(T), 468, 470(BL)

Eric Crichton: Cover, half title page, title page, back endpaper, 6, 16, 17, 20, 21(T), 22, 23, 24(T), 41, 42(T), 44, 45(T), 46, 50(T), 51, 52(T), 55, 56(BL), 73, 74(TL), 74-5(B), 76(TL), 78, 80(B), 82(B), 83(B), 84(BL), 85, 87(TL), 88, 105, 106(B), 108, 109, 110, 111(B), 112(T), 113(T), 114, 115, 117, 120, 137(T), 142, 144, 145, 148(T), 149, 150(B), 152, all

photographs in Part Two: Foliage Houseplants, 376(BR), 401

Jan van Dommelen: 370(B), 405(T), 464

Derek Fell: 147(T)

Kees Hagerman: 76(BL)

B.J. van der Lans: 19(B), 86, 151, 363(TL), 465(B)

Louise Lippold: 369(T)

Gordon Rowley: 19, 338(T), 339(B), 341(T), 364, 375(T), 394(B), 407(B), 428(B), 437, 467(TL), 469(TR), 470(TL), 471

Franz Noltee: 336(TR), 338(BL), 340(TL), 341(B), 342(TL), 344(BR), 363(B), 367(B), 374(C), 395(T), 396(BR), 399(B), 400(BL), 402, 404(B), 406, 425, 429(BL), 432(B), 439(BR), 459(TR), 463(B)

Daan Smit: Front endpaper, 10-11, 47, 75, 113(BR), 148(BL), 342(B), 362(T), 393(B), 427(T), 435(T), 438(BL), 465(TR)

Harry Smith Photographic Collection: 9, 18(B), 54, 80(B), 83(T), 106(T), 116(BL), 137(BR), 140(T), 150(T)

Michael Warren: 49(B), 107, 111(T), 330-1, 368(B), 371(BL), 398(BR), 400(TL), 430, 431(T), 440, 461(T), 466-7(B), 472

Miltonia 'Peach Blossom'